BUILDING
ZION

BUILDING
ZION

THE LATTER-DAY SAINTS IN EUROPE

BRUCE A. VAN ORDEN

Deseret Book Company
Salt Lake City, Utah

Van Orden, Bruce A.
    Building Zion : the Latter-day Saints in Europe / Bruce A. Van
    Orden.
        p.   cm.
    Includes bibliographical references and index.
    ISBN 0-87579-939-6
    1. Church of Jesus Christ of Latter-day Saints—Europe—History.
    2. Mormon Church—Europe—History. 3. Europe—Church history.
    I. Title.
    BX8617.E85V36   1996
    289.3'4—dc20   96-12654
                                                                  CIP

Printed in the United States of America

10   9   8   7   6   5   4   3   2   1

To the European Saints
for their sacrifice, faith, and devotion

Contents

Maps

Preface

This book surveys missionary work in Europe, the gathering of European converts to the American Zion in the nineteenth century, and the process of building Zion in Europe in the twentieth century. The recent miraculous developments in eastern Europe are one reason for this book. Another is that the entire history of the Church in Europe deserves to be told. More than a million Latter-day Saints in the United States and other parts of the world can trace their membership in the Church today to contacts made by missionaries in Europe, beginning in the late 1830s.

The global history of The Church of Jesus Christ of Latter-day Saints is a relatively new study. As a professor in the Department of Church History and Doctrine at Brigham Young University, I entered the field of international history when two of its pioneers, Professors James R. Moss and James R. Christiansen, died prematurely. These two men, along with Professors R. Lanier Britsch and Richard O. Cowan, had compiled a text entitled *The International Church* (Provo, Utah: Brigham Young University Publications, 1982). I am deeply indebted to Professors Moss and Christiansen and to Professors Britsch and Cowan, who have continued to inspire and encourage me with my teaching, research, and writing. Richard Cowan, my dear friend, has been especially helpful in reviewing this book.

My principal mentor for modern European history and European LDS history has been BYU history professor Douglas F. Tobler. His scholarly example, encouragement, writings, and love for the European Saints have helped me immeasurably in writing this volume.

Other colleagues who have encouraged and aided me include James B. Allen, Ted Bair, Alexander L. Baugh, Maureen Ursenbach Beecher, Howard L. Biddulph, Rodney B. Boynton, Gary L. Browning, Donald Q. Cannon, Dong Sull Choi, Larry E. Dahl, George D. Durrant, Ronald K. Esplin, Lawrence R. Flake, Sherman L. Fleek, Kenneth W. Godfrey, Leon R. Hartshorn, Matthew K. Heiss, Richard Neitzel Holzapfel, Paul Y. Hoskisson, Steven K. Iba, Kent P. Jackson, Roger R. Keller, E. Dale

LeBaron, Carol Cornwall Madsen, Robert J. Matthews, Robert L. Millet, Kahlile Mehr, Spencer J. Palmer, Paul H. Peterson, Larry C. Porter, Alvin H. Price, Stephen Ricks, Andrew Skinner, William Slaughter, D. Brent Smith, Everett Smith, Brent L. Top, James A. Toronto, Grant R. Underwood, Ronald Watt, Ronald W. Walker, David H. Whittaker, John W. Welch, and Raymond S. Wright.

I have been greatly blessed by able student research assistants and secretaries. My heartfelt thanks go to Brian (BJ) Fogg, Matthew Godfrey, Stephen Harper, Dannette Nicholes, Val Sederholm, Julie Thwaits, Jessica Top, Julie Workman, and Nanette Workman. I owe a special debt to my hundreds of students, whose term papers have often been valuable in my teaching and in my writing this and other volumes.

I thank BYU geography professor Jeffry S. Bird for preparing the maps for this book.

Writers for the *Ensign,* the *New Era,* the *Church News,* and the *International Magazine* (including *Tambuli* for the Filipino Saints—the only version in English) have researched and written numerous articles about Latter-day Saints around the globe. These have enlightened and inspired me. I cite them often in this volume and continue to be blessed by them as I teach classes on the international Church.

I value the cooperation and assistance I have received from the staffs of the Historical Department of The Church of Jesus Christ of Latter-day Saints and Special Collections of the Harold B. Lee Library at BYU.

I appreciate the cooperation of Deseret Book in the publishing of this volume, especially Sheri Dew, Suzanne Brady, and Kent Ware. Publishing with Deseret Book was made possible by the generous help of Robert L. Millet, dean of Religious Education, and the Religious Studies Center.

I express heartfelt thanks to my family. Over the past twenty-seven years my wife, Karen, has constantly encouraged me in teaching and writing. My two adult children, Stephen and Kaye, have borne with me in my BYU classes on the international Church and have contributed valuable insights from their own experience in Europe. To Michael, Rachel, and Matthew, I am glad to be their father and am thankful to find after long hours on the job that they still accept me. I thank all of my family from the bottom of my heart for accompanying me on the 1992

BYU Vienna Study Abroad—for enduring hardships as well as growing and learning together.

Most of all, I wish to thank my European friends, many of whom I met during my service in the South German Mission from 1965 to 1967. I labored under President John K. Fetzer, who has continued to be a marvelous role model. I have also become acquainted with hosts of European Saints who have traveled to Utah. Recent visits to Europe have netted yet more friends that will ever be dear to me. I have worshipped with them in many different lands and tongues, and memories of these sacred events will remain with me always.

CHAPTER 1

Introduction

n the fall of 1989, Latter-day Saints, along with the rest of the world, watched their televisions with excitement as revolutions unfolded in eastern Europe. "During a brief period of weeks, we have witnessed some phenomenal changes . . . which God-fearing men attribute to the hand of the Almighty in bringing about His glorious purposes," assessed Elder David B. Haight in the April 1990 general conference. "Walls have come down, gates have opened, and millions of voices have chorused the song of freedom! We rejoice in the dawning of a brighter day."[1]

Twenty-five years before, as a nineteen-year-old missionary in West Germany, I had labored in Coburg, a city less than ten miles from the East German border. One preparation day, three other missionaries and I cycled out to see the "iron curtain." We were not disappointed. Numerous signs warned of land mines and the possibility of being shot as we neared barbed wire fences and watchtowers. On the other side I saw farmers going placidly about their business. I prayed that the Eastern Bloc peoples would one day be free to hear the restored gospel of Jesus Christ. That same month Elder Ezra Taft Benson, then president of the European Mission, dedicated a handsome new chapel in Coburg. Testifying that people behind the iron curtain would one day hear the gospel, he declared, "Time is on the side of truth." He prophesied that eventually the new chapel would bless those people. In 1990, immediately after German reunification, Coburg became part of the Leipzig Germany Stake in former East Germany. In 1991, at a youth conference, I saw that chapel filled with fine young East German Saints, all born since my mission in Coburg.

Throughout the Cold War, Church leaders prophesied the demise of the iron curtain so the gospel could be preached in eastern Europe. "Is anything too hard for the Lord?" asked President Spencer W. Kimball in 1974. He emphasized that the Lord would break down barriers as soon as Latter-day Saints were ready and could supply enough missionaries.[2]

In April 1980, Elder Bruce R. McConkie shared what the Quorum of

The East German border near Coburg, West Germany, on
23 July 1965. The signs say "Stop! The Zone Border" and
"Careful: Mine Danger"

the Twelve Apostles saw in the Church's future: "We see congregations
of the covenant people worshipping the Lord in Moscow and Peking and
Saigon. . . . We see temples in great numbers dotting the earth."[3]

Elder Russell M. Nelson, assigned to minister to eastern Europe in
1986, privately declared many times that Communism would fall and
the gospel would be preached to millions more of our Heavenly Father's
children. Church leaders—including Elder Nelson, Elder Hans B. Ringger,
president of the Europe Area, and Thomas S. Monson of the First
Presidency—frequently negotiated with government leaders to admit
missionaries into many Communist countries well in advance of the
1989 revolutions. Those revolutions expedited what had already begun.

The circumstances in which modern European Saints find themselves differ greatly. Some members worship in extremely modest rented
quarters, their branches struggle to grow, and they themselves are ostracized by family and friends. In other places, wards flourish, with choirs,
youth programs, auxiliary activities, and stake missionaries. But the
common thread is love of the gospel and the Lord Jesus Christ.

Elder Ezra Taft Benson, speaking with the aid of an interpreter, at the dedication of the Coburg chapel, 12 September 1965

My experience with the Saints in Europe echoes that of Petrea Kelly, who visited a ward in Geneva, Switzerland. Members in that great city represented nearly a score of different nationalities: "I had expected to be overwhelmed by the differences—the languages, the cultures, the variety in ages and in experience in the Church. But as we sang hymns, prayed and worshipped together, there was a great spirit of unity. We were united by our testimonies of the Savior, by our love for the Book of Mormon, and by the knowledge that Joseph Smith was a prophet. I felt the differences melt away. The languages, the cultures, our tastes in foods and clothing were unimportant—for I had come to the place where the four corners of the world meet, and I had met my brothers and sisters."[4]

NOTES

1 David B. Haight, in Conference Report, April 1990, 28.

2 Spencer W. Kimball, "When the World Will Be Converted," *Ensign* 4 (October 1974): 7.

3 Bruce R. McConkie, in Conference Report, April 1980, 98–99.

4 Petrea Kelly, "Geneva—Unity and Diversity," *Tambuli,* November 1992, 48.

CHAPTER 2

The Kingdom Rolls Forth

fter his resurrection, the Lord Jesus Christ commanded his apostles: "Go ye into all the world, and preach the gospel to every creature" (Mark 16:15; see also Matthew 28:19). The Lord gave this same instruction to his Nephite disciples a short time later on the American continent (see Mormon 9:22). And the Lord repeated the same charge to the Prophet Joseph Smith and other latter-day prophets, seers, and revelators (see D&C 68:8; 80:1; 84:62; 112:28; 124:128). Clearly this commandment is of great importance.

The Old Testament prophet Daniel, while interpreting King Nebuchadnezzar's mysterious dream, foretold that a stone would be "cut out of the mountain without hands" and roll down the mountainside until it broke up all earthly kingdoms and "filled the whole earth" (Daniel 2:34–35, 44–45). Daniel explained to the Babylonian monarch that those wondrous events would occur "in the latter days" (Daniel 2:28).

The great latter-day prophet, Joseph Smith Jr., received divine authorization to establish the prophesied kingdom of God on earth. The Lord told his prophet: "The keys of the kingdom of God are committed unto man on the earth, and from thence shall the gospel roll forth unto the ends of the earth, as the stone which is cut out of the mountain without hands shall roll forth, until it has filled the whole earth" (D&C 65:2).

We are witnessing the fulfillment of those prophecies, for the gospel message is now going to the ends of the earth. Zion, the New Jerusalem, will be established, and a righteous people from all over the globe will await the glorious second coming of the Lord Jesus Christ to begin his millennial reign as King of kings and Lord of lords.

Prophets and Apostles Direct the Work

The mission of the Church requires ordained apostles, called to be "special witnesses of the name of Christ in all the world" (D&C 107:23). These men of the Quorum of the Twelve Apostles "officiate in the name

Two Latter-day Saint missionaries in Revolution Square with soldiers of the Red Army, Leningrad, Soviet Union, May Day 1990

of the Lord, under the direction of the Presidency of the Church, agreeable to the institution of heaven; to build up the church, and regulate all the affairs of the same in all nations" (D&C 107:33). The First Presidency and the Council of the Twelve, working in harmony, meet regularly to prayerfully discuss means to achieve their holy charge. Whenever the gospel has been taken into a new nation, the First Presidency and the Twelve have led the way.

They have also called others to help them. "It is the duty of the traveling high council [the Twelve] to call upon the Seventy, when they need assistance, to fill the several calls for preaching and administering the gospel" (D&C 107:38). "The Seventy are to act in the name of the Lord, under the direction of the Twelve," the Lord has revealed, "in building up the church and regulating all the affairs of the same in all nations" (D&C 107:34). Members of the Seventy, under the direction of the First Presidency and the Twelve, served as area presidencies in various geographical areas, including three in Europe by the mid 1990s.

America Is the Lord's Base of Operations

Nephi, the great Book of Mormon seer, foretold the formation of the

United States of America. He beheld in vision that "the wrath of God was upon all those that were gathered together against [the early Americans who fled from Europe]" and that those early Americans "were delivered by the power of God out of the hands of all other nations" (1 Nephi 13:18–19). Nephi prophesied that after Israel was scattered "the Lord God will raise up a mighty nation among the Gentiles, yea, even upon the face of this land," and in that nation the restored gospel would come forth (1 Nephi 22:7–8).

Religious liberties guaranteed by the Constitution allowed the early Church to grow, although even in the United States the Saints at first faced serious opposition and persecution. From these center stakes of Zion, headquartered in the Americas, "a land which is choice above all other lands" (Ether 2:10), the gospel would be spread abroad to fill the whole earth. Elder Ezra Taft Benson testified: "When this nation was established, the Church was restored and from here the message of the restored gospel has gone forth—all according to divine plan. This then becomes the Lord's base of operations in these latter-days. And this base—the land of America—will not be shifted out of its place. This nation will, in a measure at least, fulfill its mission even though it may face serious and troublesome days. The degree to which it achieves its full mission depends upon the righteousness of its people. God, through His power, has established a free people in this land as a means of helping to carry forward His purposes."[1]

Time and again latter-day apostles of the Lord Jesus Christ have used their influence and prestige with other nations to open doors to the Church in other countries. Isaiah prophesied that the gospel would go forth from an American Zion and other nations would gather there: "And it shall come to pass in the last days, that the mountain of the Lord's house shall be established in the top of the mountains, and shall be exalted above the hills; and all nations shall flow unto it. And many people shall go and say, Come ye, and let us go up to the mountain of the Lord, to the house of the God of Jacob; and he will teach us of his ways, and we will walk in his paths: *for out of Zion shall go forth the law*" (Isaiah 2:2–3; emphasis added).

The First Mission Outside the United States

The first international expansion of the Church was to British North America, as Canada was then officially known. From as early as 1830, missionaries, including the Prophet Joseph Smith, crossed the international border between New York and Upper Canada to proselyte. Upper Canada, what is now southern Ontario, was so named because it is the site of the upper reaches of the Saint Lawrence River. It was a productive mission field, the equal of any in the States. (No attempts were made in the Church's first decade to take the gospel into French-speaking Lower Canada, or Quebec.) Because the language and cultural roots of Upper Canada were English, neither Joseph Smith nor the elders considered these missionary journeys foreign.

But the Prophet Joseph Smith taught his associates that before long the Church would become international. A hymn composed by William W. Phelps in 1832, only two years after the Church was organized, proclaims:

> Glad tidings I bring unto you and each nation;
> Glad tidings of joy, now behold your salvation; . . .
> Around the whole world let us tell the glad story,
> And sing of his love, his salvation, and glory.[2]

In late 1830 and early 1831, when Joseph Smith was still in New York but preparing to move to Ohio, the Prophet received the following instruction in four revelations given within a few weeks of each other:

"And ye are called to bring to pass the gathering of mine elect" (D&C 29:7).

"And even so will I gather mine elect from the four quarters of the earth" (D&C 33:6).

"And from thence [Ohio], whosoever I will shall go forth among all nations, and it shall be told them what they shall do" (D&C 38:33).

"And inasmuch as my people shall assemble themselves at the Ohio, I have kept in store a blessing such as is not known among the children of men, and it shall be poured forth upon their heads. And from thence men shall go forth into all nations" (D&C 39:15).

The Prophet frequently met with the missionary elders and spoke of the possibilities awaiting the Church as it began to expand into all the world. In 1834 Wilford Woodruff, then a new convert, gathered with other brethren in the small log schoolhouse used for meetings in Kirtland. He listened with wonder to these words of the Prophet: "I want to say to you before the Lord, that you know no more concerning the destinies of this Church and kingdom than a babe upon its mother's lap. You don't comprehend it. It is only a little handful of Priesthood you see here tonight, but his Church will fill North and South America—it will fill the world."[3]

In early 1835, after the march of Zion's Camp to Missouri forged a strong group of potential leaders, Joseph Smith called the first group of Twelve Apostles in this dispensation. Through a revelation to the Prophet that outlined their duties as witnesses of Christ and regulators of the affairs of the Church in all nations, these early apostles knew that soon they would embark on their global duties (see D&C 107). England was a natural beginning for the work. Each of the Twelve had English ancestors. England had comparative religious freedom. And the language and culture would not be a significant barrier.

Through 1837 the members of the Quorum of the Twelve, ranging in age from twenty-three to thirty-five, continued to labor in eastern United States and Upper Canada. They strived for unity among themselves to fulfill the full measure of their calling. The pentecostal outpouring of the Lord's Spirit in the March 1836 dedication of the Kirtland Temple further prepared them. But many of them also drank of the spirit of apostasy that rocked Kirtland just a year later.

In June 1837, while the Church was suffering in the depths of this apostasy, the Lord revealed to Joseph Smith that "something new must be done for the salvation of His Church."[4] The Prophet directed a valiant apostle, Elder Heber C. Kimball, to lead the first mission to England. Joined by fellow quorum member Orson Hyde and five others (four of them converts from Upper Canada), Elder Kimball sailed to Liverpool. From there they journeyed to Preston, England, where they established the British Mission. This handful of men drew more than 1,500 converts into the gospel net, setting the stage for astonishing growth over the next three decades in Great Britain. The apostolic mission of 1837 and 1838, followed by another mission of nine apostles in 1840 and 1841, counterbalanced the ills of the great apostasy in Kirtland and then the Missouri persecutions and expulsion in 1838 and 1839. The training the apostles received in these two missions proved indispensable in their leading the Church after the martyrdom of Joseph Smith in 1844.

Once the Church under Brigham Young had found a refuge in the Rocky Mountains, the First Presidency and the Twelve launched in 1849 an astounding worldwide proselyting effort. Only a minority of Saints were even in Utah. Most were still in the Iowa camps or in Britain waiting to gather to Zion. Brigham Young directed three apostles—John Taylor, Erastus Snow, and Lorenzo Snow—to preach the gospel. By 1852 the Book of Mormon had been translated into Danish, German, French, and Italian; a Welsh edition followed a few years later. By 1853 the Twelve Apostles had directed the preaching of the gospel not only to England, Scotland, and Ireland but also to Wales, Denmark, Sweden, Norway, Iceland, France, Italy, Switzerland, Germany, Malta, and Gibraltar.

Between 1849 and 1853, the First Presidency and the Twelve also sent elders to South Africa, Jamaica, India, Siam, China, Chile, Australia, French Polynesia, and the Sandwich Islands (Hawaii). Though courageously undertaken, these missions were not particularly successful, except for Hawaii and French Polynesia. Nonetheless, Church leaders and members were determined to follow the Lord's command to take the gospel to all the world.

Europe proved to be the Church's most fertile international mission field throughout the rest of the nineteenth century. But not all of Europe proved equally ready for the gospel. The British Mission prospered until about 1870, when conversions declined. The Scandinavian Mission did next best, primarily because Denmark had comparatively greater religious freedom than the rest of Europe when missionaries first arrived in 1850. Switzerland was third; there again religious liberty, at least from 1864, made possible a greater harvest. In other European countries a lack of legal provisions for religious freedom combined with religious persecution from state-sponsored churches and police harassment to discourage investigators and missionaries alike. And if most of Europe was hard, the rest of the world was more difficult still. The only nineteenth-century exceptions were among Polynesians in French Polynesia, Hawaii, New Zealand, and Samoa. Not until after World War II and then the Cold War did changes in religious, political, and social conditions make preaching the gospel possible in much of Europe and the rest of the world.

Next to the two apostolic missions to Britain, the most remarkable event of nineteenth-century international Church history was the gathering to Zion of about 85,000 Saints from their homelands. Some 95 percent of them were from Europe. Though European Church units suffered from the steady drain of emigration, the influx of European Saints to Deseret provided a strong population base, a variety of skilled workers, and many loyal followers and stalwart Church leaders. More than half of the Latter-day Saints in Utah between 1870 and the end of the century were either British-born themselves or the children of British converts.[5] British immigrants composed and wrote more than half of the Latter-day Saint hymns. Such areas as "Little Scandinavia" in Sanpete County, Utah, were strongholds of cultural richness and valiant Saints. Countless immigrants contributed their skills and spiritual gifts to the fold of Christ.

Building Zion in Europe

Beginning early in the twentieth century, Church leaders began urging Saints to build Zion in their home countries. At first this change was an economic necessity: Church-sponsored colonization in "Zion" had ended, and even Church-subsidized industries and businesses, such as sugar production, did not provide sufficient employment to absorb continued immigration to the Intermountain West. President Joseph F. Smith, visiting Europe in 1906, urged Saints to stay and build up their branches and districts. European Mission presidents echoed these instructions through the *Millennial Star* in succeeding years. Thus emigration soon fell from its nineteenth-century pace.[6]

During the Great War (World War I), Latter-day Saint emigration stopped almost entirely. But in the years between the two World Wars, hosts of Saints on their own and without Church encouragement or sponsorship, made their way to the United States. Still, at least half of the European members stayed in their home branches. During the Great Depression, Utah held out little hope for employment. In fact, this was a time of migration from Utah and other predominantly Latter-day Saint areas to such places as California, primarily for economic reasons. In 1939, World War II halted emigration altogether. After the war another surge of emigration from Europe carried many Latter-day Saints to the United States.

In the 1950s circumstances were right for adding to the Church's teaching on gathering articulated by President Joseph F. Smith in 1906. President David O. McKay, who took office in 1951, had visited all the missions of the Church in 1920 and 1921 and, as British Mission president in the 1920s, had successfully implemented the slogan of "Build Zion in Britain." President McKay flew to Europe by jet eight times during the 1950s and visited all the other world regions at least once during the same decade. On his travels, he shared his international vision for the Church: The Church would bring Zion to the people. Members in other lands would have wards and stakes, the scriptures and curriculum in their own language, leadership training, meetinghouses, visits from general authorities, and, most significant, temples of their own. From 1950 to 1970, President McKay made good on these promises in Europe and laid the groundwork for similar development in other countries.

By the 1970s the doctrine was established. Building Zion now meant stakes in every land, not emigration to Utah. Subsequent Church presidents Joseph Fielding Smith, Harold B. Lee, and especially Spencer W. Kimball preached and implemented the doctrine of global Zion.

Cultural Adaptations and Challenges

The Lord Jesus Christ taught that the gospel net would gather fish of every kind (see Matthew 13:47). To preach the gospel to every nation and tongue has not been an easy assignment. Often we struggle to learn new languages and cope with cultural traditions different from our own—and each other. Gradually the Church is learning valuable lessons. We now know that we can achieve doctrinal and ecclesiastical unity while allowing and even promoting cultural diversity.

Nowhere do latter-day scriptures mandate that Saints adopt an American lifestyle. Elder John H. Groberg has said: "Our prime role . . . is not to teach people English or how to become American. Gospel standards and the message of the Atonement and the Restoration don't vary from language to language."[7] Our leaders constantly emphasize teaching the gospel principles and ordinances in their intended simplicity. Elder Dean L. Larsen explained why: "The segmenting biases that worked such a destructive influence in the church of Paul's day cannot be allowed to take root in this dispensation. . . . Latter-day Saints [must] rise above interests of nationality, culture, tradition, and politics to a higher view of their joint membership in God's eternal kingdom. This will be an ever-present challenge in a worldwide Church. To be 'fellowcitizens with the saints, and of the household of God' (Eph. 2:19) should be regarded as a privilege and blessing that supersedes all others."[8]

This ideal has been a challenge to Latter-day Saint congregations in all countries, Europe included. From the 1960s on, increasing numbers of workers, refugees, and asylum seekers have spread into western Europe. Some have accepted the gospel and joined the Church, but as cultural outsiders, they have not always been welcomed immediately into local branches and wards. Accepting others into the household of faith continues as a permanent and important endeavor.

Elder Dallin H. Oaks has explained what our missionaries can accomplish as ambassadors of peace between nations:

"Like the church that sends them forth, our missionaries have no political agenda and no specific program for disarmament or reduction of forces. They circulate no petitions, advocate no legislation, support no candidates. They are the Lord's servants, and his program for world peace depends on righteousness, not rhetoric. His methods involve repentance and reformation, not placards and picketing.

"By preaching righteousness, our missionaries seek to treat the causes of war. They preach repentance from personal corruption, greed, and oppression because only by individual reformation can we overcome corruption and oppression by groups or nations. By inviting all to repent and come unto Christ, our missionaries are working for peace in this world by changing the hearts and behavior of individual men and women."[9]

Elder Boyd K. Packer illustrates how the message of the gospel may be adapted to all cultures and languages: "Several years ago I was assigned to go to Germany to take care of some important Church business. As I looked forward to that assignment, I worried a great deal. I knew there would be some very important interviews and that I do not speak German. I knew that most of those with whom I would conduct the Church business did not speak English. I felt helpless. After taking care of some work in English for about two weeks, I was finally on the plane to Germany. As I sat there pondering and praying, the voice of the Lord came into my mind, and gave me some instructions. You know, the Lord doesn't speak in either English or German, and he can speak pure intelligence into our minds without passage of time. The message was something like this: 'What are you worried about? There is another language, the language of the Spirit. Those brethren will know that language. You know the language. There will be no problem.' I was greatly comforted. And I had a great experience on that occasion.

"As a witness that there is that universal language, the language of the Spirit, since then I have never been very anxious when I have had to go into other countries. Sometimes we will visit among people of seven or eight languages on one trip. But always there is that language of the Spirit."[10]

A high priority for Church leaders is to take the holy scriptures to all nations (D&C 90:10–11). Members of the First Presidency and the Twelve serve as a scripture committee to oversee translation of the Book of Mormon, the Doctrine and Covenants, and the Pearl of Great Price into as many of the world's languages as possible. The Church's translation projects do not include the Bible because most nations already have the Bible available in native languages. The *Church News* reported in 1992: "Church leaders have expressed a debt of gratitude and love to members of Bible societies who have literally dedicated their lives to the translation of the Bible into new languages."[11]

Prophetic Promises

The Lord has assured the Saints through his servants that his kingdom shall not fail. The Prophet Joseph Smith was adamant in his claim: "The truth of God will go forth boldly, . . . till it has penetrated every continent, visited every clime, swept every country, and sounded in every ear, till the purposes of God shall be accomplished, and the Great Jehovah shall say the work is done."[12]

The scriptures are replete with these same promises. Just before his ascension, Jesus Christ said to his apostles: "Go ye therefore, and teach all nations" (Matthew 28:19). To members of the restored Church, the Lord declared: "Zion shall flourish, and . . . be an ensign unto the people, and there shall come unto her out of every nation" (D&C 64:41–42). He instructed the Prophet Joseph: "Send forth the elders of my church unto the nations which are afar off; unto the islands of the sea; send forth unto foreign lands; call upon all nations" (D&C 133:8).

None of this expansion of the gospel into the world will be achieved without the dedication of hundreds of thousands of the Lord's servants, each willing to do his or her part. Increasingly, many missionaries serve in their own country. "For behold, the Lord doth grant unto all nations, of *their own nation and tongue,* to teach his word, yea, in wisdom, all that he seeth fit that they should have" (Alma 29:8; emphasis added).

President Spencer W. Kimball taught us that we must "lengthen our stride" and "increase our vision." In 1974, soon after he became president of the Church, President Kimball issued his clarion call to the Saints.[13] "Our goal is nothing less than the penetration of the entire world. . . . We are not promised that the whole world will believe. Evangelization of the world does not mean that all men will respond, but all men must be given the opportunity to respond as they are confronted with the Christ."[14]

President Kimball's challenge had an immediate effect. Thousands of new missionaries, a large number of them from other lands, entered their fields of labor. Many new lands were opened. Elder W. Grant Bangerter stated in 1977, "We suddenly find ourselves in a new era of the gospel. The members of the Church should recognize it for what it is. These years are decisive!"[15]

In his great sermon, President Kimball promised that all nations would reap immeasurable blessings for accepting representatives of the Lord's true Church: "I am positive that the blessings of the Lord will attend every country which opens its gates to the gospel of Christ. Their blessings will flow in education, and culture, and faith, and love. . . . There will come prosperity to the nations, comfort and luxuries to the people, joy and peace to all recipients, and eternal life to those who accept and magnify it."[16]

Beginning in 1989, revolution—for the most part so comparatively peaceful that it was called the Velvet Revolution in Czechoslovakia—

spread through the Communist nations of eastern Europe. It inspired new hope for freedom and human rights throughout the world, particularly in Central America and Africa. Members of the Church rejoiced and acknowledged the hand of the Lord. Early in that revolution, Church leaders, including Thomas S. Monson of the First Presidency, obtained permission for missionaries to enter the previously closed German Democratic Republic. President Monson spoke of those events: "The bright light of day had dawned. The gospel of Jesus Christ would now be carried to the millions of people in that nation. . . . As I reflect on these events, my thoughts turn to the Master's words, 'In nothing doth man offend God, or against none is his wrath kindled, save those who confess not his hand in all things' (D&C 59:21). I confess the hand of God in the miraculous events pertaining to the Church in the German Democratic Republic."[17]

The history of The Church of Jesus Christ of Latter-day Saints in Europe bears witness that the Lord answered the solemn prayer of the Prophet Joseph Smith given at the dedication of the Church's first temple in Kirtland, Ohio: "Remember the kings, the princes, the nobles, and the great ones of the earth, and all people, and the churches, all the poor, the needy, and afflicted ones of the earth; that their hearts may be softened when thy servants shall go out from thy house, O Jehovah, to bear testimony of thy name; that their prejudices may give way before the truth, and thy people may obtain favor in the sight of all; that all the ends of the earth may know that we, thy servants, have heard thy voice, and that thou hast sent us" (D&C 109:55–57).

NOTES

1 Ezra Taft Benson, *The Teachings of Ezra Taft Benson* (Salt Lake City: Bookcraft, 1988), 571.

2 These are stanzas from a hymn called "We Shall See Him Again," which was first published in *The Evening and the Morning Star* 1 (August 1832): 8. It was included in the first hymnal published by the Church in 1835 and also in the later Manchester Hymnal.

3 Wilford Woodruff, in Conference Report, April 1898, 57; spelling standardized.

4 Joseph Smith, *History of The Church of Jesus Christ of Latter-day*

Saints, 7 vols., 2d rev. ed., edited by B. H. Roberts (Salt Lake City: The Church of Jesus Christ of Latter-day Saints), 2:489.

5 Dean L. May, "A Demographic Portrait of the Mormons, 1830–1980," in Thomas G. Alexander and Jessie L. Embry, eds., *After 150 Years: The Latter-day Saints in Sesquicentennial Perspective* (Provo, Utah: Charles Redd Center for Western Studies, 1983), 39–69.

6 Thomas G. Alexander, *Mormonism in Transition: A History of the Latter-day Saints, 1890–1930* (Urbana, Ill.: University of Illinois Press, 1986), 79–84, 198–201, 237–38.

7 Giles H. Florence Jr., "City of Angels," *Ensign* 22 (September 1992): 36.

8 Dean L. Larsen, "The Challenges of Administering a Worldwide Church," *Ensign* 4 (July 1974): 22.

9 Dallin H. Oaks, in Conference Report, April 1990, 94.

10 Boyd K. Packer, "Language of the Spirit," *New Era* 7 (March 1977): 4.

11 "'All People' to Receive LDS Scriptures," *Church News,* 8 Feb. 1992, 3.

12 Smith, *History of the Church,* 4:540.

13 Spencer W. Kimball, "'When the World Will Be Converted,'" *Ensign* 4 (October 1974): 2–14.

14 Spencer W. Kimball, *The Teachings of Spencer W. Kimball,* ed. Edward L. Kimball (Salt Lake City: Bookcraft, 1982), 545.

15 W. Grant Bangerter, in Conference Report, October 1977, 39.

16 Kimball, *Teachings of Spencer W. Kimball,* 584–86.

17 Thomas S. Monson, in Conference Report, April 1989, 69.

CHAPTER 3

Apostolic Missions to the British Isles

JUNE 1837   HEBER C. KIMBALL IS CALLED TO LEAD
FIRST MISSION TO ENGLAND

30 JULY 1837   FIRST CONVERTS ARE BAPTIZED IN PRESTON,
LANCASHIRE, ENGLAND

SUMMER 1838   ENTIRE QUORUM OF THE TWELVE IS CALLED
ON MISSION TO GREAT BRITAIN

26 APRIL 1839   MEMBERS OF TWELVE ASSEMBLE AT TEMPLE
SITE IN FAR WEST TO FULFILL PROPHECY
BEFORE DEPARTING FOR ENGLAND

APRIL 1840   FIRST CONFERENCE IS HELD BY APOSTLES IN
ENGLAND

MAY 1840   FIRST ISSUE OF THE *MILLENNIAL STAR* IS
PUBLISHED

JUNE 1840   FIRST BRITISH SAINTS EMIGRATE TO
AMERICA

APRIL 1841   CONFERENCE IS HELD BEFORE THE TWELVE
LEAVE GREAT BRITAIN

he first apostolic mission to England began with a prophecy for Canada and a crisis in Kirtland. In April 1836 Elder Heber C. Kimball pronounced a blessing on Parley P. Pratt. He prophesied that Elder Pratt would find in Toronto, Canada, "a people prepared for the fulness of the gospel" and that "from the things growing out of this mission, shall the fulness of the gospel spread into England, and cause a great work to be done in that land."[1]

In Toronto, Elder Pratt encountered a group known as the Seekers. They had long been discussing principles of religion together, hoping to find or establish a church built on New Testament doctrines and practices. Prominent among them was John Taylor, a former Methodist preacher and a recent immigrant from England. For two weeks Elder Pratt taught them from the scriptures; most of the group, convinced that his message represented the gospel of Christ restored, accepted baptism. From Toronto the message spread to neighboring communities. Before long Elder Orson Hyde joined Elder Pratt in Canada. Their mission ended in late autumn 1836. In only a few months more than 200 converts had

Heber C. Kimball

been baptized, several branches established, and John Taylor appointed as presiding elder in that region. Elder Kimball's 1836 prophecy was fulfilled in every way. From this mission came four of the original missionaries to Britain in 1837; two elders who introduced the gospel to Scotland in 1840; and John Taylor, who returned to Great Britain as an apostle-missionary in 1840 and eventually became the third president of the Church.

Elder Pratt and Elder Hyde returned to Kirtland to find the Church suffering from apostasy, which grew to epidemic proportions by the spring of 1837. The Church-sponsored bank, the Kirtland Safety Society, failed along with most other banks in Ohio during the nationwide panic of early 1837. Unaware of national economic trends, some members blamed Joseph Smith and other leaders for their financial problems. Backbiting against the Prophet fed upon itself and drew into apostasy nearly a third of the membership of the Church, including four members of the Quorum of the Twelve.[2]

During this crisis, the Lord revealed to Joseph Smith that "something new must be done for the salvation of [my] Church."[3] On Sunday, 4 June 1837, Joseph Smith confided to Heber C. Kimball in the Kirtland Temple: "Brother Heber, the Spirit of the Lord has whispered to me: 'Let my servant Heber go to England and proclaim my Gospel, and open the door of salvation to that nation.'"[4] Heber felt overwhelmed, keenly aware of his limited education and lack of refinement. "The idea of being appointed to such an important office and mission was almost more than I could bear up under," he wrote later. "I felt my weakness and unworthiness."[5] But calling upon God for strength, he soon felt encouraged and eager. "I felt an ardent desire that my fellow creatures in other lands, as well as those of the land of my birth, might hear the sound of the everlasting gospel, obey its requisitions, [and] rejoice in the fullness and blessings thereof."[6]

Elder Kimball selected as companions a close friend, Willard Richards, a member of six months who had already served a mission in the eastern states, and Joseph Fielding, a native of England and a newcomer to Kirtland from the recent Canadian converts. When Elder Kimball was being set apart on 11 June, Elder Orson Hyde stepped into the room. Upon his return from Canada, Elder Hyde had succumbed to the spirit of apostasy rampant in Kirtland. In tears, Elder Hyde then and there requested forgiveness and a chance to accompany Elder Kimball and his companions. The First Presidency gladly acceded. Thus two apostles, Elder Kimball and Hyde, led this first foreign mission. Before they sailed for Britain, they were joined in New York by three other Canadian converts: Isaac Russell, John Goodson, and John Snyder. Like all missionaries of this period, they traveled without purse or scrip. They sought donations from Church members and others, even to pay their passage.

Planting the Seeds in England

The voyage across the Atlantic, begun on 22 June, took only eighteen days instead of the usual five to six weeks. The *Garrick* docked at Liverpool, main port of what was then the most powerful nation in the

THE BRITISH ISLES, 1840

North
Atlantic
Ocean

SCOTLAND

North
Sea

Glasgow
Edinburgh

Alston

Loughbrickland

Milnthorpe
ENGLAND

Newry

Isle
of Man
Douglas

Chatburn and
Downham

Preston
Manchester

IRELAND

Liverpool
Stoke-on-Trent

POTTERIES

Irish

Birmingham

WALES
HEREFORDSHIRE

Sea

Hereford
Bedford

Merthyr Tydfil
Ledbury

Bristol
London

English Channel

| 0 | 50 | 100 miles |
| 0 | 50 | 100 kms |

world. Britain's industrial supremacy was due mainly to the Industrial Revolution, which had begun in England in the late eighteenth century. Its most impressive developments occurred after 1815, when the invention of the steam engine transformed the cotton and textile industries. By 1837 such by-products of the Industrial Revolution as inadequate housing, poor sanitation, and oppressive working conditions plagued English cities. The missionaries were often appalled at the general squalor.[7] Nonetheless, these conditions and the economic depression of the late 1830s created hardship and the accompanying desire for change that led to an interest in religion. Most who joined the Church in the early years were factory workers or farmers with little material wealth.

Another factor that favored missionary work in England was that nation's religious freedom. Since the Glorious Revolution of 1689, the British had been free to choose religious affiliations other than the Church of England. Under the law, any qualified person could apply for a minister's license and be protected from persecution.

A religious awakening was sweeping Britain in the 1830s. Numerous denominations, such as the Methodists, already had sizable constituencies. Scores of other nonconformist groups and dissenters from the Church of England sprang up all over England in the 1830s. Many who were earnestly seeking the primitive religion of the New Testament found what they were looking for in The Church of Jesus Christ of Latter-day Saints. As LDS historian Malcolm Thorp observed: "Many people in Britain were indeed ripe for the harvest not only during the years of the apostolic mission but for many years thereafter, and between 1837 and 1852 the total number of conversions reached 57,000."[8]

At Liverpool the seven missionaries waited three days for their trunks to clear customs. "We remain in prayer and council most of the time," Elder Kimball recorded in his journal.[9] They confirmed their decision to move on to Preston, Lancashire, a crowded, grimy, industrial city of 45,000 people about thirty miles northeast of Liverpool. One missionary, Joseph Fielding, had written ahead to his brother, a reformed minister in Preston, and had been praying that his brother and other relatives would be prepared to hear the gospel.

Upon arriving in Preston on Saturday, 22 July 1837, Joseph immediately sought out his brother, the Reverend James Fielding, while the

Joseph Fielding

others waited in the street. Heber C. Kimball noticed a general election banner with the slogan, "Truth will prevail." "Amen! So let it be," he said aloud, expressing their own high hopes of success.[10]

Joseph Fielding returned with the good news that his brother wanted to hear their message. That evening in James Fielding's parlor, "we gave . . . a short account of the object of our mission and the great work which the Lord had commenced," Heber recorded. The Reverend James Fielding invited the missionaries to address his congregation the next day at the afternoon Sabbath meeting. Vauxhall Chapel was filled to capacity, and the parishioners responded with great enthusiasm, for they had heard of the Restoration already: their minister had read his brother's letters from the pulpit. The Lord had opened the way, and when Elder Kimball declared that an angel had returned to earth with the fulness of the everlasting gospel and urged his listeners to repent and prepare for the Lord's second coming, "they cried glory to God to think that the Lord had sent His servant to them."[11]

On that same day, in Ohio, the Lord revealed to the Prophet Joseph

Missionaries at Vauxhall Chapel, 1930

that the Twelve Apostles were to take the gospel to all the world. Even though it would mean "much tribulation," the Lord promised that "in whatsoever place ye shall proclaim my name an effectual door shall be opened unto you, that they may receive my word" (D&C 112:19).

He had opened a door in Preston, England. The Reverend James Fielding invited them to speak again that night and then again the following Wednesday. When Elder Hyde addressed the audience, "the power of God rested down on the congregation and many [were] pricked to the heart."[12] James Fielding, realizing he was losing his flock and not himself converted, forbade the elders to teach in his chapel. Nevertheless, they were invited to two and three homes each evening. Many believed and asked for baptism.

On Saturday, 29 July, the missionaries confronted their most vigorous opponents. "By this time, the adversary of souls began to rage," reported Elder Kimball, "and he felt a determination to destroy us before we had fully established the gospel in that land; and the next morning I witnessed such a scene of satanic power and influence as I shall never forget while memory lasts."[13] Elder Isaac Russell had come into Elder Kimball and Elder Hyde's room to ask for a blessing. Elder Kimball

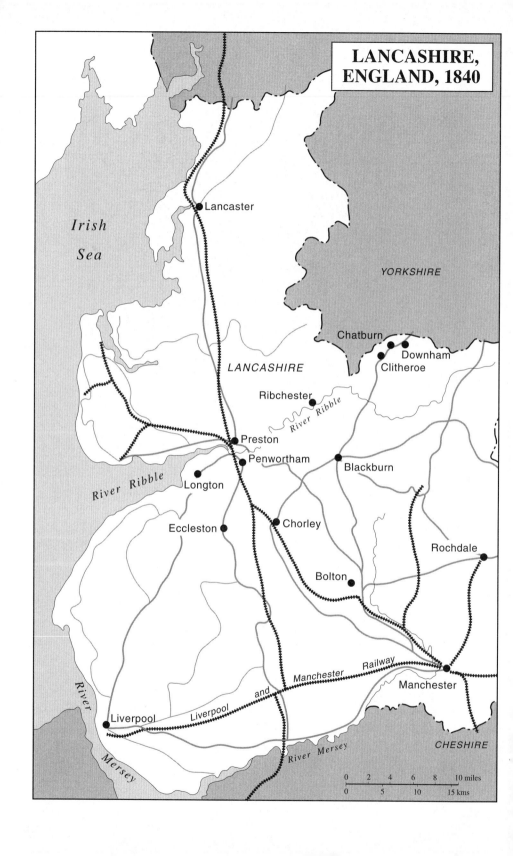

LANCASHIRE, ENGLAND, 1840

Irish

Sea

Lancaster

YORKSHIRE

Chatburn

Downham

Clitheroe

LANCASHIRE

Ribchester

River Ribble

Preston

Penwortham

Blackburn

River Ribble

Longton

Eccleston

Chorley

Rochdale

Bolton

Railway

Manchester

and

Manchester

Liverpool

Liverpool

CHESHIRE

River

River Mersey

Mersey

| 0 | 2 | 4 | 6 | 8 | 10 miles |

| 0 | 5 | 10 | 15 kms |

recorded in his journal: "I was struck with a great force by some invisible power and fell senseless on the floor as if I had been shot, and the first thing that I recollected was, that I was supported by Brothers Hyde and Russell, who were beseeching a throne of grace in my behalf. They then laid me on the bed, but my agony was so great that I could not endure, and I was obliged to get out, and fell on my knees and began to pray. I then sat on the bed and could distinctly see the evil spirits, who foamed and gnashed their teeth upon us. We gazed upon them about an hour and a half, and I shall never forget the horror and malignity depicted on the countenances of these foul spirits, and any attempt to paint the scene which then presented itself, or portray the malice and enmity depicted in their countenances would be vain."[14]

Joseph Smith rejoiced when he learned of this satanic manifestation. As he explained later to Elder Kimball: "It gave me great joy, for I then knew that the work of God had taken root in the land. It was this that caused the devil to make a struggle to kill you."[15]

Despite the terrors of the morning, the brethren proceeded to the River Ribble, which ran through Preston. A large crowd of onlookers gathered to watch. "Two of the candidates who were changing their clothes and preparing for baptism at the distance of several rods from the place where I was standing in the water," wrote Elder Kimball, "ran with all their might to the water, each wishing to be baptized first."[16] The younger one, George D. Watt, won the race and was baptized first. Nine were baptized that day, including a woman with incurable tuberculosis. Heber had promised her that if she were baptized she would live. She began to improve immediately, later emigrated to Utah, and lived to age eight-two among the Saints.

The next morning, after another baptismal service, Elder Kimball sent delegations to two more communities. Elders Russell and Snyder went to Alston, where Russell had relatives, and Elders Richards and Goodson traveled to Bedford with a letter of introduction from Joseph Fielding to his brother-in-law, the Reverend Timothy Matthews. "Thus the work of the Lord commenced in that land," exulted Elder Kimball, "a work which shall roll forth, not only in [England] but upon all the face of the earth, even 'in lands and isles unknown.'"[17]

Great Harvest in Preston and Surrounding Communities

The next weekend the three missionaries remaining in Preston confirmed nearly fifty persons and held their first sacrament meeting.

Elder Kimball baptized a young woman, Jennetta Richards, from
Walkerford, a nearby village. Jennetta convinced her father, a Methodist
minister, to open his church to Elder Kimball. When Heber arrived in the
village, John Richards treated his American guest with exceptional hos-
pitality. Heber preached three times that Sunday and recorded, "My hear-
ers seemed to manifest great interest in the things which I laid before
them. Nearly the whole congregation shed tears of joy."[18] He preached
three more times the following week. When six individuals requested
baptism, however, the Reverend John Richards closed his chapel to further preaching, although he continued to treat his visitor with respect
and kindness. As in Preston, Heber accepted invitations to preach in private homes. "The Lord was with me on my right hand and on my left."[19]

One night Elder Kimball was prompted to return to Preston by a
vision of a man telling him he was needed there. Awaiting him was an
important letter from Kirtland and some business. This done, he
returned with Elder Hyde to Walkerford to preach. Thus began Elder
Kimball's pattern of traveling back and forth to country villages from
Preston. In both city and village the call from interested persons was so
great that the three missionaries in Preston simply could not respond to
all requests. Every day they taught and baptized, despite opposition from
the local clergy. "The Standard is planted in the Land and they can't Root
it up for it has become so powerful, and it is spreading," Heber wrote his
wife. "Love casts out fear. I feel firm in the Lord, I never enjoyed myself
better than I do now."[20]

The Preston Saints met in the open air at first, but in the cooler
weather of September the brethren obtained a license to meet in a large
renovated meeting hall used for temperance meetings and preaching.
Once used for cock fighting, it was still called the Cock Pit. At a special
conference of nearly 150 members held on 8 October 1837, several new
brethren were ordained to priesthood offices and five branches were created. Each branch held Thursday prayer meetings separately, and on

Sundays all gathered in the Cock Pit to partake of the sacrament and receive general instruction.

In ensuing months, numerous new branches were established in ten villages. In his journal Elder Kimball often recorded that he felt the Holy Spirit guiding him what to say and do. Years later he recalled: "I was humble, knew nothing else but to trust in God alone . . . and his angels truly went with me."[21]

On Christmas Day 1837 the brethren convened a conference in Preston. More than 300 people from Preston and branches throughout Lancashire gathered in the Cock Pit. The apostles ordained numerous brethren, blessed approximately 100 children, and conducted other business.

Early in 1838 Elders Kimball and Hyde, on the advice of Joseph Smith, determined to leave England in April after holding a final conference. Their plan was to return to Britain as soon as possible with the missionary force of the entire Quorum of the Twelve. In their circuits to the numerous branches they continued to baptize in huge numbers. After a last visit and a great outpouring of the Spirit in Downham and Chatburn, they found saying farewell very hard. Elder Kimball wrote: "These towns seemed to be affected from one end to the other; parents called their children together, spoke to them of the subjects upon which I had preached, and warned them against swearing and all other evil practices, and instructed them in their duty, . . . etc. [T]he hearts of the people appeared to be broken, and the next morning they were all in tears, thinking they should see my face no more. When I left them my feelings were such as I cannot describe. As I walked down the street, followed by numbers, the doors were crowded by the inmates of the houses, waiting to bid us a last farewell . . . in sobs and broken accents. . . . [W]e felt as if the place was holy ground. The Spirit of the Lord rested down upon us, and I was constrained to bless that whole region of country."[22]

Labors in Alston and Bedford

Meanwhile, beyond Preston, Elders Isaac Russell and John Snyder began their labors in the beautiful little market town of Alston, set on a hill about forty miles from the Scottish border. Within a month they baptized enough converts to organize a branch there. But when local clergy vehemently opposed their work, Elder Snyder "became discouraged and could not preach and became like a drone," recorded Elder Kimball.[23] Elder Snyder returned to Preston and soon sailed for home. Elder Russell pursued valiantly his lonely mission in Alston and struggled to keep the little branch of sixty souls together. Sadly, he later apostatized during the 1838–39 persecutions in Missouri and wrote bitter letters to Alston members, negating much of the good he had done there.

In Bedford, to the south, Elders Willard Richards and John Goodson met with some success and then encountered opposition from local clergy. The Reverend Timothy Matthews, brother-in-law of Joseph Fielding, opened his chapel to the missionaries and even considered being baptized himself, but becoming confused about some deeper doctrine taught by Elder Goodson, he turned away, closed his church to the missionaries, and opposed their every effort after that. John Goodson, like John Snyder in Alston, became discouraged and returned to Preston. He and Snyder sailed to America on the same ship. Elder Richards stayed on alone in Bedford for the next five months, fasting and praying for the Lord's help. Encouraged by Elder Kimball, Elder Richards expanded his work into surrounding villages. When he finally left Bedford in March 1838, he had established two branches of the Church in the vicinity.

The Transition

The conference preceding the departure of Elders Kimball, Hyde, and Russell convened in Preston on 8 April 1838. Of the original seven missionaries, Elders Fielding and Richards would remain to preside over the mission until the apostles' return. Elder Kimball called Joseph Fielding as mission president with Willard Richards and convert William Clayton from Penwortham as counselors. Approximately 700 members were present, representing twenty-six branches. More than 1,500 individuals had been baptized during this nine-month period.

The next day, Elder Heber C. Kimball's mind wandered back to "the peculiar feelings I had when I traveled from Liverpool to Preston some months before. Then I was a stranger in a strange land, and had nothing to rely upon but the kindness and mercy of that God who had sent me there. . . . [Now] I had hundreds of brethren to whom I was united in bonds the most endearing and sacred, and who loved me as their own souls." Heber knew the change was nothing short of miraculous. "[M]y soul was humbled within me, and I had to exclaim, 'Surely this is the Lord's doings, and marvelous in my eyes!'"[24]

Elders Fielding, Richards, and Clayton held the infant Church in England together from 1838 to 1840. About 800 more members were baptized during those two years, but some were excommunicated for apostasy. Years later Joseph Smith's *History of the Church* described the period as "a general time of pruning in England." What opposition from the clergy had not prevented, apostasy might. "The powers of darkness raged, and it seemed as though Satan was fully determined to make an end of the work in that kingdom."[25] At first the presidency confined their work to visiting and stabilizing the branches. But by the fall of 1838 they were again proselyting as well and directing the labors of other missionaries.

Elder William Clayton, one of the first converts in England, was particularly successful in extending the work to Manchester, one of England's largest, most industrialized cities. Clayton selflessly left his family in Penwortham and labored nearly two years in Manchester "without purse or scrip." He described his sense of discipleship in a letter to Elder Richards: "I feel I am not my own. I am bought with a price, even the blood of Jesus Christ, and as a servant I must soon give up my account. I desire and strive, brethren, to keep my account right with the Lord every day that I may meet him with joy."[26] Before he left Manchester, the branch in that city numbered about 240, rivaling the number in Preston.[27]

The two other members of the mission presidency were single when they began their missions, and they married English converts during this period. Elder Joseph Fielding married Hannah Greenwood, and Elder Willard Richards married Jennetta Richards, the daughter of the Reverend John Richards of Walkerford.[28]

Preparations for the Apostles' Second Mission Abroad

When Elders Kimball and Hyde arrived in Kirtland in May 1838, they found few Saints there. The First Presidency had moved to Missouri because of widespread apostasy and persecutions in Ohio. Most faithful Saints were following the Prophet from Kirtland to the new Church headquarters in Far West, Missouri. The two apostles and their families joined the exodus. Once in Missouri, they reported the good news of their mission to the Saints.

The Prophet Joseph was especially pleased. He agreed with Elders Kimball and Hyde that the entire Quorum of the Twelve should go to Britain to further the work; however, four of the original Twelve had fallen into apostasy. That summer of 1838, the Lord instructed: "Let a conference be held immediately; let the Twelve be organized; and let men be appointed to supply the place of those who are fallen. . . . And next spring let them depart to go over the great waters, and there promulgate my gospel, the fulness thereof, and bear record of my name. Let them take leave of my saints in the city of Far West, on the twenty-sixth day of April next, on the building-spot of my house [temple in Far West], saith the Lord." In this revelation, the Lord named "my servant John Taylor, and also my servant John E. Page, and also my servant Wilford Woodruff, and also my servant Willard Richards" to be called to the apostleship (D&C 118:1, 4–6).

Everything seemed in order for the second apostolic mission to the British Isles the following spring. That summer and fall, however, differences festered between the Latter-day Saints and their enemies in Missouri. Open warfare broke out when Governor Lilburn W. Boggs issued his infamous Extermination Order on 27 October 1838, requiring the immediate departure of all Latter-day Saints from the state. Joseph Smith, his counselors, and numerous others were incarcerated in Missouri jails. Other Church leaders apostatized, including Thomas B. Marsh, president of the Twelve. Another apostle, David W. Patten, died in battle defending the Saints. George A. Smith, who at age twenty-one remains the youngest man in this dispensation to be ordained an apostle, filled the vacancy. Three of the Twelve—Brigham Young, Heber C. Kimball, and John Taylor—dedicated their all to rescuing the stricken Saints and delivering them to safety as exiles along the Mississippi River in Illinois.

Despite all the despair, persecution, and chaos, the faithful members of the Twelve did not forget England and their call to a mission there. On 26 April 1839, the day appointed, Brigham Young, Heber C. Kimball, Orson Pratt, John E. Page, John Taylor, Wilford Woodruff, and George A.

Smith met under cover of darkness in Far West, laid a large stone at the temple site, and officially designated this meeting as the beginning of their mission to Britain. Two months later the Saints, under the direction of their escaped prophet, identified a new gathering place at Commerce, Illinois, soon renamed Nauvoo. Thus by June, Church matters had settled enough for the Twelve to embark.

In late June and early July the Prophet met twice with the Twelve to instruct them and to bless the apostles and their wives. On Sunday, 7 July, the Twelve spoke at a farewell meeting. Each bore powerful witness of the work. Then a malaria epidemic hit Nauvoo, postponing the apostles' departure. A month later, some of the brethren, still not fully recovered, nevertheless set out.

In all, nine apostles served in Britain. The Prophet's brother William remained behind to defend the Church as editor of a pro-Latter-day Saint weekly newspaper and member of the Illinois legislature. In 1840 Orson Hyde and John E. Page, who had not yet departed for England, were called instead to dedicate the Holy Land for the return of the Jews. Elder Hyde joined his brethren in England for a few months in 1841 while en route to Jerusalem. Elder Page forsook his mission and later apostatized. The vacancy created in the Quorum of the Twelve by the apostasy of Thomas B. Marsh was filled by Lyman Wight in 1841; after years of misery, Marsh returned to the Church in 1857.

Leaving their families was exceedingly difficult for the missionary apostles. Wilford Woodruff wrote: "Early upon the morning of the 8th of August, I arose from my bed of sickness, laid my hands upon the head of my sick wife, Phoebe, and blessed her. I then departed without food or the necessaries of life. She suffered my departure with the fortitude that becomes a saint, realizing the responsibilities of her companion."[29]

Brigham Young and Heber C. Kimball were also ill and left sick family members behind. As the men drove off, Heber said he felt that "my very inmost parts would melt within me at leaving my family in such a condition, as it were almost in the arms of death. I felt as though I could not endure it. I asked the teamster to stop, and said to Brother Brigham, 'This is pretty tough, isn't it; let's rise up and give them a cheer.' We arose, and swinging our hats three times over our heads, shouted: 'Hurrah, hurrah for Israel.' Vilate, hearing the noise, arose from her bed

Wilford Woodruff

and came to the door. She had a smile on her face. Vilate and Mary Ann Young cried out to us: 'Goodbye, God bless you.' We returned the compliment, and then told the driver to go ahead. After this I felt a spirit of joy and gratitude, having had the satisfaction of seeing my wife standing upon her feet, instead of leaving her in bed, knowing well that I should not see them again for two or three years."[30]

Early Labors of John Taylor and Wilford Woodruff

John Taylor and Wilford Woodruff, the first to leave Nauvoo, arrived in Liverpool in January 1840. They hastened to Preston to meet with the mission presidency. From Preston Elder Taylor returned to Liverpool with Joseph Fielding, and Elder Woodruff traveled south with another missionary, Theodore Turley, to the Staffordshire Potteries.

In Liverpool Elders Taylor and Fielding baptized their first converts the following month, February 1840. Those baptized included the entire family of George Cannon, brother of John Taylor's wife, Leonora. Among them was George Q. Cannon, a boy of twelve, who later became first an

John Taylor

apostle and then counselor to four Church presidents, including his uncle John Taylor. The work in that port city grew so steadily that the members of the Twelve who arrived in Liverpool that April were welcomed by a branch of the Church.

Elder Woodruff successfully organized several branches in the small towns of the Potteries. In March he left Elder Turley in charge of them and heeded a prompting to go farther south to Herefordshire, accompanied by the new convert William Benbow. They contacted William's brother and sister-in-law, John and Jane Benbow and a group of six hundred people who had formed their own religious society called the United Brethren. Eventually the leader of the group, Thomas Kington, and all but one of the six hundred members accepted the restored gospel. Hundreds of others in the vicinity also joined the Church.

As the work prospered, opposition mounted from the local clergy. A constable was sent to arrest Elder Woodruff for preaching without a license, but instead he chose baptism after hearing an inspiring sermon. Later two clerks sent to discover what Elder Woodruff was teaching were

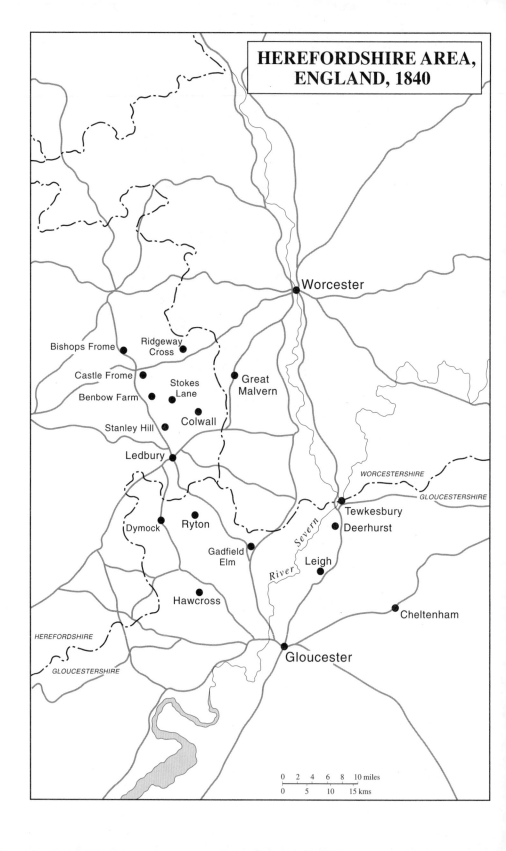

HEREFORDSHIRE AREA,
ENGLAND, 1840

Worcester

Bishops Frome

Ridgeway
Cross

Castle Frome

Stokes
Lane

Great
Malvern

Benbow Farm

Stanley Hill

Colwall

Ledbury

WORCESTERSHIRE

GLOUCESTERSHIRE

Dymock

Ryton

Tewkesbury

Deerhurst

Gadfield
Elm

River

Severn

Leigh

Hawcross

Cheltenham

HEREFORDSHIRE

GLOUCESTERSHIRE

Gloucester

0	2	4	6	8	10 miles
0		5		10	15 kms

baptized as well. Members of the clergy finally wrote to the Archbishop of Canterbury, ecclesiastical head of the Church of England, requesting that he use his influence to ban the Mormons from Britain. But recent British laws prescribed religious tolerance, and the archbishop counseled the ministers to solve the problem by becoming more dedicated pastors. Instead, the clergy preached anti-Mormon sermons and agitated the local press to harass the Latter-day Saints.

Such opposition did not deter Elder Woodruff. Ever since he joined the Church in 1832, he had been an exceptional missionary. He courageously led individuals to the waters of baptism through the midst of mobs. More than once he and his congregations were stoned. Through his and the efforts of many others, some 1,800 people were converted in the three adjoining counties of Hereford, Worcester, and Gloucester. "The whole history of this Herefordshire mission," he wrote, "shows the importance of listening to the still small voice of the spirit of God, and the revelations of the Holy Ghost. The people were praying for light and truth, and the Lord sent me to them."[31]

The Twelve in Great Britain

In April 1840, when the other apostles arrived in England, Brigham Young, the president of the Twelve, summoned the brethren to Preston for a conference. Nearly 1,600 members, representing thirty-three branches, attended. Willard Richards, named an apostle in the 1838 revelation, was ordained to that office. Elders Fielding, Richards, and Clayton were released as the mission presidency, and Brigham Young was sustained as president of the British Mission and of the Twelve. The conference also approved President Young's proposal to publish the Book of Mormon, a hymnbook, and a monthly periodical. Elder Woodruff suggested its title, *The Latter-day Saints' Millennial Star,* and Elder Parley P. Pratt was chosen as editor.

President Young's style of leadership showed "concern for the feelings of others" and an ability to supply "leadership without being overbearing." According to historian Ronald Esplin, "In England, Brigham Young consciously strove to . . . build unity among the apostles and the Saints. . . . Expecting a great deal of himself and others, Young could be both firm and demanding. But rather than dictating to his peers or to the

Brigham Young

Saints, as quorum leader he consciously sought to promote the collegial fellowship that meant so much to him."[32] Brigham Young was also an example of faith. He exercised the gift of healing on many occasions and prayerfully sought revelation to solve problems and direct missionaries where they should labor.

Heber C. Kimball was eager to visit Preston, where he had previously served, to strengthen the Saints who had remained faithful and work to reconvert those who had fallen away on account of persecution and apostasy. Brigham sent Willard Richards to assist Wilford Woodruff in southern England. John Taylor, having had some success in Liverpool with Irish immigrants, sailed with three Irish companions to Ireland. Although they had little success there, they laid an important groundwork. Upon his return to Liverpool, Elder Taylor felt impressed to expand the work to the Isle of Man, where many relatives of his wife, Leonora, lived. He soon baptized several people and organized a branch on that island.

Orson Pratt was assigned to Scotland. In 1839 two Scottish converts—Samuel Mulliner and Alexander Wright—had returned to their homeland from Canada to share the gospel with their families and friends. So a small group of twenty converts awaited Elder Pratt's arrival. Orson organized a branch in Paisley, a few miles from Glasgow, on 8 May 1840. Late that same month he ascended Arthur's Seat, a prominence overlooking Edinburgh, the capital of Scotland, where he dedicated Scotland for the preaching of the gospel. In his prayer he asked for 200 converts. Elder Pratt proselyted vigorously, holding as many as seven street meetings in one day. He also published a pamphlet, called *An Interesting Account of Several Remarkable Visions*, which included the first published account of Joseph Smith's first vision. By the time Elder Pratt left Scotland in March 1841, membership in the Edinburgh Conference numbered 226.

In July Brigham Young sent Elders Heber C. Kimball, Wilford Woodruff, and George A. Smith to open the work in London, the world's most populous and prosperous city. These brethren were awed by the great mass of humanity. London was the only city of the world at that time with more than a million inhabitants. They prayed to preach with power and struggled to secure places to preach to larger audiences. Local officials often curtailed their efforts, and people bent on materialism failed to heed the gospel message. Then one night, remembered Elder George A. Smith, Satan and his legions "fell upon us to destroy our lives and [we] would have been killed, apparently, had not three holy messengers come into the room with light. . . . They laid their hands upon our heads and we were delivered, and that power was broken, so far as we were concerned."[33]

Eventually the brethren made small inroads, converting a few individuals each week, and in February 1841, when their efforts in London drew to a close, they organized the London Conference with 106 members. The apostles left the young Elder Lorenzo Snow from Ohio in charge of the work in the city. The seeds had been well planted, for in succeeding months, the number of conversions swelled manyfold, and Elder Snow presented two beautifully bound copies of the Book of Mormon to Queen Victoria and Prince Albert.

Parley P. Pratt's missionary labors focused on the writing and publishing of Church literature vital to the success of all the missionaries. Besides missionary tracts, Elder Pratt edited the monthly *Millennial Star*, in which the Saints in England read the first published accounts of Joseph Smith's revelations and history. The *Star* also printed general news from the Church in America. And Parley wrote nearly fifty hymns for the new Manchester Hymnal. The Church's 1985 hymnbook opens with one of his enduring and much-loved hymns of the Restoration:

> The morning breaks, the shadows flee;
> Lo, Zion's standard is unfurled!
> The dawning of a brighter day,
> The dawning of a brighter day
> Majestic rises on the world.[34]

Effects of the Mission of the Twelve to Britain

Early in 1841 the Prophet Joseph wrote to the Twelve to return to Nauvoo that spring. Parley P. Pratt remained to edit the *Millennial Star* and preside over the mission, which now had many local missionaries as well as a few American elders. The Church had grown phenomenally in the year between Brigham Young's arrival in April 1840 and the following April, when nearly all the Twelve returned to America. At the conference held in Manchester in April 1841, Church membership in Britain stood at 5,814. Total growth in the year's time was 4,143 new members, 102 elders, 251 priests, 131 teachers, sixty deacons, and two patriarchs.[35] This count did not include converts who had emigrated to America.

The emigration of British Saints to America had begun with the arrival of President Young. On 1 June 1840, Brigham Young and Heber C. Kimball met with forty-six Saints ready to embark from Liverpool. John Moon, a faithful convert from Elder Kimball's previous mission, was appointed to preside over the group during their passage. The Saints in Nauvoo wrote letters to their friends encouraging the gathering. Most British members needed no urging to emigrate, however. They desired to see the Prophet and live in a community of Saints. As President Brigham Young wrote, "They have so much of the spirit of gathering that they would go if they knew they would die as soon as they got there or they knew that the mob would be upon them and drive them as soon as they got there."[36] Approximately 1,000 Saints emigrated by early 1841, and a shipping agency was established to oversee travel arrangements. Over the next decades many thousands more sailed to America.

The 1840–41 apostolic mission was perhaps the single most productive in the Church's history. On no other occasion were so many of the Twelve joined in one missionary endeavor. The trials and sacrifices in Britain united them and proved a signal time of training and maturing. Brigham Young soon needed his strengthened leadership skills in Nauvoo as well as the loyalty of his fellows. The British Mission of 1840–41 assured the Church of strong leadership in the years ahead: four future presidents of the Church served on this mission—Brigham Young, John Taylor, and Wilford Woodruff of the Twelve and Lorenzo Snow, not then an apostle.

When the apostles returned to Nauvoo, the Saints looked to them as proven and trustworthy leaders. In August, Joseph Smith told them that the Council of the Twelve would assume a new leadership role in the Church directly responsible to the First Presidency. They were to supervise Church business in Nauvoo and surrounding regions, previously a responsibility of the Nauvoo high council. Heretofore the duties of the twelve had been restricted to mission fields as a traveling high council. "Emerging from the shadows after their successful British mission, in Nauvoo the Twelve would serve prominently as Joseph Smith's right hand."[37] As president of the Quorum of the Twelve, Brigham Young continued to develop in testimony and leadership so that he was prepared to lead the Church after the martyrdom of Joseph Smith in 1844.

The two apostolic missions to Britain saved the Church from destruction in the successive disasters of expulsion from Ohio, Missouri, and Illinois. Wave after wave of stalwart Saints from abroad bolstered the young Church. "The 4,700 converts who immigrated from England to Nauvoo by 1846 strengthened the church during the Illinois period, and the more than 19,000 British converts who went to Utah between 1847 and 1856 proved a necessary force in taming the desert and establishing a viable Kingdom in the Great Basin."[38] By 1870, some 38,000 British immigrants had come to America and most adults in Utah were natives of the British Isles. Other parts of the world also benefited from the work in Britain. The far-flung British Empire became an avenue for the gospel when British converts emigrated or traveled on business or military duty.

NOTES

1 Parley P. Pratt, *Autobiography of Parley P. Pratt* (Salt Lake City: Deseret Book, 1985), 110.

2 Milton V. Backman Jr., *The Heavens Resound* (Salt Lake City, Deseret Book, 1983), 310–41.

3 Joseph Smith, *History of The Church of Jesus Christ of Latter-day Saints*, 7 vols., 2d rev. ed., edited by B. H. Roberts (Salt Lake City: The Church of Jesus Christ of Latter-day Saints, 1932–51), 2:489.

4 Orson F. Whitney, *Life of Heber C. Kimball*, 3d ed. (Salt Lake City: Bookcraft, 1967), 104.

5 *Heber C. Kimball's Journal* (Salt Lake City: Juvenile Instructor Office, 1882), 10.

6 Ibid., 13.

7 See James B. Allen, Ronald K. Esplin, and David J. Whittaker, *Men with a Mission, 1837–1841: The Quorum of the Twelve Apostles in the British Isles* (Salt Lake City: Deseret Book, 1992), 10–19; Malcolm R. Thorp, "The Setting for the Restoration in Britain: Political, Social, and Economic Conditions," in V. Ben Bloxham et al., eds., *Truth Will Prevail: The Rise of The Church of Jesus Christ of Latter-day Saints in the British Isles, 1837–1987* (West Midlands: Corporation of the President of The Church of Jesus Christ of Latter-day Saints, 1987), 44–70.

8 Malcolm R. Thorp, "'The Field Is White Already to Harvest,'" in Allen et al., *Men with a Mission*, 323. See the same source, pages 323–44, and Malcolm R. Thorp, "The Religious Backgrounds of Mormon Converts in Britain, 1837–1852," *Journal of Mormon History* 4 (1977): 51–65, for a discussion of the religious climate in Britain during this era.

9 Stanley B. Kimball, ed., *On the Potter's Wheel: The Diaries of Heber C. Kimball* (Salt Lake City: Signature Books, 1987), 7; spelling standardized.

10 *Heber C. Kimball's Journal*, 17.

11 Kimball, *On the Potter's Wheel*, 8–9; spelling standardized.

12 Ibid., 9; spelling standardized.

13 *Heber C. Kimball's Journal*, 19–20.

14 Ibid., 20.

15 Whitney, *Life of Heber C. Kimball*, 145–46.

16 *Heber C. Kimball's Journal*, 21.

17 Ibid.

18 Ibid., 24.

19 Kimball, *On the Potter's Wheel*, 12.

20 Heber C. Kimball to Vilate Kimball, 12 November 1837 and 2 September 1837, Archives of The Church of Jesus Christ of Latter-day Saints, Salt Lake City, Utah.

21 *Millennial Star* 25 (17 October 1863): 669.

22 *Heber C. Kimball's Journal*, 37.

23 Kimball, *On the Potter's Wheel*, 18.

24 *Heber C. Kimball's Journal*, 49.

25 Smith, *History of the Church*, 3:162.

26 James B. Allen, *Trials of Discipleship: The Story of William Clayton, a Mormon* (Urbana, Ill.: University of Illinois Press, 1987), 1.

27 James B. Allen and Thomas B. Alexander, eds., *Manchester Mormons: The Journal of William Clayton, 1840 to 1842* (Santa Barbara: Peregrine Smith, 1974).

28 Allen et al., *Men with a Mission*, 61–66.

29 Matthias F. Cowley, *Wilford Woodruff* (Salt Lake City: Bookcraft, 1964), 109.

30 Whitney, *Life of Heber C. Kimball*, 266.

31 Cowley, *Wilford Woodruff*, 120.

32 Ronald K. Esplin, "The 1840–41 Mission to England and the Development of the Quorum of the Twelve," in Richard L. Jensen and Malcolm R. Thorp, *Mormons in Early Victorian Britain* (Salt Lake City: University of Utah Press, 1989), 78.

33 Bloxham et al., *Truth Will Prevail*, 156–57.

34 *Hymns of The Church of Jesus Christ of Latter-day Saints* (Salt Lake City: The Church of Jesus Christ of Latter-day Saints, 1985), no. 1.

35 V. Ben Bloxham, "The Apostolic Foundations, 1840–1841," in Bloxham et al., eds., *Truth Will Prevail*, 149.

36 Leonard J. Arrington, *Brigham Young: American Moses* (New York: Alfred A. Knopf, 1985), 94; spelling standardized.

37 Esplin, "The 1840–41 Mission," 91.

38 Stanley B. Kimball, *Heber C. Kimball: Mormon Patriarch and Pioneer* (Urbana, Ill.: University of Illinois Press, 1981), 48.

CHAPTER 4

The Work Expands: Britain, Scandinavia, and the Continent

1846 THREE APOSTLES ARE SENT TO BRITAIN TO HANDLE MISSION MISMANAGEMENT

1848 DEMOCRATIC REVOLUTIONS ERUPT THROUGHOUT EUROPE

OCTOBER 1849 JOHN TAYLOR, ERASTUS SNOW, AND LORENZO SNOW ARE CALLED TO TAKE THE GOSPEL TO CONTINENTAL EUROPE

1850 THE CHURCH IS ESTABLISHED IN DENMARK, ITALY, AND FRANCE

1851 THE CHURCH IS ESTABLISHED IN SWITZERLAND AND GERMANY

1851 THE BOOK OF MORMON IS PUBLISHED IN DANISH, THE FIRST FOREIGN LANGUAGE TRANSLATION

1852 THE BOOK OF MORMON IS PUBLISHED IN FRENCH, GERMAN, AND ITALIAN

 n the 1840s and 1850s Latter-day Saint missionaries strengthened the Church in England and Scotland and introduced the gospel to Wales, France, Denmark, Sweden, Norway, Germany, Italy, Switzerland, Malta, and Gibraltar. Again, as with the first missions to Britain, the apostles led the way in bringing new souls to the fold of Christ.

Britain, 1841–46

Elder Parley P. Pratt, editor of the *Millennial Star,* presided over the British Mission from April 1841, when Brigham Young and the others of the Twelve returned to Nauvoo, to October 1842. The mission had about ten American and twenty British elders, and through their enthusiastic labors, conversions continued at a rapid pace, miracles abounded, and new communities were opened to the ministry. Parley printed inspiring materials for missionaries and members in the *Star,* including an account of Elder Orson Hyde's labors in Jerusalem. He also transferred the mission offices from Manchester to Liverpool to assist the many Saints emigrating from this seaport city.

By 1842 the Church in England had drawn unwelcome notice. In a letter to Joseph Smith, Elder Pratt reported: "The Church is Generally in union, and increasing in Confidence, and in Numbers; but it makes but slow progress because . . . Discussions, Contentions, Lectures, Sermons, play cards, tracts, Books, Papers, pamphlets, etc., etc. are flooding the Country in Great number, all containing Little else than Lies and foolishness of the Grossest kind against the Cause of truth."[1]

Missionaries and members in Britain also struggled under the harsh, grinding poverty brought on by the Industrial Revolution. Elder Pratt wrote to the Prophet: "Millions of Laborers are out of employ, and are starving in this country, and among others hundreds of the most faithful Saints, and hundreds more are laboring like slaves on about half what they can eat. This pains my heart." Parley longed to "take them all on my shoulders and . . . carry them to Zion; but alas, the means is Wanting." Church leaders encouraged the wealthier Saints to help the less fortunate. They were given recommends to emigrate only if they assisted the needy to pay passage also. "Yet we are enabled to Work the deliverance of many by humbling the rich and exalting the poor," Elder Pratt continued.[2]

When Elder Pratt sailed from Liverpool, he left the mission in the hands of mission clerk Thomas Ward, an Englishman who had assisted him in editing the *Millennial Star.* A year later Joseph Smith sent Reuben Hedlock to preside over the British Mission, and Brother Ward became Elder Hedlock's counselor.

From October 1842 to February 1845, under Elders Ward and Hedlock, Church growth in Britain fell on account of emigration and numerous excommunications. In those formative years, persons considered troublemakers were cut off in an attempt to strengthen and purify the organization. That policy remained in effect in all missions around the world throughout the nineteenth century. Charges leading to excommunication included "neglect," "bad conduct," "apostasy," "adultery or fornication," and "swearing." Also during this time, the 27 June 1844 martyrdom of Joseph Smith, the Prophet, and Hyrum Smith, the Patriarch, rocked the Church.

When Church members in Nauvoo sustained the Twelve Apostles to act in the office of the First Presidency after the martyrdom, President Brigham Young promptly sent Elder Wilford Woodruff to Liverpool. Elders Hedlock and Ward then became President Woodruff's counselors. Elder Woodruff threw himself into the work with his typical devotion. He felt that British laws and culture favored preaching the gospel and generally increased receptivity among the people. He traveled to each conference, or district, to strengthen the members and encourage the missionaries, and baptisms rose to nearly 2,000 in a year's time. Church membership in Britain soared to more than 11,000 souls, despite emigration.

President Woodruff attached great importance to continuing Church publications from Liverpool. He arranged for the publication of the first British edition of the Doctrine and Covenants and printed twenty thousand copies of an official proclamation of the latter-day work to kings and rulers of the world, thus fulfilling a divine mandate (see D&C 124:2–11). In January 1846, Elder Woodruff returned to the States, leaving the British Mission again in the hands of Elders Hedlock and Ward.

Without direct apostolic leadership, the British Mission soon declined. Brigham Young had charged Reuben Hedlock in 1844 to gather funds and set up a shipping agency to assist the British and European Saints in emigrating. Under President Woodruff, mission funds were judiciously managed. But as soon as Elder Hedlock became the presiding officer, he and Elder Ward mismanaged the funds and overextended the agency. They also used considerable money on private affairs. As a result, thousands of dollars worth of funds were squandered or lost. "This [mismanagement] was peculiarly distressing because the money was taken from the hard earnings of many poor people, struggling in the midst of depressed industrial conditions, and was obtained by the pressure of religious influence upon them," lamented Church historian B. H. Roberts.[3]

Word of these financial irregularities reached Brigham Young at Council Bluffs, Iowa, in the summer of 1846. He immediately dispatched three apostles—Orson Hyde, Parley P. Pratt, and John Taylor—to England. They arrived to find that Brother Hedlock had deserted his mission and fled to London. After investigating the situation, the apostles disbanded the stock company and restored order to Church affairs. Elder Hedlock was excommunicated and Elder Ward disfellowshipped. The latter was repentant but took ill and died before he could visit Church officials in America to make restitution and seek forgiveness.

Elder Hyde stayed in Liverpool to edit the *Millennial Star* while Elders Pratt and Taylor traveled the mission, restoring harmony and confidence. In the *Star* Elder Hyde wrote of the Saints' larger unifying purpose: "The time has now come for us to lose sight of our national and political feelings, and unite in one spirit and enterprise, men of every nation, kindred, tongue, and people, . . . and to know no distinction except in character and conduct, and . . . let the kingdoms of this world become the kingdom of our God."[4] Once again apostles had revived and invigorated the work abroad.

A Mighty Harvest in Wales

In early 1845 when Brigham Young sent Wilford Woodruff to England, he also sent Elder Dan Jones, a native of Wales. Dan Jones had been a Mississippi River steamboat captain who transported emigrants upriver from New Orleans to Nauvoo on the *Maid of Iowa.* The captain became a stalwart convert and was among those who accompanied the Prophet Joseph Smith to Carthage Jail. The Prophet promised him that he would survive persecution and fill a mission to his native land. In 1846 Elder Jones became the Church's presiding officer in Wales, and under his inspired leadership lasting through 1849, nearly 4,000 of his countrymen joined the Church. Many prepared to emigrate to Zion.[5]

The first Welsh converts joined the Church during Wilford Woodruff's 1840 ministry to Herefordshire, twenty miles from the English-Welsh border. Missionary work in Wales officially began later that year but only in the English language. Small branches were established in North and South Wales, and some Welsh converts emigrated to America, but Church growth in the coal-mining region of Wales was slow because the gospel was not being preached to the Welsh in their own language. That changed with the arrival of Dan Jones.

Elder Jones wrote at a furious pace, publishing numerous pamphlets in his native tongue. The first year was filled with frustration, but the next year, 1846, doors began to open. He was called to preside, and the work prospered. The missionaries encountered severe persecution from the nonconformist clergy, principally Baptist, and were chagrined by scurrilous anti-Mormon editorializing in the press. When the newspaper editors refused to print anything in defense of the Latter-day Saints, Elder Jones began his own periodical, *Prophwyd y Jubili (Prophet of the Jubilee)*. This publication, along with a stream of pamphlets, led to a lively print war between the Church and its foes, led by Baptist minister W. R. Davies. Davies labeled the Saints "Latter-day Satanists" and frenetically attacked Church doctrines. His diatribes served in many instances to create interest in the Church. Soon more than 100 people were joining the Church every month.

Several persons important in Church history joined during the heyday of the Welsh mission, including William Howells, the first missionary to France; John Parry, who upon arriving in Utah formed a choir, mostly of Welshmen, that became the renowned Mormon Tabernacle Choir; William S. Phillips, who succeeded Dan Jones as the Church's presiding officer in Wales in 1849; John S. Davis, a prolific pamphleteer who also translated the Book of Mormon, the Doctrine and Covenants, and the Pearl of Great Price into Welsh.

Before Elder Jones left Wales, he became the target not only of hostile polemics but of serious threats. Eventually he needed round-the-clock protection. The Welsh Saints loved Captain Jones, as they affectionately nicknamed him, and relied heavily on his testimony and counsel. A large contingent of emigrants accompanied him to Zion when he was released in 1849. Sadly, 20 percent of this company died from cholera on the trip upriver from New Orleans.

Church membership reached its peak in Wales in 1851 with 5,244 members. Conversions continued steadily throughout the 1850s but did not equal the surge of the late 1840s. Dan Jones returned to serve in Wales from 1852 to 1856. The Welsh publication *Prophwyd y Jubili* continued through 1862. Historian Ronald Dennis has noted: "From the mid-1860s until the middle of the twentieth century, very few Welsh converts would come into the Church. Yet, because of the extraordinary success of the Church's early proselytizing efforts in Wales, there are today tens of thousands of Latter-day Saints who can point with pride to a Jones, Thomas, Davis or Williams line on their pedigree charts and thank the Lord for the courage of their ancestors who accepted the restored gospel somewhere in the hills of Wales."[6]

British Mission on a Firm Footing

After the brief ministry of Elders Hyde, Pratt, and Taylor in 1846 and 1847, Brigham Young sent Orson Spencer to preside over the British Mission. Elder Spencer, a college graduate and former Baptist minister, had devoted his scholarly talents to service in the Church since joining in 1841. His wife died at Winter Quarters, Nebraska, shortly before he was called to England. He left his six children, all under thirteen years of age, in the care of a trusted friend. His presidency lasted only until the summer of 1848, when Elder Orson Pratt of the Twelve Apostles arrived in Liverpool to succeed him. Elder Pratt served as mission president until the end of 1850.

The British Mission swelled during this period from 10,894 members in 1846 to 30,747 in 1850.[7] Since the mission began in 1837, an estimated 51,000 had been baptized into the Church in the British Isles. At first most were converts from such splinter groups as the Primitive Methodists and the United Brethren, but these nonconformist chapels were soon closed to LDS missionaries. The elders resorted to open-air preaching in the late 1840s, which attracted a wider audience, and a greater number of converts started to come from the mainstream churches—the Church of England, the Methodists, Baptists, Congregationalists, and Presbyterians, in that order.[8] The years 1846 to 1850 were the zenith of missionary work anywhere in the Church in the nineteenth century.

Elder Orson Pratt particularly instilled zeal among his growing corps of missionaries. It was, he told them, their duty to warn every living soul in Britain within a year. Biographer Breck England observed, "His main voice was the *Millennial Star,* the periodical inaugurated by [his brother] Parley nearly ten years before. It had a big circulation, and the Mormons drank in every word; Orson took over this organ with all the pent-up energy of an evangelist . . . printing a series of pamphlets on . . . Mormonism to be dumped in the laps of the orthodox Christian establishment."[9] Elder Pratt also oversaw the publication of ten thousand hymnbooks, new printings of the Book of Mormon and Doctrine and Covenants, and reams of his own writings on Church doctrines.

The Gospel Is Taken into Europe

Once he had established a refuge for the Saints in the Rocky Mountains, President Brigham Young reestablished the outward reach of the Church. In February 1849 President Young called Charles C. Rich, Lorenzo Snow, Erastus Snow, and Franklin D. Richards, all proven missionaries and leaders, to fill vacancies in the Quorum of the Twelve. In the October 1849 General Conference, the First Presidency called numerous missionaries to foreign fields.

The newly called apostle Franklin D. Richards and seven elders were called to the still strong British Mission. Elder Richards was to aid and eventually replace Orson Pratt. In a general epistle "to the Saints Scattered Throughout the Earth," the First Presidency announced the calling of three other apostles and others to preach on the continent of Europe: "Elder John Taylor, accompanied by Curtis E. Bolton and John Pack, goes to France; Elder Lorenzo Snow to Italy, accompanied by Joseph Toronto; Elder Erastus Snow to Denmark, accompanied by Peter Hanson [Hansen], . . . Elder John Forsgreen [Forsgren] will go out at the same time on a mission to Sweden."[10] Adventure lay ahead for these missionaries who stepped into languages and cultures foreign to them.

This 1849 call coincided with revolution that rocked continental Europe. In February 1848 King Louis Philippe of France had been forced to abdicate. Liberal French views and their accompanying revolution quickly spread to the Austrian Empire, the various German states, the Italian states, Denmark, and other smaller European countries. In nearly every country, however, the uprisings were quashed sooner or later and the former rulers reinstated. But the absolute rule of monarchies and the aristocracy had been challenged, and Europe was no longer the same. These "revolutions that failed" led eventually to the establishment of freedom of the press, freedom of religion, and freedom of assembly in several European nations.

Beginnings in Scandinavia

The earliest Scandinavian converts to the Church were Norwegian immigrants who were baptized in Illinois, Iowa, and Wisconsin in the early 1840s. Traveling elder George Parker Dykes went to Fox River, Illinois, in 1842 and in a year's time organized a branch of fifty-eight. Some of these new Norwegian Saints then visited and converted friends and family in Wisconsin Territory and in Sugar Creek, Iowa, directly across the Mississippi River from Nauvoo. Joseph Smith rejoiced at these conversions and spoke of missionary work being taken to Scandinavia in the near future. One of the Norwegians, Endre Dahl, took to Nauvoo money collected for the temple. "Brother Joseph" met him on the street and invited Brother Dahl to his home. Brother Dahl declined, saying he was "a very simple Norwegian, unworthy to enter a prophet's dwelling." Joseph was deeply touched. Not long afterward, he prophesied to Elder George A. Smith that the Scandinavians would play a significant role in the Church.[11]

Two other Scandinavians, Dane Hans C. Hansen and Swede John E. Forsgren, both sailors, had embraced the gospel in Boston in the early 1840s and migrated to Nauvoo. Brother Hansen wrote of his conversion to his younger brother, Peter O. Hansen, in Copenhagen. Peter, finding no Latter-day Saints in Denmark, set out at once for America and joined the Church after arriving in Nauvoo. After the martyrdom of Joseph Smith, Brigham Young assigned Peter Hansen to work on a Danish translation of the Book of Mormon.

Scandinavia is a general term for the countries of Denmark, Sweden, Norway, and Iceland. Scandinavians descend from both the ancient Norsemen who first settled Iceland in A.D. 870 and the Teutons. Throughout most of the Middle Ages, Denmark, Norway, Iceland, and the southern tip of Sweden were united, usually under Danish royalty. When Denmark supported Napoleon, who was defeated in 1815, Danish rule was ended in Norway, although Iceland remained under Danish control until 1918. Norway was technically part of Sweden until 1905.

Denmark, Scandinavia's smallest country, occupies the Jutland Peninsula, between the tips of Norway and Sweden, and includes some five hundred islands. Seaside terrain defines much of the country: its highest point is only 568 feet above sea level; no Dane lives more than thirty-five miles from the coast. Norway, which shares the Scandinavian peninsula with Sweden, is also a country of coasts. Eleven hundred miles

Erastus Snow

of craggy coastline extend three hundred miles north of the Arctic Circle, and 70 percent of Norway is uninhabitable. Sweden, to the east, is the largest and most populated Scandinavian country. Iceland lies east of Greenland in the north Atlantic Ocean and touches the Arctic Circle.

The 1848 revolutions in Europe coincided with the death of the Danish king, and the Danes seized the opportunity to reform their government. The heir to the throne was not crowned until a new constitution was agreed upon, signed, and proclaimed in June 1849. This constitution secured for the people new freedoms, including freedom of religion—a first in continental Europe. Without it the Church would not have grown so rapidly in Denmark and missionaries would have suffered imprisonment or banishment as did their brethren in other countries on the Continent.

Elder Erastus Snow, a stocky Vermonter, deliberate in speech and action, was only thirty-two when he, as an apostle, was sent with John Forsgren and Peter Hansen to Scandinavia. Elders Snow and Forsgren stopped in England for two months. There they enlisted the aid of George Parker Dykes, now a missionary to Britain, who had been the first elder sent to the Norwegian settlements in Illinois. Meanwhile Elder Hansen went on without them to Denmark and wrote the first LDS tract in Danish: "En Advarsel til Folket" ("A Warning to the People"). He preached to his family and friends but to no avail. Elders Snow, Forsgren, and Dykes joined him in Copenhagen on 14 June 1850 and officially opened the Scandinavian Mission. After a few days Elder Forsgren left on his own for his native Sweden.

The missionaries wasted no time. On their first Sunday in Copenhagen they attended a Baptist meeting of reformer Peter C. Mönster, a dissenter from the state religion (Lutheran) who welcomed them as allies. The elders first taught Mönster's followers in various meetings and then some of them in their homes. In less than two months, baptisms began on 12 August, and a month later the first branch of more than fifty converts was established. Most were former members of Mönster's congregation, although the pastor himself did not accept the gospel. The missionaries also drew converts of German heritage using Elder Orson Hyde's tract "Ein Ruf aus der Wüste" ("A Call from the Wilderness"), written nine years earlier. In time some Lutherans in Copenhagen joined as well. Members of the Copenhagen branch were blessed with many spiritual gifts. "Several manifestations of the power of God, especially in the healing of the sick, strengthened and comforted the believers and inspired them to renewed effort."[12]

In October Elder Snow assigned Elder Dykes to begin the work in the north in Aalborg. Elder Dykes reported stirring results: "I began to raise my warning voice to a very superstitious people, and soon I had enough to do, for the spirit that had for ages lulled the people to sleep under their ancient customs and dead ceremonies, was now awakened, and arose like the old lion from his slumbers. . . . The people were astonished, their sleep was disturbed by night and their labors by day. There was something new

Anthon H. Lund

in the land, it was the voice of God from on high—a message from that God whom they or their fathers had not known."[13] Again, as in Copenhagen, reformation broke ground for restoration, and breakaway Baptists were the earliest converts and leaders in the new Aalborg branch. Among the first baptized was the Lund family, one of whom, Anthon H. Lund, later became an apostle and a member of the First Presidency of the Church. By the end of 1850 there were 135 members in Denmark in the two branches.

In 1851 Elder Snow launched the infant Church in Denmark on two courses of action that would create a strong base of faith and strengthen the Danish Saints to withstand persecution at the hands of the mobs. He set them to printing vast stores of literature, including scriptures, in the Danish language and directed the calling of local elders to lead the branches and to serve as missionaries.

Elder Peter O. Hansen was the chief translator of Church materials into Danish. He had begun translating the Book of Mormon before his mission, and his manuscripts aided in the earliest conversions. But he had forgotten many Danish language nuances, so in Denmark an educated Danish woman, a Miss Mathiesen, was hired to assist him. After careful revision supervised by apostle Erastus Snow, the Danish Book of Mormon was published in Copenhagen in May 1851. This was the first foreign language edition of the Book of Mormon. (Today there are more than one hundred.) Elder Snow had also supervised the earlier publication in Danish of several tracts and a hymnbook that included selections from the Doctrine and Covenants as well as the Articles of Faith. Then in October, Elder Snow commenced publishing the *Skandinaviens Stjerne (Scandinavian Star)*. This newspaper, first a monthly and later a bimonthly, bolstered the Danish Saints into the twentieth century.

Because Church leaders colonizing the Utah territory could ill afford to send very many elders to Denmark, Elder Snow simply trained and then ordained numerous young Danes to the work. That proved to be a providential decision, solving communication problems and multiplying the missionary force. By the end of 1851, despite intense persecution, Church membership in Denmark soared to more than 500 members in twelve branches organized into three conferences.

Persecution intensified in Denmark throughout 1851. Elder Snow reported to Brigham Young early in 1851: "It seemed, indeed, as though the powers of earth and hell were combined to crush the work of the Lord in that land, but through prayer and fasting we received strength, and the clouds began to disperse."[14] But the respite was only temporary, for persecution grew as the year progressed. The Lutheran clergy perceived the Latter-day Saints to be stealing their flock, a source of tax revenues from the government. Until 1849, Lutheran leaders had dictated the religious lives of the people. The ministers were, for some reason, particularly incensed at the Latter-day Saints' midweek meetings. They even started their own midweek gatherings to thwart interest in Latter-day Saint teachings. They next resorted to violence against the missionaries and then native Danes who had converted.

At year's end Elder Snow reported to Church leaders in Utah: "The difficulties we have to encounter cannot be realized by those who have only labored in England. . . . In many places here, to embrace the gospel is almost equal to the sacrifice of one's life; and to travel and preach it, a man carries his life in his hands. The Danish Constitution guarantees the right, but . . . the priests [wish] to keep the people ignorant of the fact, and their influence in the country towns and settlements is almost boundless. The masses are not a reading people. We have to preach the constitution to prepare the way for the Bible, and the Bible to prepare the way for the Book of Mormon."[15]

During Erastus Snow's presidency, missionaries also took the gospel to Sweden, Norway, and Iceland, although with much less fruitful results. John E. Forsgren arrived in Sweden in June 1850, less than two weeks after he and Erastus Snow had arrived in Copenhagen. Members of his family readily accepted the gospel, and Elder Forsgren had little difficulty in interesting individuals of the lower classes in his message, but Swedish laws forbade his preaching. Undaunted, Brother Forsgren taught as many groups as he could but was soon taken prisoner and was ordered to be deported to America by the Swedish government. Before he left, however, Elder Forsgren baptized and organized into a branch seventeen Swedes who planned to emigrate. Fortunately, he was allowed to disembark in Denmark, where he rejoined his brethren and continued his ministry there.

Two natives of Iceland, Thorarinn Haflidason Thorason and Gudmund Gudmundson, joined the Church in Copenhagen early in 1851. The two were craftsmen who had gone to Denmark to improve their skills. Shortly before they returned to Iceland, Elder Snow ordained them to the Aaronic Priesthood so they could preach and baptize. They baptized two persons in Iceland before the authorities prohibited further public preaching. In December 1851, Brother Thorason accidentally drowned. Elder Snow tried to send a Danish elder to assist in Iceland but the necessary papers were denied. Brother Gudmundson was on his own until 1853, when Dane Johan P. Lorentzen arrived and ordained him an elder. The missionaries organized a small branch that June. Soon afterward, nearly all the Icelandic members emigrated to America. No other missionaries served in Iceland during the 1850s and 1860s.

The first Norwegian convert, ship captain Svend Larsen, approached Erastus Snow in Copenhagen in September 1851 about Latter-day Saint teachings. Brother Larsen accepted President Snow's testimony with gladness, was baptized, and returned to seafaring and his homeland. Accompanying him to Norway was Danish elder Hans F. Petersen. They left well supplied with Danish translations of the Book of Mormon and various tracts because Norwegians and Danes share common written language roots. As soon as Elder Petersen began preaching in Norway, he was arrested and forbidden to preach. When he persisted in talking privately with interested persons and baptized some in the community of Österrisör, he was accosted by mobs and forced to leave Norway. On his way, however, he met in private with individuals in Mandal and Bergen and baptized several more. As for Captain Larsen, as he traveled he shared the gospel wherever he docked his ship. Although he encountered constant harassment from the law, he dubbed his boat *Zion's Lion* and flew from the mast a pennant upon which was painted a golden lion. His "Mormon" boat helped keep the Church's profile high.

The Scandinavian Mission held a special conference on 22 February 1852 to honor and be instructed by Erastus Snow, who had been called home by the First Presidency. The Saints were sad to see their apostle leave. They had grown attached to this noble leader who had stood by them through oppressive persecution. In less than two years, despite great opposition, the Scandinavian Mission had recorded more than 700 baptisms. Elder Snow left the mission in the hands of John E. Forsgren and during the conference called new missionaries to Sweden and Norway. Elder Snow also prepared the first Scandinavian emigrants to travel to Liverpool, there to join other emigrants and make their way to Zion.

Persecution continued throughout the 1850s. In Sweden and Norway missionaries were repeatedly imprisoned or banished from the country or both. But the mission stabilized and even prospered because of the many receptive souls among the poor as well as the persistence of the missionaries, most of whom were either local elders or Scandinavian emigrants who returned to their homeland as missionaries. With its relative religious freedom, Denmark produced most of the converts during this decade. In 1857, when missionaries were temporarily called home for the "Utah War," there were 3,353 Saints in Scandinavia: 2,317 Danes, 726 Swedes, and 310 Norwegians.[16] Approximately 25 percent of the Scandinavian converts emigrated to Utah in the 1850s. Denmark had become the leading baptizing nation after England and remained such through 1870.

Beginnings in France

In the mid nineteenth century, the most powerful nation in the world next to Great Britain was France. Naturally, Church officials desired to begin proselyting efforts there. But the great religious awakening that swept through England in the 1830s had not crossed the Channel. In fact, the so-called enlightened secularism had dimmed the desire of many people to learn about God and religion. Church efforts were also thwarted by government suspicion of new groups in France that might prove revolutionary. A third obstacle was the powerful Roman Catholic Church, still the state religion.

In 1847, British mission leaders asked for volunteers to accept a call to France. No one offered, but the next year William Howells, a Welshman, accepted a call to be the first missionary across the English Channel. He took with him as a companion his nine-year-old daughter Ann. Elder Howells arrived in the port city Le Havre in July 1849, carrying English pamphlets and a flyer he had composed in rudimentary French entitled "L'Evangile" ("The Gospel"). Because his French was very limited, William distributed numerous tracts but visited mostly English families in Le Havre. His first convert was August Saint d'Anna, a young man who spoke several languages. Elder Howells and Ann then took ship to one of Britain's Channel Islands, the Isle of Jersey, to deliver tracts to Elder William C. Dunbar. Elder Dunbar had been preaching to both English and French. On the way back to France, Howells preached in Saint Servan and Boulogne. In the latter seaside city, he organized the first branch of the French Mission on 5 April 1850. Even with Ann at his side, Elder Howells had frequently faced mob persecution and unkind treatment from both Catholics and Protestants, so in Boulogne he welcomed the news that other missionaries were even then on their way from Utah. John Taylor, an apostle, and Curtis E. Bolton and John Pack would officially open the French Mission. Elder Howells returned with his daughter to England to await their arrival.

In June 1850 John Taylor and his companions arrived in Boulogne. Missionaries and members gathered at the seashore to hear Elder Taylor dedicate the nation of France to receive the gospel.

The missionaries were dedicated and enthusiastic, but numerous obstacles blocked their early attempts to find converts. First was the language barrier. Curtis Bolton had been to France years before as a student, but his French was far from fluent. Elder Howells' French was halting at best. The others, including Elder Taylor, were no better. Hence their teaching was limited to people who could speak English. Second, the French were generally skeptical of all religions, even their own. Third, in 1850 the government of France, still in upheaval since the 1848 revolutions, considered all public meetings a threat to the new head of state, Louis Napoleon. Consequently, government officials forbade any substantial meetings of the Saints.

Within a month, three English ministers who had followed the missionaries to France challenged Elder Taylor to a debate. In three successive evenings, the apostle defended the integrity of Joseph Smith against anti-Mormon libel and charges that the Prophet was an imposter. Afterwards Elder Taylor wrote a tract based on the debate for distribution in Boulogne. This was one of many occasions in Elder Taylor's decades-long ministry when he distinguished himself as a formidable defender of the faith.

Leaving Elder Pack in charge of the work in Boulogne, Elder Taylor proceeded to Paris. Though the brethren succeeded in finding a few interested persons in that huge city, baptizing six and establishing a branch, their first priority was to translate the Book of Mormon and write and translate various tracts. Curtis Bolton began the work and was soon aided by new converts, including Louis Bertrand, an experienced journalist, and some non-Latter-day Saints who were willing to assist. They also began a monthly periodical entitled *Etoile du Deseret (Star of Deseret)* containing instruction on doctrine and Church history. It ran from May 1851 to April 1852.

Meanwhile missionary work was progressing reasonably well on the Channel Islands. Because so many island inhabitants were French, the Channel Islands Conference was transferred to the French Mission, and several French converts became missionaries in their native land.

But missionary work flagged. It was hard to interest people without public meetings, and government officials kept a watchful eye on the missionaries. Elder Bolton even spent three months in prison in Paris. Elder John Taylor described conditions in France to the Saints in Deseret:

"'Liberty, Equality, Fraternity, and Brotherhood,' was written almost upon every door. You had liberty to speak, but might be put in prison for doing so. You had liberty to print, but they might burn what you had printed, and put you into confinement for it. . . . Infidelity [to any religion] prevails there to a great extent. . . . You will find [only] women in the places of worship there, while on the other hand, if you go out to the public promenades, and theatres, and public amusements on Sunday, you will see men by [the] thousands; and if you judge of their religion by their actions, you would consider that the theatre and public amusements are their places of worship."[17]

In March 1852 Louis Napoleon, who had just proclaimed himself Emperor Napoleon III, imposed martial law. Missionary work effectively came to a stop. Elder John Taylor, ordered out of the country, retreated to England with the manuscript of the French translation of the Book of Mormon. He left Curtis Bolton in charge of the mission.

When obstacles persisted, the few missionaries remaining in France were finally withdrawn in 1855, and a handful of French converts made their way to Zion. In 1859 Louis Bertrand returned to France as mission president, but when he could not obtain government permission to preach, he resorted to the pen. Formerly a propagandist for the Communist Party, he wrote well, and many of his articles were published and reviewed favorably in a prestigious literary magazine. Nevertheless, his efforts did not spark the interest that led to conversion, and he wrote in frustration to Brigham Young that the French infidels were all spiritually dead. He also wrote a letter to Napoleon III, who responded by ridiculing the Latter-day Saints. In 1864, Elder Bertrand emigrated, and the French Mission was closed, not to open again until 1912. The Channel Islands Conference, which included a few Saints in France, reverted to the British Mission.

Beginnings in Germany

When Elders Erastus Snow, John Taylor, and Lorenzo Snow were called on missions to Europe in 1849, they had not expected to proselyte in Germany, but events involved all three in founding the German Mission as well.

Germany at that time was not a single country but rather thirty-nine separate kingdoms, duchies, and city-states bound by a common language and culture and, since 1815, loosely connected in the German Confederation. Prussia was the most powerful of the German states when the three apostles went to Europe. (In the 1860s, Otto von Bismarck of Prussia engineered the consolidation of the German states except Austria into one powerful state, finally achieving his ends in 1871.) From 1815 to 1871, state churches, either Roman Catholic or Evangelical Lutheran, dominated the German states in religion. Both were exceedingly suspicious of other religions. For three hundred years Germany had been the scene of countless wars and controversies over religion.

During the 1840s some groundwork was laid for preaching the gospel in Germany. James Howard, a convert from England who went in 1840 to Hamburg to work in a foundry, was instructed to do missionary work. His stay was brief, and no baptisms are recorded. In 1841 Elder Orson Hyde of the Quorum of the Twelve went through Germany en route to Jerusalem. A quick learner, he absorbed much of the German language and on his return trip spent many months in Regensburg, Bavaria. He published a pamphlet "Ein Ruf Aus der Wüste" ("A Cry from the Wilderness"), the oldest extant foreign language publication in the Church archives. Elder Hyde also did not baptize in Germany in 1841–42.

Numerous German immigrants to Britain and America embraced the gospel message, however, and settled in Nauvoo. Their devotion impressed the Prophet Joseph Smith, and he learned some German and studied the Luther German Bible. In 1843 the Prophet called Johann Grünig to return to Germany as a missionary. Elder Grünig organized a small branch in Darmstandt, but no letters or other records detail his year-long mission.

The more permanent presence of the Church in Germany began with Elder George Parker Dykes, one of the original missionaries to Denmark. He had gone in the course of his labors to the province of Schleswig, an area of dispute between Denmark and German rulers for centuries. Elder Dykes, who spoke some German as well as Danish, baptized a few German converts in Schleswig. In September 1851 he was banned from the province and to avoid arrest fled to the city-state of

Hamburg. At the same time Elder John Taylor had been banned from Paris but was looking for a place to continue his mission to Europe and to publish the Book of Mormon in French. Elders Taylor and Dykes learned of each other's situation, met in London, and then traveled to Hamburg in October 1851. There they commenced a German translation of the Book of Mormon and a monthly periodical, *Zions Panier (Zion's Banner)*. In the first number, Elder Taylor expressed his belief that many thousands of German-speaking people would flock to Zion. This prophecy was not immediately fulfilled, but in the 1920s Germany for several years became the most productive of all Church mission fields.

Hamburg officials forced Elder Taylor to leave in December. He made his way back to Utah, taking with him sugar refinery equipment he had acquired in various parts of Europe—a boon to the economy in Deseret. Elder Taylor left to Elder Dykes the commission to finish their project, and in May 1852 the Book of Mormon was published in both German and French, side by side in a single volume.

Meanwhile, President Brigham Young had appointed Daniel Carn, a native German who had been a stalwart member in Nauvoo and early Utah, to be the first German Mission president. He arrived in Hamburg in 1852 after meeting with Elder John Taylor in England. Elder Carn labored alone at first, boldly proclaiming his message, and by August had organized a branch of twelve members in Hamburg. Terrific opposition from both Lutherans and Roman Catholics soon accompanied the success. Priests and newspapers warned the people that if they even listened to Mormons they would be cut off from their churches. Both were powerful denominations supported by government taxation as state churches. Neither was willing to allow any other church, especially one considered to be a dangerous American sect, to gain a foothold in their midst.

In August 1852, Elder Carn organized seventeen Saints from Hamburg to emigrate to Utah. Later the same year, Carn, still laboring alone, reported that the work was progressing in Hamburg. The branch had twenty-one new members who possessed "much faith, unity and love . . . [and] the gift of healing . . . wonderfully manifest in several instances."[18] But in December, police ordered Elder Carn to leave Hamburg. When he refused, he was stripped of all his possessions and imprisoned. They released him on the condition that he leave Hamburg. He complied by moving to Altona, a suburb not in Hamburg's jurisdiction. He also strengthened Elder Dyke's German-speaking branches in nearby Schleswig province.

In 1853, seven more missionaries arrived. One of these, Elder Orson Spencer, British Mission president in 1847–48, traveled with a companion to Berlin in the kingdom of Prussia to see King Wilhelm IV, who had asked his ministers about the curious Mormons. But the King's curiosity was not benign. In Prussia they were summoned before a police court and questioned about Mormon marriage practices. The judges were not interested in the missionaries' message nor were they advocates of religious freedom. They banished the elders, and the Prussian government issued a decree against the Mormons. Besides religious intolerance, the document revealed the Prussians' fear that their countrymen would emigrate to America and then speak out against the Prussian state.[19] Other missionaries tried other Germanic areas but were similarly rebuffed.

But despite constant persecution, as in Sweden and Norway during these same years, there were conversions in Germany. At the end of 1853, after two years of missionary work, 128 persons had been baptized, forty-six of whom had emigrated. The main reason the Church did not give up on Germany, Sweden, and Norway, even though there was virtually no religious freedom there through the 1850s, is that the steady trickle of conversions promised many more, if only political conditions became favorable.

One exceptional convert, Karl G. Maeser, came from the German kingdom of Saxony. In 1855, Maeser, a schoolteacher, found an anti-Mormon tract that aroused his curiosity. He read elsewhere that the Latter-day Saints had a mission headquarters in Copenhagen and wrote asking for information. The Scandinavian Mission president replied that no one there could communicate in German, so he suggested Maeser write to President Daniel Tyler of the Swiss Mission. At first Maeser's persistent letters to the Swiss Mission went unanswered because the brethren feared that German officials were trying to discover illegal activities. Finally, believing Maeser to be sincere, a British missionary, Elder William Budge, went to Dresden to meet him. Elder Budge, however, did not speak German. Also, foreign missionaries were outlawed in

Karl G. Maeser

Saxony. The two, meeting in secret, communicated by opening both an English and a German Bible and referring to passages. Highly motivated, Elder Budge learned the language quickly and taught Maeser and some interested friends. Under cover of darkness Karl G. Maeser and some of his friends and family were baptized. A branch was formed in Dresden with Brother Maeser as branch president. Conditions were so prohibitive, however, that they all decided to emigrate. These first converts from Dresden arrived in Salt Lake City in 1857.

In Utah Brigham Young hired Brother Maeser to tutor his children and teach in one of the city schools. In 1875 President Young sent Brother Maeser to be superintendent of Provo's Brigham Young Academy. Later Brother Maeser served as superintendent of all Church schools and as assistant superintendent of the Deseret Sunday School Union. Brother Maeser's monumental contributions to the Church over many years led Heber J. Grant to remark, "If nothing more had been or ever would be accomplished in Germany than the conversion of Dr. Karl G. Maeser, the

Church would have been well paid for all the efforts and means expended in that land."[20]

Throughout the rest of the 1850s, the Church enjoyed sporadic success in Germany, including the southern kingdoms, which opened to missionaries proselyting out of Switzerland in 1859. Swiss convert Serge L. Ballif, a former Protestant minister, formed the Karlsruhe Branch in the kingdom of Baden in 1860. But persecution of missionaries intensified in Germany rather than diminished, and Church growth there had to wait for more tolerant times.

Beginnings in Italy

Elder Lorenzo Snow of the Twelve received his call to Europe in 1849 along with Erastus Snow and John Taylor. Called to Italy as well was Sicilian native Joseph Toronto (original spelling was *Taranto*). These brethren stopped in England to visit the Saints and contemplate the best way to approach this stronghold of Catholicism. As with Germany to the north, there was no united Italy as yet. Instead Italy consisted of numerous independent political entities allied by a common language and a devout loyalty to the Roman Catholic Church.

A Protestant sect known as the Waldenses seemed a promising place to start. Elder Snow visited the public library in Liverpool to research the group. Some religious liberties had been granted this sect only two years earlier in the alpine Piedmont region of the Sardinian states. The Waldenses, like the Latter-day Saints, had suffered religious persecution and been driven to a mountain retreat. There were doctrinal similarities as well. Both emphasized a belief in an apostasy and a return to primitive Christianity. As he read, Elder Snow became convinced that he had been directed to a branch of the house of Israel.

Elder Snow learned that the founder of the Waldenses, Peter Waldo, had been a wealthy twelfth-century French merchant who became convinced that the Catholics were not practicing New Testament Christianity. In Lyons, France, Waldo took a vow of poverty and formed a group called "The Poor," which attracted many followers. They were soon excommunicated and banished from France. The Waldenses found refuge across the Alps in the Lombardy region of what is now northern

Italy. By 1850, approximately 20,000 Waldenses were living in the Piedmont.

Elder Lorenzo Snow visited several British Church conferences and called two English elders, T. B. H. Stenhouse and Jabez Woodard, to accompany him and Elder Toronto to Italy. They sailed by way of the Mediterranean to Genoa and then traveled overland to Torre Pellice, the largest Waldensian village. Elders Snow and Toronto were struck with how much the Piedmont valleys resembled the Salt Lake Valley. On 19 October 1850 the four elders ascended a high mountain, where they formally dedicated the land of Italy as a missionary field. They named the peak Mount Brigham and the rock where they stood the Rock of Prophecy.

A healing opened the door to missionary work. When the brethren blessed their innkeeper's critically ill child, the child's miraculous recovery stirred interest throughout the community. Their first baptism took place in late October. Elder Snow became convinced that further progress required written material both in French, the language of most Waldenses, and Italian. He returned to England to finish his tract, "The Voice of Joseph," and arrange for translation of the Book of Mormon into Italian. Elder Snow sent Elder Stenhouse to begin missionary work in Switzerland, and Elder Toronto went on to his native Sicily to introduce the gospel to relatives and others. Elder Toronto labored without success during his year in Sicily.

Meanwhile, missionaries from America joined Elder Woodard among the Waldenses. A few were receptive to the gospel, but most Waldensians felt that listening to representatives of another religion would be betraying their forefathers. From October 1850 to the end of 1852 only thirty-nine joined the Church. Fifty-three were added in the next year.

During these same years Elder Lorenzo Snow completed his translation projects. The Book of Mormon in Italian was published in May 1852, within weeks of the French-German edition in Hamburg. With the Danish edition, there were now four foreign language translations of the Book of Mormon. Elder Snow returned to Utah in 1852, leaving Elder Woodard as president of the Italian Mission. Elder Woodard sent missionaries to Malta, Nice, Genoa, and Turin but with practically no success. Elder Woodard faithfully prepared the Waldensian converts for emigration to America, and in January 1854 he led the first group to Liverpool and on to Salt Lake City.

In 1854 the Swiss and Italian Missions were consolidated. A few more Waldenses converted to the Church, but by 1861 the work in Italy had come to a complete standstill, and nearly all faithful members, a total of seventy-three, had emigrated. The mission recorded a total of 211 baptized in all of Italy since the opening of the mission. Outside the Waldensian Protestants, the time was not ripe for the Church in Catholic Italy, and Italy did not receive missionaries again for more than a hundred years.

Beginnings in Switzerland

The landlocked and mountainous nation of Switzerland was opened to the preaching of the gospel in December 1850. Though missionaries endured relentless persecution in Switzerland as they did in other countries on the Continent, the Swiss Mission grew, and after 1864 when religious liberty was granted, Switzerland became the third most productive European mission. Only England and Denmark produced more converts in the nineteenth century.

Elder T. B. H. Stenhouse was the British missionary who had accompanied Elder Lorenzo Snow to Italy and was set apart by him in November 1850 to introduce the gospel to Switzerland. Stenhouse knew some French, as did his wife, and he was eager to go to the beautiful lake city of Geneva, where his wife and daughter could join him in this new missionary venture. (Four western Swiss cantons are French-speaking; most of the country is German-speaking.) Armed with French language pamphlets, Elder Stenhouse braved fierce winter conditions to cross the Alps. That December he immediately began seeking people who wanted to be taught the gospel, but most rudely turned him away. He found that the Calvinist Protestants were as belligerently attached to their religion as were the Catholics. He dubbed Geneva "the Protestant Rome."

Two months later Elder Lorenzo Snow also crossed the Alps on his way to England and joined Elder Stenhouse to dedicate Switzerland for the preaching of the gospel. By the end of 1851 there were two small branches and twenty members. In 1852 Elder Stenhouse extended his labors to Lausanne and was greatly aided by the arrival of other elders and the publication of the French-German Book of Mormon in Hamburg. This edition of scripture seemed tailor-made for bilingual Switzerland. In 1853 the first German-speaking elders arrived to proselyte in the German-speaking cantons of Switzerland. Their success was gratifying but hard-won, for on every hand church and government officials persecuted the missionaries. They were sometimes imprisoned or banned from the cantons. On Christmas Day 1853 the Swiss Mission held its first conference and recorded that 144 had been baptized since December 1850. In February 1854 President Stenhouse led the first group of fifty-eight emigrating Swiss Saints to Liverpool and on to Zion.

The most notable Swiss converts of those early years were the Serge Ballif family of Lausanne. Brother Ballif was a wealthy aristocrat who gave gladly to publish tracts and support the missionaries. He served as a local missionary, baptized several families, and then emigrated to America. He later returned to Switzerland as a missionary in 1860 and as mission president from 1879 to 1881. Brother and Sister Ballif are among the progenitors of the thirteenth president of the Church, Ezra Taft Benson.

In 1854 the Swiss and Italian Missions were combined under a new president, Daniel Tyler. In 1855 he began publishing the periodical *Der Darsteller (The Representer)*. Gradually the Church became firmly established in eight branches in Switzerland. In 1859 Swiss missionaries entered the southern German kingdoms, and in 1861 the mission was renamed the Swiss, Italian, and German Mission, although work by this time was negligible in Italy. In 1864 the Swiss achieved their long-sought religious freedom, which made an immense difference in Mormon missionary labors. In 1868 the mission adopted its more permanent name of the Swiss-German Mission.

Conclusion

Entering the continent of Europe was risky for the earliest Mormon apostles and missionaries. Political, religious, language, and cultural barriers seemed almost insurmountable. These first elders bravely expounded the principles of eternal life, sacrificing earthly comforts and risking their lives to do so. Yet they persevered and established fruitful branches in Europe. The British, Scandinavian, and Swiss-German

Missions became permanent and ultimately yielded thousands of Latter-day Saints who emigrated to their new mountain home in the American West.

NOTES

1 Parley P. Pratt to Joseph Smith, 4 December 1841, in David H. Pratt, "Oh! Brother Joseph," *BYU Studies* 27 (Winter 1987): 130.

2 Ibid., 129.

3 B. H. Roberts, *A Comprehensive History of The Church of Jesus Christ of Latter-day Saints, Century One*, 6 vols. (Provo, Utah: Brigham Young University Press, 1965), 3:126.

4 *Millennial Star* 7 (15 October 1846): 119.

5 Ronald D. Dennis, "The Welsh and the Gospel," in V. Ben Bloxham et al., eds., *Truth Will Prevail: The Rise of The Church of Jesus Christ of Latter-day Saints in the British Isles, 1837–1987* (West Midlands: Corporation of the President of The Church of Jesus Christ of Latter-day Saints, 1987), 236–67; Gordon B. Hinckley, "The Thing of Most Worth," *Ensign* 23 (September 1993): 2–7.

6 Dennis, "The Welsh and the Gospel," 267.

7 Statistics cited in Richard O. Cowan, "Church Growth in England, 1841–1914," in Bloxham et al., *Truth Will Prevail*, 199.

8 Malcolm R. Thorp, "The Religious Backgrounds of Mormon Converts in Britain, 1837–1852," *Journal of Mormon History* 4 (1977): 51–66.

9 Breck England, *The Life and Thought of Orson Pratt* (Salt Lake City: University of Utah Press, 1985), 143.

10 James R. Clark, ed., *Messages of the First Presidency of The Church of Jesus Christ of Latter-day Saints*, 6 vols. (Salt Lake City: Bookcraft, 1963–70), 2:35.

11 William Mulder, *Homeward to Zion: The Mormon Migration from Scandinavia* (Minneapolis: University of Minnesota Press, 1957), 8.

12 Andrew Jenson, *History of the Scandinavian Mission* (Salt Lake City: Deseret News Press, 1927), 15.

13 Ibid., 17.

14 Ibid., 30.

15 Ibid., 43.

16 Jenson, *History of the Scandinavian Mission*, 127.

17 John Taylor, in *Journal of Discourses*, 26 vols. (London: Latter-day Saints' Book Depot, 1854–86), 1:22.

18 *Millennial Star* 14 (14 November 1852): 603.

19 Michael Mitchell, "The Mormons in Wilhelmine Germany, 1870–1914: Making a Place for an Unwanted American Religion in a Changing German Society," master's thesis, Brigham Young University, 1994, 33–36, 39–42.

20 Gilbert W. Scharffs, *Mormonism in Germany* (Salt Lake City: Deseret Book, 1970), 16.

CHAPTER 5

Gathering to Zion

JUNE 1840	FIRST BRITISH EMIGRANTS SAIL FOR AMERICA
1848	CHURCH HEADQUARTERS ARE ESTABLISHED IN SALT LAKE CITY
1849	PERPETUAL EMIGRATING FUND COMPANY (PEF) IS INCORPORATED
1856	HANDCARTS ARE FIRST USED BY THE SAINTS; TRAGEDY ON THE PLAINS
1861–68	THE CHURCH TRAINS SYSTEM OPERATES
1869	FIRST YEAR OF EXCLUSIVE STEAM AND RAIL TRANSPORTATION FOR THE GATHERING
1887	PEF DISSOLVED

he hymn "Israel, Israel, God Is Calling" was sung by many Saints who sought to leave Babylon in their native lands and gather to Zion in Utah. It was written by Richard Smyth, a convert to the Church from Dublin, Ireland, years before he emigrated to Utah in 1863.

Israel, Israel, God is calling,
Calling thee from lands of woe.
Babylon the great is falling;
God shall all her tow'rs o'erthrow.
Come to Zion, come to Zion
Ere his floods of anger flow.
Come to Zion, come to Zion
Ere his floods of anger flow.

Israel! Israel! Canst thou linger
Still in error's gloomy ways?
Mark how judgment's pointing finger
Justifies no vain delays.
Come to Zion, come to Zion!
Zion's walls shall ring with praise.
Come to Zion, come to Zion!
Zion's walls shall ring with praise.[1]

This and hosts of other gathering songs encouraged the nearly 85,000 Latter-day Saints who sacrificed and suffered to emigrate to Zion. Approximately 6,000 died along the way. More than 98 percent of the surviving Saints who gathered to America in the nineteenth century were from Europe.

The scattering and the gathering of Israel are a topic frequently repeated in the Old Testament, the New Testament, and the Book of Mormon. Latter-day prophecies of gathering began in September 1830, when the Church was only four months old: "And ye are called to bring to pass the gathering of mine elect; for mine elect hear my voice and harden not their hearts; wherefore the decree hath gone forth from the Father that they shall be gathered in unto one place upon the face of this land" (D&C 29:7–8). The next March another revelation declared: "And it shall come to pass that the righteous shall be gathered out from among all nations, and shall come to Zion, singing with songs of everlasting joy" (D&C 45:71). In November 1831 came the following injunction: "Go ye out of Babylon; gather ye out from among the nations, from the four winds, from one end of heaven to the other. Send forth the elders of my church unto the nations which are afar off; unto the islands of the sea; send forth unto foreign lands; call upon all nations. . . . Go ye out from among the nations, even from Babylon, from the midst of wickedness, which is spiritual Babylon" (D&C 133:7–8, 14).

Few doctrines of nineteenth-century Mormonism were mentioned as often as that of gathering to Zion. Time and again in sermons, in circulars from the First Presidency, and in such periodicals as the *Millennial Star*, Church leaders admonished the faithful to gather. By joining together in Kirtland, in Far West, and in Nauvoo, the Saints established a unified community of believers. Eventually, in Utah, they made the desert "blossom as the rose" (Isaiah 35:1), built temples, and established a commonwealth that could not be overthrown.

Most emigrant Saints in the nineteenth century came from Europe. Some 55,000 gathered to Zion from the British Isles. Another 21,000 came from Scandinavia. Others in fewer numbers came from Switzerland, Germany, France, Italy, Holland, Belgium, the Austro-Hungarian Empire, South Africa, Australia, New Zealand, India, and Hawaii. In the twentieth century, natives of yet other countries joined

Immigrants from Europe arriving in New York.
Drawing by early Latter-day Saint artist Frederick Piercy

the Church, and even though the doctrine of gathering eventually emphasized building the stakes of Zion in one's own land, thousands more emigrated to America to be with the main body of the Saints. Not until the late twentieth century did most members stay in their homelands, confident that the word of the Lord would go forth to all nations from Church headquarters in Salt Lake City, Utah.

"And it shall come to pass in the last days, that the mountain of the Lord's house shall be established in the top of the mountains, and shall be exalted above the hills; and all nations shall flow unto it. And many people shall go and say, Come ye, and let us go up to the mountain of the Lord, to the house of the God of Jacob; and he will teach us of his ways, and we will walk in his paths: for out of Zion shall go forth the law" (Isaiah 2:2–3). The multitudes who journeyed to Utah from all nations have helped Zion to become what she was prophesied to be.

Emigration in the Early 1840s

In 1837 Joseph Smith instructed the first overseas missionaries to "remain silent concerning the gathering."[2] This proved to be wise

A steamboat chartered to take Latter-day Saint immigrants upriver.
Drawing by Frederick Piercy

counsel, because no stable headquarters had yet been established to which British Saints could gather. During the 1830s, the first decade of the Church's existence, members had gathered to New York, then to Ohio and Missouri, and finally to Nauvoo, Illinois. It was to Nauvoo that the first British emigrants went in 1840. Soon after Brigham Young and the other apostles arrived in England that year, they determined that the time was right to encourage gathering. This they did privately, wishing to avoid controversy. Actually, many English converts had already determined from the scriptures and from answers to their own prayers the rightness of going to Zion.

While Brigham Young presided over the British Mission, he organized seven companies, totaling more than 800 emigrants. A few more Saints arranged private passage. The first official Church emigration company (forty-one Preston Saints headed by John Moon) received a blessing from Elders Young and Kimball and departed from Liverpool on the *Britannia* on 6 June 1840. They arrived at New York 20 July. Two other ships carried approximately 250 more British Saints the same year. The second of these carried Scottish converts to New Orleans, from which point they took a steamboat up the Mississippi River. That soon became the preferred route. In early 1841, four more ships left Britain with some 500 emigrants headed for Nauvoo.

The Prophet Joseph Smith enthusiastically greeted these British converts. Their conviction and devotion tremendously blessed the Church. The British members wrote back to family and friends exciting testimonials of Joseph Smith and stories of new opportunities in America. Their stories, many of them published in Elder Parley P. Pratt's *Millennial Star,* encouraged others to consider emigrating. Life was exciting but not easy in America, for many immigrants had to learn farming instead of practicing their trades or performing factory work. Some helped develop industry in Nauvoo, and Church leaders were grateful to receive an influx of skilled tradesmen and laborers. Over the next five years, while the Church was headquartered in Illinois, twenty-six more companies, tallying nearly 4,000 more converts, arrived in Nauvoo. Nearly all traveled through New Orleans and up the Mississippi River.

British Emigration, 1846–51

Wilford Woodruff, then president of the British Mission, embarked for America in January 1846. Before leaving he arranged the formation of the "British and America Commercial Joint Stock Company." Stated company goals were to raise capital by selling export machinery to Church headquarters in America and import foodstuffs for British stockholders to use or sell to others. The company's unstated purpose was to facilitate emigration: the ships carrying machinery could also transport Saints. Prospects seemed bright for the enterprise.

Complications soon arose, however. Mission leaders had to hire an expensive solicitor to incorporate the company legally. That put off operations for a time. Second, the location of Church headquarters in America became uncertain, because the Twelve were seeking a new gathering place, perhaps in the Rocky Mountains. Nevertheless, mission leaders preached support of the joint-stock company. They made tentative plans to charter a ship to New Orleans, but the plan never came to fruition. Meanwhile, Reuben Hedlock, acting mission president, and Thomas Ward, his counselor, mismanaged company funds. When word of their actions reached Brigham Young at Council Bluffs, Iowa, he immediately sent Elders Orson Hyde, Parley P. Pratt, and John Taylor to Liverpool. They dissolved the company and distributed its remaining assets to stockholders.

These brethren explored other alternatives for subsidizing emigration. They prepared a petition to Queen Victoria and members of Parliament, requesting that the British government assist poor Latter-day Saints to emigrate to Vancouver Island and to the British portion of Oregon. The government was generally interested in peopling their foreign holdings with new colonists, but The British Colonial Office decided against allotting funds to emigrants to North America. During this same time (1846–47), confusion remained about where exactly Church headquarters would be. Still, British members held out hope that an organized, subsidized program of emigration could be arranged. Meanwhile, they turned their energies to sharing the gospel with neighbors and relations. From 1847 to 1851, convert baptisms nearly tripled, from about 11,000 to more than 30,000.

In February 1848, Brigham Young sent word of settlement in the valley of the Great Salt Lake. Mission leaders encouraged Saints to emigrate to Council Bluffs, Iowa, by way of New Orleans and to continue onward to the Valley as soon as they could arrange overland transportation. The Quorum of the Twelve admonished all "who could be called Saints" to gather and carry with them seeds, implements, educational materials, and any items that might adorn a new temple to be built in the new Zion.

Brigham Young sent Elder Orson Pratt to preside over the British Mission and supervise emigration. Elder Pratt brilliantly organized and refined emigration procedures, regularizing the flow of emigrants through Liverpool, and standardizing preparations for the voyage. He also recruited as many artisans, mechanics, and textile workers as possible. He scoured shops in Liverpool for equipment to build a civilization, purchasing everything from clock-making tools to engineering apparatus.

Between 1846 and 1851 the Church organized passage for approximately 6,000 emigrants to New Orleans on twenty-seven sailing vessels. Companies ranged in size from 10 to 466 passengers. Emigration accelerated considerably under Elder Pratt's presidency. He estimated that wealthy British Saints assisted nearly 200 of their poorer brothers and sisters in the spring of 1849, a practice that continued for another two years.

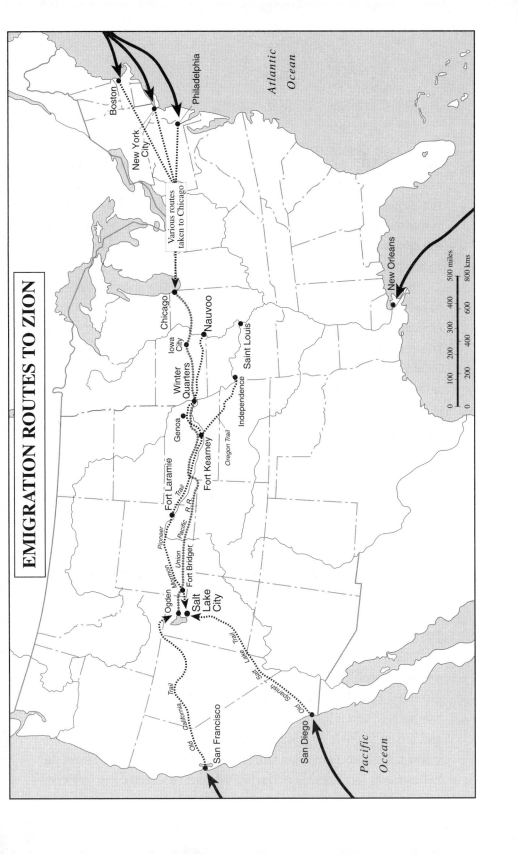

EMIGRATION ROUTES TO ZION

Atlantic Ocean

Boston

New York City

Philadelphia

Various routes taken to Chicago

Chicago

Iowa City

Nauvoo

Winter Quarters

Genoa

Saint Louis

Independence

Fort Kearney

Oregon Trail

Fort Laramie

Pioneer Trail

Union Pacific R.R.

Fort Bridger

Mormon Trail

Ogden

Salt Lake City

Old California Trail

San Francisco

Salt Lake Trail

Old Spanish Trail

San Diego

Pacific Ocean

New Orleans

| 0 | 100 | 200 | 300 | 400 | 500 miles |

| 0 | 200 | 400 | 600 | 800 kms |

The Perpetual Emigrating Fund Company

In October 1848, President Brigham Young arrived with his family and a large company of Saints to settle in the Great Salt Lake Valley and establish Church headquarters there. President Young called the settlement "Deseret," a Book of Mormon term meaning "honey bee" and connoting industry and devotion. Church leaders applied to the Congress of the United States to admit Deseret as a state but were instead granted status as a territory. In 1850, Senator Stephen A. Douglas, chairman of the Senate Committee for Territories, named the new territory "Utah" in honor of the Ute Indians who lived in the Great Basin.

In the spring of 1849, Brigham Young and the Twelve faced an enormous task. They needed to arrange for the safe arrival in Deseret of approximately 14,000 Saints still scattered through some forty camps in western Iowa. The solution was to establish the Perpetual Emigrating Fund Company (PEF) and a committee to collect funds Churchwide to gather all poor members to Great Salt Lake City. In an October 1849 general epistle to the Saints, the First Presidency explained that Church leaders had covenanted in the Nauvoo Temple in 1846 to "never cease our exertions, by all the means and influence within our reach, till all the Saints who were obliged to leave Nauvoo should be located at some gathering place of the Saints."[3] The PEF was created to fulfill that covenant. The committee had raised almost six thousand dollars by fall, and Presiding Bishop Edward Hunter went to Iowa and purchased wagons, livestock, and provisions to outfit numerous Saints for the trek to Zion. By 1852 most Saints in Iowa, including thousands of British Saints, had moved out of the camps. Church leaders then directed PEF resources to the 30,000 Saints still in Britain and other new converts on the European continent.

Over time the PEF became an impressively efficient operation with agents stationed at such strategic spots along the emigration route as Liverpool, Saint Louis, and Council Bluffs to help the emigrants on their way west. Church leaders also encouraged members in Utah to assist specific individuals by contributing cash, or items that could be converted to cash, to a European family member or friend in the care of the PEF office in Salt Lake City. The PEF office then directed agents abroad to send the persons named under the care of the company. The passage of some European Saints was paid for completely by PEF funds; others paid part or all of their own way. Immigrants using PEF funds signed a contract to pay back the amount lent to them, thus keeping the fund "perpetual." Because cash was scarce in Utah, many were unable to pay all their PEF debts. Some immigrants paid off part of their debt by laboring on community projects at Temple Square or other Church facilities, public roads, canals, and fences. The PEF, though successful as an organization, always struggled financially.

From 1852 to 1855, approximately 10,000 European Saints sailed from Liverpool to New Orleans. Each company maintained strict discipline during the lengthy voyages and was presided over by a returning mission president or other assigned missionary. Historian Leonard Arrington summarized their activities en route:

"The companies arose at an early hour, made their beds, cleaned their assigned portion of the ship, and threw the refuse overboard. At seven they assembled for prayer, after which breakfast was had. All were required to be in their berths ready for retirement at eight o'clock. Church services were held morning and evening of each day, weather permitting. Many of the companies had excellent choirs which sang for the services. During the time of passage, which occupied something like a month, concerts, dances, contests, and entertainments of various types were held. Schools were held almost daily for both adults and children. The classes were particularly popular with Scandinavians who learned English en route."[4]

During this period of emigration, three ships sailed from Australia and one from Calcutta to California carrying new converts. Strong winds swept one of these vessels, the *Julia Ann,* into a coral reef, causing the death of five Latter-day Saint passengers. This was the only sailing vessel disaster in the course of Latter-day Saint migration.

From New Orleans, the European immigrants traveled by steamboat up the Mississippi and Missouri Rivers to Council Bluffs, which usually took another week or two. Although the possibility of contracting cholera on the waterways was a concern, only one serious disaster took place. In 1852, ninety Mormons traveled on the *Saluda,* a dilapidated steamship whose machinery was tired and worn. In the thaw of early

Handcarts crossing the plains in 1856. Drawing by Grant Thorburn

April, the *Saluda* reached Lexington, Missouri. Steaming through float-ing chunks of ice, her boilers overheated and suddenly exploded, hurling people into the air. About 100 of the 175 passengers were killed, including between twenty-five and thirty Latter-day Saints. The residents of Lexington quickly organized a rescue. Some Saints were soon on their way to Council Bluffs; others remained in Lexington to recover. Several orphaned children were adopted by Lexington's citizens and grew up in that Missouri town far from England and from Utah. This freak steam-boat disaster, the worst in the history of Missouri River travel, was the greatest cause of death by accident during the entire Latter-day Saint migration.[5] To avoid the risk of contracting cholera, Church officials advised against travel through New Orleans after 1855, when rail trans-portation became available from the eastern seaboard all the way to Iowa.

Handcarts to Zion

A grasshopper plague in 1855 and severe weather the following win-ter created a famine and economic crisis in Utah in 1856. These factors spurred Brigham Young to invent an even more economical mode of transport—handcarts. His unique idea was to have the immigrants cross the plains on foot, pushing or pulling two-wheeled handcarts. They could carry with them very few belongings and only necessary provisions, but they could travel more quickly and certainly less expensively. A few ox-drawn wagons with camp supplies would accompany them. He estimated that the cost of emigration from Britain could be cut by two-thirds. Fewer provisions meant an earlier start, so they might also avoid some of the sickness that had beset earlier companies.

The first emigrant company to try this new system, some 534 strong, set sail from Liverpool 23 March 1856. After a pleasant voyage that witnessed four births and only two deaths on board, the *Enoch Train* arrived in Boston on 30 April. They divided into two companies in Iowa City, and the first company left on 9 June, the first handcart pioneers. Their carts had been constructed so that the immigrants could either push or pull a load of between one hundred and five hundred pounds of food and clothing. Elder J. D. T. McAllister, who helped outfit the first company, composed a merry song for the Saints to sing as they crossed the plains:

> Ye Saints who dwell on Europe's shore
> Prepare yourselves with many more
> To leave behind your native land,
> For sure God's judgments are at hand.
> Prepare to cross the stormy main
> Before you do the valley gain
> And with the faithful make a start
> To cross the plains with your hand cart.
>
> *Chorus*
> Some must push and some must pull
> As we go marching up the hill,
> As merrily on the way we go
> Until we reach the valley, oh.[6]

Both companies paused at Florence, Nebraska, on the Missouri River, to make repairs. They "walked" the distance to Salt Lake City, often suffering from painful blisters and exhaustion. Both companies arrived the same day, 26 September 1856. Everything had gone as planned. Another company of 320 handcart pioneers arrived in Salt Lake City on 2 October at the end of the immigration season. Their journey by sea, then railroad, and finally crossing the plains met with even fewer mishaps than the first two companies. The new handcart venture appeared to be a resounding success.

But only days later, on the first day of general conference, returning

British Mission president Franklin D. Richards arrived with bad news. Two additional handcart companies of about 500 each and two ox-train companies with another 385 immigrants were still on the plains, desperate for food and clothing to finish the journey.

The James G. Willie and Edward Martin companies had started late from Liverpool. PEF agents in the Midwest had not been prepared for so many—some 1,400 British immigrants. Many decided to spend the winter in Iowa, but the more zealous Saints insisted on pressing on to the Valley. They first had to wait for handcarts to be constructed, and then, because the wood had not been properly seasoned before they left, extensive repairs in Florence, Nebraska, meant another delay. They were thus not ready to press on from the Missouri River, nearly a thousand miles from Salt Lake City, until 4 September.

Some experienced leaders at Florence argued that passing through the mountains in October would probably be unsafe, but the immigrants were eager to press on. Levi Savage reportedly consented with these words: "Brethren and sisters, what I have said I know to be true; but seeing you are to go forward, I will go with you, will help you all I can, will work with you, will rest with you, will suffer with you, and, if necessary I will die with you. May God in his mercy bless and preserve us."[7]

Elder Richards caught up with these handcart pioneers on the Platte River, and seeing that their provisions were insufficient to make it to the Valley, hurried ahead to dispatch supplies from Salt Lake. By the time the Willie and Martin companies reached what is now Wyoming, their scant clothing was inadequate to protect them in the cold mornings. Early snows trapped the Willie Company a few miles east of South Pass and the Martin Company further back near the last crossing of the North Platte River.

When Brigham Young learned that these companies were on the plains, he urged the Saints assembled at conference to immediate action: "I shall not wait until to-morrow, nor until the next day, for 60 good mule teams and 12 to 15 wagons. . . . Go and bring in those people now on the plains."[8] The response was impressive. Twenty-seven hardy young men, known as Brigham Young's "Minute Men," departed Salt Lake City on 7 October with the first provisions. More relief teams left each week, and by the end of October, 250 rescuers from throughout Utah Territory were on their way.

Relief parties finally found the Willie Company 19 October and the Martin Company nine days later. The immigrants in both companies were freezing, listless, and near starvation. More than a hundred had died already, and even after the rescue, nearly a hundred more perished. Many adults had lost their spouses, and children, their parents. Several could not walk because of frozen feet and legs. The Willie and Martin companies dragged into Salt Lake City on 9 and 30 November respectively, greeted by crowds of cheering Saints. More people died in this tragedy than in any other group crossing the continent in United States history.

President Brigham Young, who had taken special interest in the handcart project, was dismayed at the tragic turn it had taken. Poor judgment and early winter storms had led to needless disaster. He sternly directed that no future immigrants should leave outfitting stations so late. Brigham maintained high hopes for the handcart program, but tensions between the United States government and the Church led to the Utah War, which put an end to most emigration from 1857 to 1860. Only five more handcart companies, totaling a little more than 1,000 immigrants, crossed the plains during those years of political stress for the Church.

The Church Trains System

Brigham Young learned from the Utah War that the Church should strive to be as independent as possible from outside, or "gentile," economic sources. He encouraged self-sufficiency in transportation across the plains as well as in public works, communications, settlements, agriculture, and industry. In 1860 Joseph W. Young, a nephew of Brigham, spoke in general conference on "the science of Ox-teamology." Previously it had been believed that oxen could not be driven more than a thousand miles in one season. But Joseph Young had captained an ox-team company of thirty wagons to Council Bluffs in 1860 and returned to Salt Lake the same fall with a load of machinery and merchandise. He proposed a new scheme of regular ox-team travel between Salt Lake and the Missouri River, transporting Utah-produced goods east to sell and returning to Utah with immigrants.

Church Trains

The proposal had many advantages. It preserved scarce Church monies in Utah. Food for the immigrants was produced in Utah rather than purchased in the east. Local units provided mules, oxen, horses, and team drivers, young men who were considered missionaries. Often unmarried men volunteered as teamsters hoping to meet prospective brides among the European immigrants. (Many romances blossomed on the plains.) Surplus Utah products were taken to the Midwest to be sold. The trains reached the Missouri River in July and returned with ten to twenty immigrants per wagon.

During the eight years of Church Trains, from 1860 to 1868, approximately 2,000 wagons went east to receive the immigrants and employed about 2,500 men and 17,500 oxen. More than 20,000 European immigrants crossed the plains in the Trains. Donations of labor, teams, supplies, and provisions made money practically unnecessary to the operation. All this proved providential, because the United States was embroiled in a wrenching civil war from 1861 to 1865, and had the Church relied on outside supplies, the gathering to Zion would have stopped almost entirely. As it turned out, Utah's population doubled from about 40,000 to more than 80,000 between 1861 and 1868.

One of the largest emigrant parties during this period, nearly 900 people strong, sailed on the *Amazon* in 1863.[9] Departing from London rather than Liverpool, they excited considerable curiosity among Londoners. Numerous onlookers—government officials and clergymen included—went to the docks for a firsthand look at so many America-bound emigrants leaving Britain for religious reasons. Author Charles Dickens went on board to question British Mission president George Q. Cannon and observe the Saints. Dickens fully expected to write harshly against the Latter-day Saints, but he was impressed by their thoroughgoing organization, calmness, sobriety, and quiet self-respect. He declared that these people were "the pick and flower of England."[10]

Most families on the *Amazon* had saved money for their passage an average of thirteen years; some had saved for as long as twenty-three years, as in the case of Ishmael and Mary Phillips, converted in Herefordshire by Wilford Woodruff in 1840. Brother Phillips had served either as a branch president or a missionary for most of that time. William Fowler, author of the hymn "We Thank Thee, Oh God, for a Prophet" was also on board this vessel with his family. A few single adult emigrants on board were leaving ahead of their families.[11] One of these, twenty-three-year-old William Waddoups, went alone to Utah, found work in Bountiful, and contributed money to the PEF in his family's name to allow his parents and younger siblings to emigrate by 1868.[12]

Harsh weather on the Atlantic subjected the *Amazon* to an unusually long voyage of forty-four days (the average was twenty-eight).[13] Because of difficulties related to the American Civil War, the company rode in cattle cars for four days from New York to Florence, Nebraska. En route they heard shots fired between Union troops and proslavery bushwhackers. "We were packed in like a lot of sheep, and the journey was anything but pleasant," remembered Waddoups.[14]

At Florence, the *Amazon* immigrants divided into several companies for the final leg of their journey. When they arrived in Salt Lake City, Elder George A. Smith of the Quorum of the Twelve sent Charles Dickens a final report: "The whole company arrived in this city, and encamped on the Union square on Saturday & Sunday Oct. 3rd & 4th, in good health and fine spirits. After attending the General Conference, they distributed themselves among the people of the Territory, like the water of a river as it empties into the sea, and could now only be found by searching 25,000 square miles of country, and by their industrious habits, they . . . will soon put themselves in possession of the necessary comforts of life."[15]

The Scandinavian Saints who emigrated during the 1860s struggled more than their British counterparts because they required at least two weeks' additional travel time and hence more money. First they assembled in Copenhagen to travel by ship to Kiel or Lübeck in Germany and then by rail to Hamburg. In Hamburg they secured passage to Hull or Grimsby, England, and finally by rail to Liverpool. Their rate of sickness exceeded that of the British emigrants as well. "Scandinavians seemed particularly susceptible to measles; common killers were cholera and dysentery." Very few Scandinavian families reached Zion without losing at least one of their children.[16]

The Church Train phase of immigration and freighting ended with the completion of the transcontinental railroad in 1869.

Steamships and Railroad

In 1869 emigration from Europe underwent a revolutionary change. Steamships that were faster and safer than the older sailing vessels had already been plying the seas since the early 1860s, but the cost had been prohibitive. Nevertheless, when Brigham Young needed numerous able-bodied men to build the transcontinental rail lines through Utah by contract with the Union Pacific Railroad, he directed British Mission president Franklin D. Richards to contract passage on steamships. After that venture Latter-day Saint European emigrant companies never used sailing vessels again.

In May 1869, the wedding of the rails took place at Promontory Summit, Utah, changing forever transportation and commerce in America. Thereafter all Latter-day Saint immigrants traveled by rail from New York or other eastern harbors. So, in the same year, 1869, gathering to Zion changed simultaneously from sailing ships to steamers and from ox wagons to the railway.[17]

Significant advantages existed for the new system. The Saints could travel much faster—in about three weeks from Liverpool to Utah, compared to about five months previously. Deaths were fewer en route. Gone were the days of high mortality aboard ship and on the plains, particularly among infants and children. The safer, faster system also allowed for flexible departure schedules. No longer was it necessary for agents to send all emigrants from Liverpool in April and May in order for them to arrive in Utah before the October mountain snows.

Historian Richard Jensen noted: "Reliance on the railroad instead of the Church teams for the final leg of the journey freed manpower, teams, wagons, and other resources for the building of temples and other community development. In earlier years, those who had helped bring home the immigrants had missed both planting time and harvest time."[18]

Financially, however, the Saints made greater initial sacrifices. Although Church agents secured favorable rates from the Guion Line, a British shipping company, payment was required up front. The same was true for rail fares in the United States. Overall costs were not much different, but European members had to have more cash in hand before they could emigrate.

By the 1880s most emigrants did not rely on PEF funds to journey to Zion, though they did use PEF services, because the Latter-day Saints conducted a safer, shepherded migration. For example, PEF agents steered the Saints clear of the notorious "Liverpool pirates" who robbed thousands of unsuspecting European immigrants.

PEF sponsorship of emigration ended in 1887 when the United States government, under the Edmunds-Tucker antipolygamy law, dissolved the Perpetual Emigrating Fund Company. During the rail-steam era from 1887 to the end of the century, European emigrants totaled about 35,000. Latter-day Saint emigration during the previous twenty-nine years had yielded about 50,000. Then, at the beginning of the twentieth century, Church leaders counseled European members to remain in their own countries. The era of organized gathering to Zion was essentially over.

Effects of the Gathering

Compared with all immigration to America in the nineteenth century, Latter-day Saint immigration was a drop in the bucket. Yet to the Church, this migration was vital. It solidified Zion in the United States in the Intermountain West. In 1840, when emigration began from Europe, Church membership was about 18,000. Sixty years later, in 1900, the total was 284,000. Most lived in Latter-day Saint communities in North America.

Immigrants to Utah brought a variety of well-honed trades and skills. The Scandinavians, Welsh, and a few other language groups colored the English spoken in the colonies of Zion. The immigrants also brought their customs to add to Latter-day Saint society.

Only a small proportion of the immigrants were well educated. A few, notably Karl G. Maeser and Jacob Spori, were educators who taught Church youth in Utah. The words and music of more than half of all Latter-day Saint hymns were written or composed by British immigrants. Countless immigrants contributed to the construction of temples, tabernacles, and other buildings and provided essential community services.

Many general authorities were born in Europe, including John Taylor, third Church president, and his nephew, George Q. Cannon, who served in the Twelve and in four First Presidencies. Three other First Presidency members from Great Britain were Charles W. Penrose (who also served as an apostle), Charles W. Nibley, and John R. Winder (both of whom also served in the Presiding Bishopric). Other English members of the Twelve included Elders George Teasdale and James E. Talmage. Elder Charles A. Callis hailed from Ireland, Elder John A. Widtsoe from Norway, and Elder Anthon H. Lund from Denmark (Elder Lund later served in the First Presidency). Elders B. H. Roberts and George Reynolds from England and Christian D. Fjelsted from Denmark served in the presidency of the Seventy. The contribution of these brethren and thousands of other immigrants cannot be overstated.

NOTES

1. *Hymns of The Church of Jesus Christ of Latter-day Saints* (Salt Lake City: The Church of Jesus Christ of Latter-day Saints, 1985), no. 7. This hymn first appeared in a Latter-day Saint hymnal in 1863.

2. Joseph Smith, *History of The Church of Jesus Christ of Latter-day Saints*, 7 vols., 2d ed. rev., edited by B. H. Roberts (Salt Lake City: The Church of Jesus Christ of Latter-day Saints, 1932–51), 2:492.

3. James R. Clark, ed., *Messages of the First Presidency of The Church of Jesus Christ of Latter-day Saints*, 6 vols. (Salt Lake City: Bookcraft, 1965–75), 2:34.

4. Leonard J. Arrington, *Great Basin Kingdom* (Lincoln: University of Nebraska Press, 1983), 103.

5 Conway B. Sonne, *Saints on the Seas* (Salt Lake City: University of Utah Press, 1983), 103–4.

6 LeRoy R. Hafen and Ann W. Hafen, *Handcarts to Zion* (Glendale, Calif.: Arthur H. Clark, 1960), 272.

7 Ibid., 96–97.

8 "Remarks," *Deseret News*, 15 October 1856, 252.

9 Richard L. Jensen and Gordon Irving, "The Voyage of the *Amazon*," *Ensign* 10 (March 1980): 16–19.

10 Ibid., 16.

11 Ibid., 16–18.

12 Bruce A. Van Orden, "William Waddoups: Case Study of a Prominent British Immigrant and Cache Valley Entrepreneur, Bishop, and Patriarch," paper delivered at the annual Mormon History Association meetings, Logan, Utah, May 1988, 10–11.

13 Sonne, *Saints on the Seas*, 84.

14 Van Orden, "William Waddoups," 9.

15 Jensen and Irving, "Voyage of the *Amazon*," 19.

16 William Mulder, *Homeward to Zion: The Mormon Migration from Scandinavia* (Minneapolis: University of Minnesota Press, 1957), 167; Carsten Gram, "Copenhagen," *Church News*, 18 September 1993, 8.

17 Richard L. Jensen, "Steaming Through: Arrangements for Mormon Emigration from Europe, 1869–1887," *Journal of Mormon History* 9 (1982): 3–23.

18 Ibid., 22.

Europe to World War I

n 1850 Elders John Taylor, Erastus Snow, and Lorenzo Snow of the Quorum of the Twelve Apostles took the gospel to the continent of Europe; that same year the administrative headquarters for the European Mission was established in Liverpool, England. Its first president, Elder Franklin D. Richards of the Twelve, served simultaneously as British Mission president. While the pioneer missionaries to the Continent struggled during the 1850s, the British Mission remained the Church's most productive mission field, although it did gradually decline from its halcyon days of the 1840s. Throughout the 1860s, however, thousands of converts provided Utah with a steady stream of British immigrants. After 1870 the British Mission was no longer the leading mission for new converts.

During these same years, from 1850 to 1870, missionary work on the Continent settled into a pattern of a few missionaries facing persistent opposition and persecution from government and religious leaders but nevertheless baptizing steadily, if not bountifully. Only three continental European missions survived the 1860s: the Scandinavian, the

Swiss-German, and the Netherlands. Attempts to take the gospel to the Austrian Empire, Finland, and Russia failed as courageous missionaries were imprisoned or deported. The much publicized antipolygamy crusade in America contributed substantially to the difficulties of the missionaries during this time in Europe.

Fresh optimism for the European missions dawned with the 1890 Manifesto, which ended the practice of plural marriage. The Church in America resolved its differences with the federal government of the United States, and President Lorenzo Snow proclaimed a revitalization of the Church's worldwide outreach. Zion's leaders urged the European Saints to stay in their homelands. Both the Swiss-German and Scandinavian Missions were divided, allowing Germany and Sweden to have their own missions. In 1906 for the first time a president of the Church, Joseph F. Smith, visited the missions in Britain and on the Continent. Gradually the pace of missionary work picked up, and with less emigration to Utah, local units increased in strength. This lengthy period of slow growth jolted to an end in August 1914 with the outbreak of war in Europe, which eventually affected the entire world.

Britain in the 1850s

In 1850 Elder Franklin D. Richards, who had been called to the Quorum of the Twelve only the year before, was sent to preside over the British Mission. He had been a stellar missionary in England and Scotland from 1846 to 1848 and returned at the peak of the mission's productivity under Elder Orson Pratt, who had led this mission to new successes. Hundreds were joining the Church every month. In 1851 more than 32,000 members of the Church resided in Britain; this figure, an all-time high for the nineteenth century, exceeded the total membership of the Church in all of North America—including Utah. President Richards recognized that the thousands of converts needed basic instruction in Church doctrine and procedures. He therefore launched an extensive publication program to provide Church literature, including new printings of the Book of Mormon, Doctrine and Covenants, and hymnbook. "It is quite inexcusable for the Saints to remain ignorant of their [latter-day scriptures'] precious contents."[1]

Publishing facilities were far more readily at hand in England than in frontier Utah, so locating the Church's principal publishing efforts in Liverpool made good sense. Elder Richards's most important new publication was an 1851 pamphlet containing several of the Prophet Joseph Smith's doctrinal contributions, such as the Vision of Moses, the Book of Enoch, and the Book of Abraham, previously printed in the Nauvoo *Times and Seasons*, but otherwise unavailable. He entitled this small compilation *The Pearl of Great Price*, alluding to Jesus' parable of the merchant who sold his entire collection of gems to acquire a most precious pearl (see Matthew 13:45–46). The book soon became a treasured volume. Emigrating British Saints took their copies to Utah, and in 1878 Elder Orson Pratt published a Utah edition of it. In 1880 the Pearl of Great Price was officially canonized as one of the standard works of the Church by vote in general conference.

Another splendid contribution to Church literature was the work of Elder George D. Watt, who in 1837 had been the first person to be baptized in England. In 1853, with the approval of the First Presidency, Elder Watt began a sixteen-page, twice-monthly periodical called the *Journal of Discourses*. This Liverpool publication contained speeches given by Church general authorities in Utah. The issues were bound into annual volumes. The *Journal of Discourses* continued through 1886, a total of twenty-six volumes. The British Mission continued publishing the *Millennial Star*, the Church's longest-lived periodical, which ran continuously until 1970, when the *Ensign* became the standard Church magazine in English. The British Mission president was always the editor of the *Star*. Because most of the British Mission presidents throughout the nineteenth century were apostles and presidents of the European Mission, their inspiring editorials and articles are an invaluable resource for Latter-day Saint history. Even Utah events were reported more completely in the *Star* than in any Utah publication. In June 1851 Elder Richards as the European Mission president called the first conference of European mission leaders. Four apostles met in London: Elders Franklin D. Richards, John Taylor, Lorenzo Snow, and Erastus Snow. Two other missionaries from the Continent, Elders T. B. H. Stenhouse and George P. Dykes, also attended, along with thirty-nine British conference presidents (who presided over several branches within a conference district) and twenty-nine traveling elders. This conference purposely coincided with London's Great Exhibition of technological advances. From this exhibit, the apostles took ideas back to Utah in the 1850s to be implemented in the Church's unique economic system.[2]

Beginning in the 1850s, the European-British Mission president kept in closer touch with Church leaders and missionaries on the Continent, helped to arrange emigration to America, and from time to time visited various missions and the new members. Many apostles served several terms as European-British Mission president.

In 1856 and 1857, the years of the Utah Reformation movement, two apostles, Orson Pratt and Ezra T. Benson, were in Britain. Those years of renewal and reform bolstered the Saints' faith and cleansed the Church of some iniquity that had arisen. Seeing the profit of this movement in Zion, President Brigham Young directed Elders Pratt and Benson to launch a similar program first in the British Isles and then in continental Europe. The Mormon Reformation in Europe lasted only six months, but its effects were considerable. Reformation historian Paul Peterson observed: "Mission leaders and presidents of the various pastorates, districts, conferences, and branches were to reform first, then lay members. Those willing to recovenant to keep the commandments more diligently were eligible for rebaptism. Members reluctant to enter into this pledge were not."[3] The Reformation had its desired effect. Most members increased their zeal for keeping the commandments, prepared righteously for emigration, and submitted to rebaptism; others fell in the general housecleaning and were cut off from the Church.

Tithing was often a crucial test. "The principle had been but recently introduced in England and prior to this time Saints had not been cut off for noncompliance. Pratt instructed the elders that Church members unwilling to covenant to pay tithing were not to be grafted in."[4] Brigham Young explained: "One hundred good and faithful brethren" were better than "millions of half-hearted milk-and-water adherents who continually seek to serve both God and the devil."[5] In 1857, as the Reformation finished its sifting, membership in the British Mission hovered around 20,000, down more than 12,000 from its peak six years earlier. Massive emigration, hundreds of excommunications, and a slightly lower conversion rate were all factors in the lower figure.

When Brigham Young learned in July 1857 that the federal army was en route to Utah, he called Elders Pratt and Benson to return quickly to help plan for a possible war. He dispatched Elder Samuel W. Richards, who was not an apostle, to England as the new European Mission president. Historian Richard Poll noted that President Young's instructions show his pressing concern for Zion: "The message from President Young was succinct: The Mormon emigration from Europe was to stop, except for Saints who might wish to go to Canada on their own and there wait until the way to Zion was open again. The American elders were to come home, 'except one or two that would be required to take charge of the *Star*' and other business in England. The returning elders were to 'bring as many good faithful men with them' as they could, but not delay to recruit them."[6] The most substantial effect of the Utah War upon the Church in Britain was to place greater leadership responsibilities on local priesthood bearers. Emigration and conversions fell to a trickle through 1860 because there were far fewer missionaries.

One local British missionary during the 1850s was Charles W. Penrose, who received his call in 1851. Even though he yearned to gather to Zion with other members and missionaries, a series of mission presidents extended his call time and time again until he had served as a missionary for ten full years. During the decade, he presided at different times over the London, Cheltenham, Herefordshire, and Birmingham conferences. Elder Penrose developed a reputation as a gifted, powerful speaker and poet. An incident from his biography also shows a man of determined kindness. "Just before his 1861 missionary release, a situation arose that greatly troubled Elder Penrose. A missionary, unnamed, began to circulate 'a sort of quiet slander' against him. There was not a word of truth to the story, and it greatly angered him. He said he had grown used to the enemies of the Church accusing him of all sorts of mischief, but it cut him 'to the heart' to have a Church member slander him. Instead of retaliating, he sat down and wrote a poem 'School Thy Feelings, O My Brother.' The writing of the poem, which was later put to music, seemed to calm Elder Penrose, and he was able to forgive the offending missionary while continuing to love and serve God."[7] Elder Penrose went on to serve the Church in such prominent positions as European Mission president, editor of the *Deseret News*, apostle, and member of the First Presidency.

Britain in the 1860s

In 1860 the Church had sufficiently recovered from the Utah War to be anxious to rejuvenate the various missions. The First Presidency sent not just one apostle to preside over the combined European-British Missions but three: Elders Amasa M. Lyman, Charles C. Rich, and the newly ordained George Q. Cannon, who eighteen years earlier had joined the Church after being taught by his uncle John Taylor in Liverpool. The three apostles arrived in England by late summer 1860 and soon invigorated the missionaries and strengthened members in the conferences and branches. Baptisms increased, and plans were formed for the next season's emigration.

During this renaissance of the British Mission, ominous events were shaping towards war in the United States. Abraham Lincoln won the presidential election of 1860, and in April 1861 civil war broke out between the northern and the southern states. Elder George Q. Cannon editorialized often in the *Millennial Star* about the portent of this conflict and Joseph Smith's prophecy of it (see D&C 87).

As dreadful as the American Civil War was, the Church was not directly affected. The terrors of war did not reach Utah or Britain, where most members lived during this period. Emigrating British Saints skirted war zones en route to Zion, and the Church actually suffered less persecution during the war (1861 to 1865).

In May 1862, Elder George Q. Cannon was left in sole charge of the European and British Missions and remained so until 1864. Elder Cannon's service as mission president stands as a hallmark in Latter-day Saint history. This gifted apostle, who later served as counselor to four Church presidents, brought both spirituality and organizational efficiency into the mission. Despite lagging religiosity in Britain during the 1860s, Elder Cannon's innovations kept the Church a vital force in that country through the entire decade.[8]

Elder Cannon had already proved himself a skilled printer, publisher, and writer. He had published the Book of Mormon in Hawaiian and edited the *Western Standard* in San Francisco and the *Deseret News* in Utah. In Liverpool, President Cannon supervised the creation of the Church's own printing office, purchasing type, a steam-driven press, and

Liverpool headquarters for both the European and the
British Mission for approximately one hundred years

other needed items. Besides writing numerous editorials, President
Cannon with unusual business acumen turned the printing office into a
financial success. Subsequent mission leaders had no need to alter his
efficient system.

President Cannon also reorganized the emigration process and
improved contacts with shipping companies. During his four years as
mission president, Elder Cannon supervised the emigration of more than
13,000 European Saints. "His belief in the principle of gathering, his skill
in organizing emigrant companies, and his ability to charter the best
ships all worked together for the good of the Saints." Emigrant companies rose from an average size of 266 per vessel in the 1850s to 424 during
the early 1860s.[9]

President Cannon set high standards for his missionaries, many of
whom were married and in their thirties or forties. "He required the
elders to be clad in a black suit and wear a silk hat. He urged them to
earnestly seek the Spirit of the Lord and to preach by that same Spirit.
He warned them about the evils of the world which would undermine
their effectiveness."[10]

Throughout the rest of the decade other mission presidents followed President Cannon's lead in Europe: Daniel H. Wells, Brigham Young Jr., Franklin D. Richards, and Albert Carrington. Both conversion and emigration statistics remained high, although slightly declined from their peak.

Decline of the British Mission

After 1870 the British Mission shrank to a fraction of its former self. In 1863 Saints in Britain numbered 12,851; in 1871, membership had dropped to 7,206, and by 1874 to 5,423. Gathering to Zion was not the cause; emigration also declined. During the 1860s, an average of 992 members left Britain each year. Between 1870 and 1875, an average of 697 emigrated per year, even though steamship and railroad made the journey much easier.[11]

Events in Utah contributed to the decline of the British Mission. Conflicts between Mormons and non-Mormons in Utah, hostility toward the Saints from the Radical Republicans, and differences with the federal government had been intensifying throughout the 1860s and 1870s. The Radicals came to power in 1869 with President Ulysses S. Grant, and the year 1870 marked the beginning of the antipolygamy crusade by the United States government, an endeavor that damaged the reputation of the Church and weakened its political and economic base in Utah. One unsuccessful bill proposed dissolving the territory of Utah and annexing portions to neighboring territories and states. The anti-Mormon crusade lasted twenty more years before declining after President Wilford Woodruff issued the Manifesto in 1890 to halt the practice of plural marriage. This conflict did not go unnoticed in the British Mission. The *Millennial Star* defended the Church and predicted eventual victory for the Saints over all their foes, but the intense antipolygamy campaign in the States eroded the reputation of the Church in the British Isles.

Other events in Utah in the early 1870s also caused some stir in the British Mission. First was the April 1873 resignation of seventy-two-year-old Brigham Young as trustee-in-trust for the Church and president of Deseret National Bank and ZCMI. President Young wished to devote his energies more fully to counseling the Saints and visiting the settlements.

The press in Great Britain foresaw in the withdrawal of this powerful leader from the public sphere an end to Mormonism and the "Mormon problem." Second and more significant was the panic of 1873 in the United States. That nationwide depression increased joblessness and tightened the money supply in Utah, thus curtailing both the number of missionaries able to go to Britain and the money available to help British Saints emigrate.

The Saints in Britain in the 1870s had also drifted into comparative apathy. George Reynolds, back in his native land as a missionary, observed: "Many of the folks have degenerated into good old singalong sectarians. Apparently not a spark of the true living spirit of the gospel is with them. They would make mighty good Methodists perhaps. They are always glad to see an elder, but there's not the true ring about them, they are so fast asleep you can't wake them up."[12]

The decline of the Church in Britain after 1870 reflected a general apathy toward religion in the country at that time. Although numerous waves of religious awakening had swept Britain since 1780, the last noticeable one was in 1859. The gradual secularization of society, including religion itself, had supplanted religious devotion. Science, especially Darwinism, challenged the worldviews of traditional religions, and "enlightened" modern thought dismissed as superstition or myth the biblical accounts of the Creation, the Flood, and the wondrous events in the life of Jesus. Modern, secular British society had lost faith in the Bible, and by the end of the century agnosticism seemed not only acceptable but almost universal.[13]

Despite these difficulties, the mission continued its uphill battle to win converts and send them to Zion. Joseph F. Smith, John Henry Smith, Daniel H. Wells, George Teasdale, Brigham Young Jr., and Anthon H. Lund served one or more terms as mission president. Each presided over a strong group of American and British elders, but baptisms for the rest of the century rarely reached more than 500 per year. The glory years for the British Mission were over until the end of World War II.

The Scandinavian Mission through 1900

Next to the British Mission, the most productive European mission during the nineteenth century was the Scandinavian Mission.

Throughout the 1860s it averaged 1,289 convert baptisms and 456 emigrants to Zion per year.[14] Those numbers are approximately half those of the British Mission and are an astounding yield, given that three different languages were spoken in the mission and in Norway, Sweden, and Iceland government persecution was intense.

Comparative religious freedom in Denmark afforded that nation more baptisms and Church growth throughout the 1860s than in either Norway or Sweden. Elder Anders Christensen reported in January 1861 from Aalborg, a stronghold of the Church in Denmark: "Greater numbers have been baptized here, according to its population, than in any other place I know of, and there are still greater numbers who believe the gospel; and in general the Elders are treated very kindly by a great many people here. A good many of those who embrace the gospel have been in possession of means, and been very liberal in assisting the Elders to send off the poorer class to the Valley. All the Elders who come here admire the freedom of spirit, and in general feel desirous of proclaiming the gospel."[15]

The various European Mission presidents visited Scandinavia two or three times per year to strengthen the elders and Saints and to supervise emigration arrangements. Their visits were times of rejoicing and spiritual rejuvenation. In 1862 President George Q. Cannon wrote of his most recent visit to Denmark: "The Saints all seemed to vie with one another to make the Elders who visited them feel comfortable. . . . We do not recollect ever having had greater liberty in speaking, and more of the spirit of instruction. . . . The people appeared to listen with eager attention to all that was said. . . . It is to be hoped that the time is not far distant when the Elders will be able openly to preach the principles of the gospel . . . without fear of molestation. If that day shall come, thousands will come forward and readily embrace the principles of truth. . . . Scandinavia will doubtless furnish her quota to make up this mighty [latter-day] kingdom."[16] Both in Europe and in Utah, the steady infusion of Scandinavian Saints substantially benefited the Church.

In late 1863, several Danish elders quickly emigrated to Zion to avoid being drafted into military service in a war that was threatening between Prussia and Denmark. The following year, the Prussian army invaded Denmark, and the invading Germans even took over the Saints' meeting hall in Aalborg.

The war slowed missionary work in Denmark for two years but led to increased effort in Sweden, where religious freedom was gradually increasing. Thus in the last half of the 1860s, Sweden matched and then in the 1870s often exceeded the productivity in Denmark. European Mission president Joseph F. Smith noted in 1875: "The elders and Saints in Scandinavia to-day, as a rule, enjoy equal rights, and liberties with all or any other denominations of professing Christians, not but what they occasionally meet with opposition and sometimes ill-treatment from bigoted priests and magistrates, but comparatively speaking, they enjoy immunity from the harsh treatment and bitter animus that so persistently followed them in these countries a few years ago."[17] In 1878 the Book of Mormon was published in Swedish. Twenty years later, in 1898, a specially bound copy was presented to the king of Sweden by Elder Janne M. Sjodahl, a Swedish emigrant who had risen to prominence in the Church in Utah. From 1880 to 1900 Sweden led the Scandinavian Mission in convert baptisms.

In Norway in the 1860s, the Church established a foothold in the capital city of Christiana (now called Oslo). In rural areas, the elders continued to be arrested and imprisoned, a situation that lasted throughout most of the century. Nevertheless, the missionaries baptized an average of 100 converts each year.

In 1873 missionaries from the Scandinavian Mission returned to Iceland for the first time since 1854. A few converts were baptized, and a branch was organized. Small companies of Icelandic Saints joined other emigrants from Scandinavia in the 1870s and 1880s. Nearly all these Icelandic immigrants settled on the east bench of Spanish Fork, Utah, where many Icelandic traditions still survive among their descendants.

Elder Erastus Snow, who opened the Scandinavian Mission in 1850, returned to visit in 1873. He rejoiced over the stronger organization in Scandinavia and the contribution of the Scandinavian Saints to the Church as a whole.

When strict antipolygamy laws began to be enforced in America in the 1880s, the State Department instructed United States ambassadors in Europe not to protect American citizens engaged in "Mormon" missionary work. This edict was felt most distinctly in Denmark, where the missionaries had recently been enjoying relative freedom. Anti-Mormon propaganda in the press also increased, and various Danish civil authorities banished elders from their jurisdictions. After the Manifesto in 1890, when the question of plural marriage was essentially settled, the situation of Latter-day Saints in Scandinavia began to improve.

By 1900 the Church's missionary harvest had diminished in Scandinavia. The membership rolls of the Church in Scandinavia listed 4,535 members, a number that had changed very little over the previous forty years.[18] Many members had gradually emigrated to Zion, and those members still in Scandinavia in 1900 yearned to emigrate.

The Swiss-German Mission through 1900

In 1861, the year the American Civil War began, a consolidated Swiss-Italian-German Mission came into being. Proselyting in Italy or the German states was a hope rather than a reality, however. Italy was included in the mission because a few Waldensian members still lived in the Piedmont, but active proselyting there had ceased. And by 1861 in the German states persecution had become so intense that most members had gathered to Zion and missionary work there was close to nonexistent. Elder George Q. Cannon visited southern Germany and concluded that only the power of the Almighty could break the iron yoke of the laws repressing the work of the Church. Thus during the early 1860s only Switzerland saw progress in this three-pronged mission.

The Swiss had enjoyed political independence since 1291, and during the revolutions of 1848, guarantees of freedom of religion and of assembly were added to the country's federal constitution. Missionaries and members were still persecuted during the 1850s and 1860s, however, because the Church was not considered Christian and its adherents were therefore denied constitutional protection. In 1858 mission president Jabez Woodard reported of difficulties in Switzerland: "I never saw such stormy times as the last few weeks. Some of the weak Saints have gone overboard; and if it keeps on blowing, we shall soon be rid of the chaff, and light wheat also."[19]

In 1864 the Federal Council of Switzerland ruled that the Latter-day Saints had as much right to constitutional protection as members of any other faith. This ruling only gradually lessened antagonism toward the Church, but at least the elders could hold meetings and baptize converts relatively unmolested—something that was next to impossible in both Italy and Germany. Throughout the 1860s, some 600 converts joined the Church in Switzerland and another 600 emigrated to Zion.[20]

In 1867 Italy was dropped from the mission, and a native German was called as president of the Swiss-German Mission. The arrival of Karl G. Maeser was a turning point in the Swiss-German Mission. When thirty-eight-year-old President Maeser took over, only two elders remained and the 469 members were scattered. Morale was low, and prospects for the future seemed bleak. But President Maeser was undaunted. Four new elders arrived from America, and missionary work revived. Within a year, 226 persons were baptized.

Among President Maeser's most significant contributions were his writings and publications. On 1 January 1869, the first issue of the monthly periodical *Der Stern (The Star)* appeared. This magazine, later a semimonthly, has powerfully influenced the German-speaking Latter-day Saints since its founding. Maeser wrote most of the early material for *Der Stern* himself. The charismatic mission president also wrote various tracts and gave lectures in Germany and Switzerland.

Despite having no more than six missionaries laboring at any one time, the Swiss-German Mission baptized about 600 people during President Maeser's administration, which lasted through June 1870. More new members were baptized during those three years than during the preceding ten years. The mission president ascribed success to "a new Spirit that came over the mission. This happened at the same time in many areas, with hardly any human effort . . . that they could not attribute it to their own doing, rather the God of Israel moved the hearts of the people. Many of the brethren who had become idle came forth again, also many who had remained aloof from the service of God."[21] Most of the new converts prepared themselves to gather to Zion as soon as they could.

In 1870 the ambitious Prussian leader Otto von Bismarck unified the various German states into one powerful nation under Prussian domination by enlisting their support in a war with France. The united Germany states won easily, and in 1871 a new German kingdom was formed.

Together with the industrial revolution that was sweeping Germany, the politically adept Bismarck molded the country into the most powerful nation on the Continent. But Germany was not founded on the same principles as were some other European nations. The new German constitution guaranteed religious liberty, but local governments, prodded by state Lutheran and Catholic religions, continued to harass Latter-day Saint elders.

Two other factors led to a decline in Church growth in Germany during the 1870s. One was an excessive national pride that hovered over the country during the period. Another was the emerging antipolygamy crusade in the United States, which fueled intolerance and bad press against the Saints in Germany.

During the 1870s, the Swiss-German Mission averaged about 180 baptisms a year, most of them in Switzerland. An average of eighty-five converts emigrated each year.[22] In contrast to German intolerance, Switzerland in the 1870s was more open-minded toward the Church. Elder Joseph F. Smith, while president of the European Mission, visited Switzerland in 1873 and commented on the increase in religious liberty. Missionaries had no trouble organizing public meetings, which were attended by large numbers of non-Latter-day Saints.[23] In 1875, President Smith directed the elders to stop asking permission from local German authorities to preach but simply to preach and build up branches.[24] A rotation system kept missionary efforts in Germany alive. When one missionary was persecuted or banished, he left for Switzerland and another arrived to replace him. Very gradually persecution of the Latter-day Saints diminished in Germany. Though hardly perceptible from year to year but noticeable over several years, baptisms increased in Germany. In 1875 German converts represented 10 percent of the mission total; by 1880 the percentage had risen to 33.

Between 1855 and 1881, the northern German areas of Hamburg and Schleswig-Holstein had been assigned to the Scandinavian Mission. Little proselyting was done in those years. In 1881 these areas were incorporated into the Swiss-German Mission. Numerous converts were baptized in the entire country, especially in Nürnberg. For the first time Germany had more new members than Switzerland, and exponential growth appeared imminent. New branches sprang up throughout the country, and new Church publications appeared in the German language. Church members were still wary of local police, however, and often held meetings in forests where they could sing and preach aloud.

Then antipolygamy activity in the United States was set off by passage of the 1883 Edmunds Act. That alone took a severe toll in both Germany and Switzerland. Officials reasoned that if the United States government was legislating against the Church, why should they do less? Conversions decreased throughout the mission, and members met even more secretly to avoid arrest or harassment. The Swiss-German Mission was shored up in 1889 by the arrival of a host of new missionaries, and after President Wilford Woodruff stopped the practice of plural marriage in 1890, the mission's fortunes again improved.

In the early 1890s the gospel was taken for the first time into the far eastern reaches of Germany, areas now part of Poland and Russia. This region blossomed quickly and for the next forty years was by far the most productive German-speaking area in the Church. The baptismal rate increased year by year in Germany as many new cities were opened. The First Presidency decided to divide the mission, and on 1 January 1898 the German Mission was created.

Other Nineteenth-Century Pioneering Efforts in Europe

From time to time the First Presidency and the Quorum of the Twelve Apostles sent representatives to other countries in Europe. Because of persecution, however, most such attempts ended soon after they began. Courageous missionaries and equally brave converts worked to help the Church fulfill its divine mandate.

One country that after 1860 was opened permanently to the Church was the Netherlands, a small kingdom also known as Holland that lies on the North Sea in northwestern Europe. The Dutch established their kingdom in 1814 after a long struggle for independence against the French and Spanish. During the revolutions of 1848, the Dutch adopted a new constitution that tolerated all religious denominations.

Elder Orson Hyde visited Rotterdam and Amsterdam in 1841 en route to Palestine to dedicate Jerusalem for the return of the Jews. In those two cities Elder Hyde contacted Jewish rabbis and left copies in Dutch of his *Address to the Hebrews.* Twenty years later, in 1861,

Church officials in Salt Lake City set apart two elders to preach the gospel in the Netherlands as part of the Swiss-German Mission. The senior elder was Paul Schettler, a Prussian immigrant to the United States baptized by Elder George Q. Cannon in New York City in 1860. His companion was A. W. van der Woude, the first Dutch convert to the Church, who had been baptized in Wales in 1852 and emigrated to America with his family the following year.

These two elders separated during their first months in Holland to take the gospel to their relatives. Both met considerable opposition, but each also succeeded in baptizing three converts before year's end. By May 1862, fourteen members had joined the Church in Amsterdam, and the first Dutch branch was organized. False rumors from a Dutch anti-Mormon pamphlet repeated in newspapers inhibited early missionary efforts. "The national character of the Dutch is to stick to the traditions of their fathers more than other nations," observed Elder Schettler. "This spirit is manifested in all their customs and fashions."[25]

In 1863 Elder van der Woude left Holland, taking two converts to Zion with him. At the end of that year Elder Schettler also departed for Utah with a convert who had been serving as a missionary. Thirty-three members were on the Church records, and no missionaries replaced Elders van der Woude and Schettler.

During 1864 Dutch members taught the gospel message to a small religious sect called New Lighters. About fifty of these people, who believed in the communal brotherhood practiced by the early disciples of Christ as described in Acts 2:44, joined the Latter-day Saints. Shortly after their conversion, the entire group of New Lighters and a few other Dutch converts emigrated to America.

In November 1864, the Netherlands Mission was organized. The First Presidency called Joseph Weiler to be its first president, and when he arrived, he found twenty-five members, three of whom were elders and one an ordained teacher.[26] Elder Weiler labored at first without a companion, and his work was hampered by a severe illness, difficult new customs, a lack of Church literature in Dutch, and a shortage of suitable places for the Saints to meet. But during his three-year presidency, he supervised the baptism of twenty-six converts and organized three branches.

Over the next two decades, the Netherlands Mission held together—barely. The few missionaries tried to deter prejudice, but they faced constant threats of mob activity incited by the clergy and by unrelenting attacks in the press. The antipolygamy crusade in America further undermined the Church's reputation in Holland, and prejudice became so widespread that proprietors refused to rent halls to the Saints for meetings. It was not unusual during the 1870s and 1880s for a year to go by with no baptisms.

After the 1890 Manifesto ended the practice of plural marriage, the Church sent more missionaries to the Netherlands. The number of converts and emigrants rose dramatically. During the 1890s some 1,400 converts joined the Church, and 289 gathered to Zion. Membership in the mission stood at 1,664 in 1900.[27]

Although the Church did not establish a permanent presence elsewhere in Europe in the nineteenth century, a few pioneering missionaries attempted to extend gospel frontiers into other nations. The largest and most powerful was the Austro-Hungarian Empire, in the heart of Europe. This sprawling political entity spawned numerous countries in the twentieth century. But in the nineteenth century, Austria-Hungary was an amalgam of more than a dozen ethnic groups that spoke as many languages. Most of the Austrian peoples were Germanic, and because the Church had the Book of Mormon in German and some stalwart German-speaking converts, the First Presidency decided to begin missionary efforts in Austria. In 1865 Elder Orson Pratt of the Twelve Apostles, one of the greatest missionaries and leaders of the British Mission, arrived with Elder William Ritter in Vienna. They remained seven months, but they soon discovered that the emperor, an ardent Catholic, dictated religious practice in Austria. He absolutely forbade a license to preach to anyone not of accepted Christian faiths. Discouraged, the two brethren were expelled from Austria without a single convert.

Eighteen years later, two elders from the Swiss-German Mission, Elders Thomas Biesinger and Paul Hammer, made another attempt in Vienna. Elder Biesinger was well aware of the powers arrayed against their hopes. When he arrived in the Austrian capital, he uttered a prayer in which he conversed with Vienna: "Thou City of Vienna, thou boasteth thyself as being one of the proudest cities of the East and the beauties of thy gardens and parks are perhaps not excelled in the world. Thou [art] also . . . the abode of a monarch who sways his proud sceptre over a dominion containing nearly forty millions of inhabitants."[28]

The Austrian Empire was still not a land of freedom. The emperor, attempting to hold his various peoples together in peace, governed a police state that forbade the preaching of new ideas, political or religious. The elders began holding meetings in the home of a widow, but the police soon warned the courageous Frau Mahrburg that she would be prosecuted and the missionaries arrested if the meetings did not cease. The elders decided to separate for safety but not before they baptized three converts. Elder Hammer remained in Vienna, and Elder Biesinger went to Prague in Bohemia (now part of the Czech Republic but then part of the Austrian Empire).

Elder Biesinger struck up many gospel conversations with German-speaking people in Prague. But under duress, two of his most promising investigators signed complaints against him, and Elder Biesinger found himself in a foreign prison without friends or companion. In a court hearing, Elder Biesinger learned that local newspapers had run articles about him, with his picture, accusing him of seeking to trap people into Mormon slavery. Finally, after two months in jail, the missionary was freed. Soon he ran into his two accusers, previously investigators, who begged forgiveness. Elder Biesinger could not stay in Bohemia, but he baptized and confirmed one of his contacts before he left for Switzerland.

This same missionary tried other places in the Austrian Empire including Budapest, Hungary, but the outcome was the same: newspapers carried his picture and a warning. So Elder Biesinger left Austria altogether and finished his mission in Bavaria, in Germany. In the 1920s, the eighty-year-old Thomas Biesinger returned to Austria as a missionary to finish the work he had started with a prayer in Vienna on a cold winter morning in 1883. As for Elder Hammer, he was banished from Vienna and then went to the Austrian-held Germanic province of Silesia, where he miraculously recovered from a near-fatal case of smallpox.[29]

The most prominent convert from the Austro-Hungarian Empire in the nineteenth century was a Serb named Mischa Markow, who was living in Hungary.[30] Reared in the Serbian Orthodox faith, as an unmarried man in his thirties Markow traveled on a pilgrimage to Jerusalem and

Mischa Markow, 1854–1934

Constantinople in 1887. In Constantinople, by a miraculous series of events, he met and was baptized by Jacob Spori, president of the Near East Mission of the Church. Soon Brother Markow became an elder, commissioned to preach and baptize. He found no success with his family in the Empire, so in 1888 he tried Antwerp, Belgium, preaching to the German-speaking community there. After he taught and baptized the entire family of Karl Beckhaus, he contacted leaders of the Swiss-German Mission to request more missionaries be sent. By the time his three reinforcements arrived in Antwerp, Brother Markow and the Beckhaus family had lined up referrals that resulted in eighty baptisms.

After returning to his homeland of Serbia and earning enough money, Brother Markow emigrated to Salt Lake City, where he became a United States citizen. In 1899 he was called on his first official mission. Because he could speak five languages, his call was simply "to Europe." He courageously preached until he was banished from Serbia, Hungary, and Constantinople. In Romania he baptized eleven people and set up a multilingual branch in Bucharest. (His converts in that city spoke four different languages.) Soon Elder Markow was arrested again, but he felt the power of angels protecting him. Banished from Romania, he next went to Bulgaria. Banished once more, he returned to Hungary and received a German-speaking companion. The two missionaries baptized twelve converts and ordained two brethren to watch over the little branch of thirty-one. Elder Markow left Hungary before being arrested and completed his mission as a branch president in Munich, Germany.

Meanwhile, in Belgium, Elder Markow's earliest efforts with the Beckhaus family in Antwerp led to the inclusion of Belgium in, first, the Swiss-German Mission and then, in 1891, the Netherlands Mission. Missionaries remained in Belgium continuously until they were evacuated at the beginning of World War I. Most of the early Belgian converts were Flemish, a people who spoke a language similar to Dutch. Branches were established in Antwerp, Brussels, and Liege.

Another country that was pioneered for missionary work in the late nineteenth century was Finland, then under czarist rule from Russia. This Nordic nation lies east of Sweden, and its west coast had a sizable Swedish-speaking population. The Scandinavian Mission sent two Swedish elders in late 1875, but Finland, like most other countries in Europe, afforded its inhabitants no religious liberty. At the request of local clergymen, the police prevented the elders from holding meetings and threatened them with beating, jail, and expulsion to Siberia. Nevertheless, the missionaries baptized their first convert in Saint Nikolaistad in early 1876. A few missionaries arrived in Finland during the next four years and, despite government harassment, established a branch of twenty-four members. One elder was heavily fined and imprisoned for four weeks on bread-and-water rations for circulating tracts and baptizing on Sunday night, which was considered breaking the Sabbath. In 1880 Russian authorities confiscated books and pamphlets and banned all Latter-day Saint missionaries. Scandinavian Mission leaders were able to do no more in Finland throughout the rest of the century except on rare visits to nurture existing members.

The rest of the huge Russian Empire was also on the minds of the brethren. As far back as 1843, Joseph Smith began preparing Elder Orson Hyde for a mission to Russia, but too many adversities intervened.[31] The desire of the Twelve to take the gospel to the millions in that empire was first fulfilled by a Finn. In 1879 Johan Lindlof, the twenty-two-year-old son of a recently baptized Finnish woman, went to Saint Petersburg, Russia, to be an apprentice.[32] He returned to Finland, and in 1887 married Alma Holmberg. Three years later, in 1890, the couple moved to Saint Petersburg and there reared their family. In 1895 Elder Joel Hoglund of the Scandinavian Mission visited the Lindlofs by invitation, taught them the gospel, and baptized them. After carefully schooling the Lindlofs in gospel principles and Church procedures, Elder Hoglund ordained Johan an elder. The Lindlofs, all alone, faced the task of living and preaching the gospel in isolation from the rest of the Church. Over the next several years, missionaries made infrequent visits to Saint Petersburg, offered the family much needed encouragement, and supervised the baptisms of the Lindlof children.

In 1903 Elder Francis M. Lyman of the Twelve, then president of the European Mission, visited Russia at the behest of the First Presidency and stayed with the Lindlofs. Elder Lyman arranged for two missionaries to go to Russia: the Serb Mischa Markow—the bold, multilingual missionary "to Europe"—and J. A. Hedrikson.

Elder Markow preached to a colony of Germans in Riga, Latvia. He learned that anyone openly challenging the authority or doctrine of the Russian Orthodox Church could be sent to Siberia for two years and that baptizing a person into another faith carried a penalty of twelve years. The ethnic Germans in Latvia were fortunately not under such restrictions, but Elder Markow's success alarmed the German clergymen, and he was soon once again back in court. The judge banned Elder Markow from Russia.[33]

Elder Hedrikson, laboring in Saint Petersburg, could preach only to people who were not Russians. He left Russia in 1905 when Russia became embroiled in war with Japan. The Lindlofs lived in Russia as isolated Church members through much turmoil. In 1918 the Bolsheviks confiscated their property and sentenced the Lindlof children to imprisonment and hard labor. Finally, in 1928, Brother and Sister Lindlof were able to return to Helsinki, Finland, where they lived out their lives, always faithful to the gospel, until they died, in 1939 and 1944, respectively. Their "story remains a legacy of endurance for all who seek to sustain their faith in a world so often callous to the workings of the Spirit."[34]

Europe before World War I

As the twentieth century dawned, Church officials in Utah sent gospel emissaries to many nations. Elder Lyman's 1903 attempt to establish the Church in Russia is one example. Another is Elder Heber J. Grant's pioneering mission to Japan in 1901. But the times were not yet ripe for a rich harvest of souls. Throughout Europe existing missions limped along under the adversities of persecutions by government and clergy, lurid attacks in the press, and widespread religious apathy. But as leaders began urging the Saints to remain in Europe instead of emigrating, the branches gradually gained stability and strength.

The First Presidency continued to send apostles to preside over missions in Europe. This policy assured the missions the best leadership the Church had. And for the first time a president of the Church visited Europe. President Joseph F. Smith's visit in 1906 was a turning point in international Church history. He appealed to the Saints to stay in their homelands. His visit symbolized that the era of organized gathering to America was over. Building Zion all over the world could commence.

The Church faced serious problems in the first decade of the twentieth century. Charges of Church-sanctioned plural marriages being performed in secret and of Church interference in Utah politics flooded the American press. The climax was the Reed Smoot hearings in the United States Senate from 1904 to 1907. Senator Smoot had been duly elected, but because he was not only a Latter-day Saint but also a member of the Quorum of the Twelve Apostles and therefore a member of the Church's second-highest presiding body, many senators were persuaded by powerful lobbying interests that Smoot should be denied his seat in Congress. The argument centered on allegations that the Church promoted un-American practices. President Joseph F. Smith and other general authorities were required to testify before an antagonistic Senate committee, and the Church's beliefs and practices were ridiculed publicly over a period of three years. The Church's reputation plummeted in the United States and in Europe. Attacks in the press on both sides of the Atlantic were unrelenting and vicious. Wherever the Church had missionaries in Europe—and at this point they were in the British Isles, Denmark, Norway, Sweden,

Germany, Austria, Hungary, Switzerland, the Netherlands, and Belgium—
the work suffered immensely.

Elder Heber J. Grant was the president of the European and British
Missions at the beginning of the Smoot hearings. President Grant tried
to counter accusations that the Saints were strange and licentious by asking various British newspapers for space to answer the prevailing argu-
ments. Only occasionally was his request granted, and his rebuttals did
not stanch the onrushing tide of prejudice against the missionaries.

Tensions were equally high on the Continent. Entrenched opposition to the Church by German government officials in the capital city of
Berlin forced the First Presidency in 1904 to reincorporate the German
Mission back into a Swiss-German Mission with headquarters in Zürich.
This way elders could retreat to more tolerant Switzerland when
tensions mounted in their fields of labor in Germany. Ugly reports in
the German press led to the banishing of four elders from Leipzig
and Dresden in the province of Saxony. Hoping to remain in Germany,
the missionaries changed their passport registration from clerical to
student status. This ruse backfired, however, because German officials,
when they learned of it, levied more severe punishment upon the
missionaries.

In contrast, the image of the Church did not become an important
issue in Switzerland between 1900 and 1910. The work fared better in
that country and resulted in many more baptisms than in Germany.[35]

Swiss-German Mission officials continued to try to establish the
Church in Austria and Hungary, though only among ethnic Germans,
but with few results. They also sought to establish legal status for the
Church but to no avail. Missionaries often pursued their work through
teaching English. A few small branches were established, but about half
the few converts emigrated to Zion before 1914. After 1909 mission leaders authorized preaching the gospel in Hungarian; this undertaking
gleaned only a handful of baptisms.

Though not inundated by success, the Netherlands Mission, which
also included Belgium, actually improved during the first ten years of the
twentieth century. In some years, the Netherlands had the most baptisms in the European missions.

In Scandinavia, the Church remained stable during the early 1900s.

As in the rest of Europe, elders encountered unenthusiastic responses from a people whose religious traditions had eroded. Religion had become a relatively insignificant part of Scandinavians' lives by 1900. One administrative change did occur in Scandinavia during this period. In 1905 Norway had separated from Sweden, so the First Presidency divided the mission into the Swedish Mission, the most productive of the three, and the Scandinavian Mission, consisting of Denmark and Norway.

From 1910 to 1914, circumstances worsened for the Latter-day Saints, especially in Britain. Not only did the press reports become more viciously anti-Mormon, but missionaries also suffered "violence and mobocracy," reported mission president Elder Rudger Clawson. For the first time since 1837, elders faced concerted hostility in England. Such labels as "Mormon Peril" and "Mormon Menace" indicate the irrationality that surfaced among the British people.

The Latter-day Saints may well have served a scapegoat function in the community. Britain was undergoing a rapid change that was unsettling to many groups in society. Domestic political chaos, labor unrest, feminist agitations, and the volatile Irish Question led many to feel that religion, the family, decency, social stability, and the country itself were all in danger. This prevailing unrest gave opponents of the Church an opportunity to unite diverse political, religious, and economic groups against a common enemy—the Latter-day Saints.[36]

The most prolific and persuasive crusader against the Church was Winifred Graham, a popular novelist who imaginatively portrayed the Saints in a series of lurid novels as the personification of evil. "I found it thrilling to fight with voice and pen this mighty kingdom working for self-interest," Graham wrote, "a vampire in fact, sucking the blood of Europe with its wolf-like emissaries in sheep's clothing hot on the heels of British womanhood."[37] All of her novels had similar plots, in which a beautiful but naive heroine, deceived by crafty Mormon missionaries, is rescued only moments before falling victim to a villainous polygamist.

The Church of England, caught up in the general rant, called upon Parliament to banish all Latter-day Saints from the shores of Britain. Although a sizable number in Parliament sympathized with the anti-Mormon sentiment, the House of Commons as a whole did not support legislation. The Home Office, headed by Winston Churchill, sent questionnaires to police commissioners in important cities, but when he failed to turn up any evidence against Latter-day Saint elders, official action against the Church was dropped. Hostile demonstrations eventually ended. By the spring of 1913, the crusade had peaked, and missionary activity, after a two-year lull, began to show signs of recovery.[38] But for many years the Church faced the damage to its reputation brought on by this hysterical crusade.

Hopeful signs also appeared in Germany from 1901 to 1914. Despite extreme governmental opposition, missionaries began baptizing in record numbers, foreshadowing the tremendous success that followed World War I.

During this period, the Church also reestablished a mission in France. By 1907 there were enough French-speaking members in Switzerland and Belgium to warrant a new French-only edition of the Book of Mormon. The following year, missionaries started preaching in French cities across the borders from Switzerland and Belgium. In 1912 the First Presidency decided to reopen the French Mission, and on 15 October elders who had been serving in Switzerland or Belgium met in Paris. The work progressed slowly, but sixty-two baptisms in the mission by July 1914 showed significant promise.

Then every missionary effort in Europe suddenly came to a halt in August 1914. From 1910 to 1914, like petulant children, the powerful and militaristic nations of Europe—Britain, France, Germany, Austria, and Russia—all committed diplomatic blunders and antagonized one another. In a quick succession of events in July and August 1914, Germany and Austria aligned themselves against Russia and France, who were soon joined by Britain. War broke out. Latter-day Saint missionaries received telegrams ordering them to leave their fields of labor immediately and return to America. This startling development marked the end of a long chapter and the beginning of a new one in European Church history.

NOTES

1 Richard O. Cowan, "Church Growth in England, 1841–1914," in V. Ben Bloxham et al., eds., *Truth Will Prevail: The Rise of The Church of Jesus Christ of Latter-day Saints in the British Isles, 1837–1987* (West Midlands: Corporation of the President of The Church of Jesus Christ of Latter-day Saints, 1987), 205.

2 T. Edgar Lyon Jr., "In Praise of Babylon: Church Leadership at the 1851 Great Exhibition in London," *Journal of Mormon History* 14 (1988): 49–61.

3 Paul H. Peterson, "The 1857 Reformation in Britain," in Richard L. Jensen and Malcolm R. Thorp, eds., *Mormons in Early Victorian Britain* (Salt Lake City: University of Utah Press, 1989), 216.

4 Ibid.

5 Ibid., 223.

6 Richard D. Poll, "The British Mission During the Utah War, 1857–58," in Jensen and Thorp, *Mormons in Early Victorian Britain*, 230.

7 Kenneth W. Godfrey, "Charles W. Penrose: The English Mission Years," *BYU Studies* 27 (Winter 1987): 118.

8 Donald Q. Cannon, "George Q. Cannon and the British Mission," *BYU Studies* 27 (Winter 1987): 97–112.

9 Ibid., 103–6.

10 Ibid., 107.

11 Bruce A. Van Orden, "The Decline in Convert Baptisms and Member Emigration from the British Mission after 1870," *BYU Studies* 27 (Spring 1987): 97–105.

12 Ibid., 102.

13 Alan D. Gilbert, *The Making of Post-Christian Britain: A History of the Secularization of Modern Society* (London: Longman Group, 1980), 76–80; Jeffrey Cox, *The English Churches in a Secular Society: Lambeth, 1870–1930* (New York: Oxford University Press, 1982), 3–20; Horton Davies, *Worship and Theology in England: From Newman to Martineau, 1850–1900* (Princeton, N.J.: Princeton University Press, 1962), 173–211; Owen Chadwick, *The Secularization of the European Mind in the Nineteenth Century* (Cambridge: Cambridge University Press, 1975), 161–88; David L. Edwards, *Christian England from the 18th Century to the First World War* (Grand Rapids, Mich.: William B. Eerdmans Publishing Co., 1984), 295–301.

14 Andrew Jenson, *History of the Scandinavian Mission* (Salt Lake City: Deseret News Press, 1927), 533.

15 Ibid., 153–54.

16 Ibid., 169–70.

17 Smith, *Millennial Star* 37 (21 June 1875): 394.

18 Ibid., 533.

19 Woodard, *Millennial Star* 20 (29 May 1858): 347.

20 Dale Z. Kirby, "History of The Church of Jesus Christ of Latter-day Saints in Switzerland," master's thesis, Brigham Young University, 1971, 51, 196.

21 Gilbert W. Scharffs, *Mormonism in Germany* (Salt Lake City: Deseret Book, 1970), 27.

22 Kirby, "History of the Church in Switzerland," 51, 196.

23 Ibid., 42.

24 Smith, *Millennial Star* 37 (21 June 1875): 394.

25 Keith C. Warner, "History of the Netherlands Mission of The Church of Jesus Christ of Latter-day Saints 1861–1966," master's thesis, Brigham Young University, 1967, 17–18.

26 Ibid., 21.

27 Ibid., 154.

28 William G. Hartley, "A Missionary's Two Months in Jail," *New Era* 12 (November 1982): 8–9.

29 Ibid., 11–12.

30 William Hale Kehr, "Missionary to the Balkans: Mischa Markow," *Ensign* 10 (June 1980): 29–32; and Kahlile Mehr, "The Eastern Edge: LDS Missionary Work in Hungarian Lands," *Dialogue* 24 (Summer 1991): 28–33.

31 Joseph Smith, *History of The Church of Jesus Christ of Latter-day Saints*, 7 vols., 2d rev. ed., edited by B. H. Roberts (Salt Lake City: The Church of Jesus Christ of Latter-day Saints, 1932–51), 5:417.

32 Kahlile Mehr, "Johan and Alma Lindlof: Early Saints in Russia," *Ensign* 11 (July 1981): 22–24.

33 Kehr, "Mischa Markow," 32.

34 Mehr, "Johan and Alma Lindlof," 24.

35 Ronald W. Walker, "Heber J. Grant's European Mission, 1903–1906," *Journal of Mormon History* 14 (1988): 21–22; Kirby, "History of the Church in Switzerland," 52, 196; Michael Mitchell, "The Stony Ground and the Peculiar Institution: The German Government and the Mormons Prior to World War I," unpublished paper delivered at the annual meetings of the Mormon History Association, Claremont, California, May 1991.

36 Malcolm R. Thorp, "'The Mormon Peril': The Crusade against the Saints in Britain, 1910–1914," *Journal of Mormon History* 2 (1975): 70.

37 Ibid., 75.

38 Ibid., 87–88.

CHAPTER 7

Two World Wars and the Depression

AUGUST 1914	**WORLD WAR I BEGINS**
NOVEMBER 1918	**ARMISTICE ENDS WORLD WAR I**
1920S	**GERMANY BECOMES CHURCH'S LEADING MISSION FIELD**
1929	**CZECHOSLOVAKIA IS OPENED TO MISSIONARY WORK**
1929-39	**GREAT DEPRESSION LIMITS NUMBER OF MISSIONARIES**
1933	**ADOLF HITLER AND NATIONAL SOCIALISM COME TO POWER IN GERMANY**
SEPTEMBER 1929	**WORLD WAR II BEGINS; MISSIONARIES ARE WITHDRAWN FROM EUROPE**
MAY 1945	**WORLD WAR II ENDS IN EUROPE**

n Sarajevo, Bosnia, on 23 July 1914 Slavic nationalists, trying to wrest part of Serbia away from the Austro-Hungarian Empire, assassinated the Archduke Franz Ferdinand, heir to the Austrian throne. European political alliances stiffened, and military forces were mobilized. On 29 July Austria declared war on Serbia. Within days Germany, ally to Austria, declared war on Russia, Serbia's protector, and on Russia's ally, France. Britain joined the war on 4 August on the side of Serbia, France, and Russia. No one realized how long or how terrible the war would be but imagined that the decisive battles would be fought within a few months and peace would be restored by 1915. Instead, the war escalated into numerous fronts on three continents. Brutal trench warfare ensued for nearly four years. Finally in 1918, a year and a half after the United States entered the war, the Allied Powers (primarily Britain, France, and the United States) convinced the Central Powers (Germany and Austria-Hungary) that further fighting would be disastrous. A truce was signed in November and the Great War, as it was called, came to an end. The number of war dead approached nine million, about fourteen times as many casualties as in any previous war in world history.

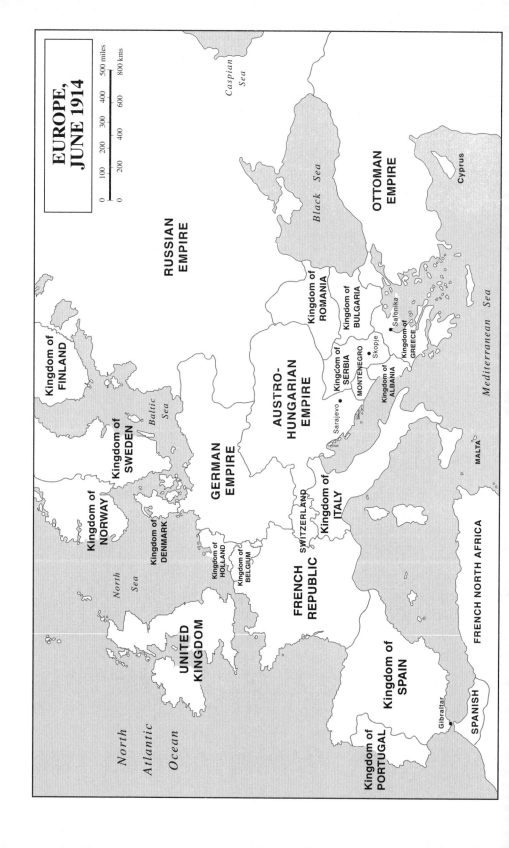

EUROPE,
JUNE 1914

500 miles
800 kms

Caspian
Sea

RUSSIAN
EMPIRE

Kingdom of
FINLAND

Baltic
Sea

Kingdom of
SWEDEN

Kingdom of
NORWAY

GERMAN
EMPIRE

Kingdom of
DENMARK

Kingdom of
HOLLAND

Kingdom of
BELGIUM

SWITZERLAND

FRENCH
REPUBLIC

Kingdom of
ITALY

AUSTRO-
HUNGARIAN
EMPIRE

Kingdom of
ROMANIA

Kingdom of
BULGARIA

Black Sea

OTTOMAN
EMPIRE

Cyprus

Sarajevo

Kingdom of
SERBIA

MONTENEGRO

Skopje

Kingdom of
ALBANIA

Kingdom of
GREECE

Salonika

Mediterranean Sea

MALTA

North
Sea

Kingdom of
PORTUGAL

Kingdom of
SPAIN

Gibraltar

SPANISH

FRENCH NORTH AFRICA

UNITED
KINGDOM

North

Atlantic

Ocean

Naturally the Great War affected The Church of Jesus Christ of Latter-day Saints. For the first time, some Church members engaged in battle against each other. The calling of full-time missionaries worldwide came nearly to a standstill. The European Mission Office, headquartered in Britain, remained intact, but American missionaries became scarce in England and were almost nonexistent on the Continent. European Church units learned to rely on local leadership. For the first time sister missionaries assumed a primary role in proclaiming the gospel. Some members lost their lives during the war or were lost from the Church. Other surviving members suffered incredible hardship and deprivation.

The war did not draw in the neutral states of Holland, Switzerland, Denmark, Sweden, and Norway. Hence the Church did not change as much in these countries during the war.

The Church in Britain during World War I

The Great War proved to be a great divide for Britain. Over the previous century, Great Britain, or the United Kingdom, held undeniable world leadership in every category—commercial, industrial, military, and colonial. After the war, Britain faced increased competition from other nations and never again regained its dominance as a world power. Before the war, Britain was the greatest source of converts in the worldwide Church. After the war, other countries had greater missionary productivity for many years.[1]

Elder Hyrum Mack Smith, son of Church president Joseph F. Smith and a member of the Quorum of the Twelve Apostles, presided over the British and European Missions from 1914 to 1916. He deftly guided the mission during that difficult time. For instance, although both Britain and the United States were hostile toward the German people with whom they were at war, President Smith passed on to the British Saints the teachings of the prophet that they should love their enemies. Though many British members were entering the battlefields, they should do so "pure in heart" and with the attitude of elders of Israel preaching the gospel.[2]

As the horrors of the war escalated, many British Saints wondered, as did Christians the world over, how a loving God could permit such slaughter. President Hyrum Mack Smith saw in this war one more fulfillment of Joseph Smith's prophecy that war would be "poured out upon all nations" before Christ's second coming (see D&C 87:2). And he was convinced that this particular war came about because the world in general had rejected the gospel of Jesus Christ.[3]

The number of missionary elders declined drastically when the war began. In Britain the full-time missionary force of 258 in 1913 dropped to just 31 by 1919. So few missionary elders plus the wartime shortage of adult priesthood bearers in the branches severely handicapped Church organization. Yet the number of baptisms, 399 in 1914, was the highest it had been for several years, and the yearly average remained at about 300 throughout the war. An important reason for this success was the calling of hundreds of sisters to serve part-time as missionaries. Church membership in Britain remained at about 8,000 during the war years.

The British Mission Relief Society also bloomed during the war as the sisters met the challenge of the national war effort. They sewed and knit clothing for British soldiers and sailors, collected books and magazines for convalescing soldiers, and cared for the wounded and ill in war hospitals.

At war's end, the *Millennial Star* recorded 65 British Latter-day Saint war dead, most of whom lost their lives in the brutal trench warfare on the continent.

One irritant during this time was Winifred Graham, whose lurid anti-Mormon novels again made headlines occasionally with sensational accusations, including the patently false notion that the Mormons were behind the German war effort. British Mission spokesmen refuted Graham's falsehoods in the *Millennial Star* and in local newspapers, often the same ones that had printed her stories.

The Church on the Continent during World War I

Despite a huge death toll among the German people, Church membership actually rose from 7,000 to 7,500 by 1918. The faithfulness of the German Saints during this adversity set the stage for the stupendous growth that followed the war.

When the war began, all American missionaries were evacuated from Germany and nearly all from other parts of the continent. But the Swiss-German Mission president, Hyrum W. Valentine, remained in

Basel, Switzerland. He took under his wing the few members of the French Mission and proselyted in Switzerland with a dozen native missionaries. Success among the Swiss increased during the war. President Valentine also corresponded with the 65 German branches and continued publishing *Der Stern* to bolster the morale of the German Saints. "Letters from the Field," a regular section of the magazine, featured many stories of faith written by German soldiers while serving their fatherland. Local German Church leaders also sent letters of encouragement and packages to their soldiers and sailors. Hardly an issue of *Der Stern* went by that did not name a few more Saints who had died in battle. In July 1916, military authorities stopped the distribution of the magazine in Germany. By war's end about 75 German Church members had lost their lives.[4]

Holland remained technically neutral, but baptisms decreased sharply in the Netherlands Mission during the war years. Shortly before the outbreak of the conflict, local members were called to preside over branches and districts in case the missionaries returned to America. Local sisters strengthened the depleted missionary ranks. Food was scarce, and Dutch members held collections to provide for the poor and unemployed. During the war, 393 members, including many in leadership positions, decided to leave for America.[5]

The Scandinavian countries also remained neutral during the Great War, but missionary work suffered in Denmark, Norway, and Sweden as well. Most missionaries were withdrawn in compliance with instructions from Church headquarters. The Swedish parliament then banished most of the remaining missionaries as "Mormon agents." More local missionaries were called, and some of them performed with "great efficiency," according to historian Andrew Jenson. Numbers of baptisms declined significantly, however.[6]

In 1915 the First Presidency announced a "Zion's Emergency War Fund" to aid needy members in Germany and other parts of Europe. President Joseph F. Smith and his counselors sought repeatedly to stave off prejudice against the German people. "Their leaders are to blame," the prophet explained, "not the people. The people that embrace the gospel are innocent of these things, and they ought to be respected by Latter-day Saints everywhere."[7]

In November 1918, when the terrible war finally ended, *Der Stern* summed up the survival of the Church in Europe: "The rains fell, the storm came, and the winds blew against the house, but the house did not fall, because it was built upon a rock."[8]

Aftermath of World War I

The war ended late in 1918, leaving European society in total disarray. Severe shortages of fuel, clothing, and food plagued every country, but people were finally safe to resume their lives. In the aftermath of the war many European members emigrated to America to join fellow Saints in Utah, looking for happiness and stability.

The First Presidency's desire to send American missionaries back to the European missions was thwarted by various governments, who would grant only a handful of visas. The situation was especially puzzling in Britain, where over the previous eighty-two years British authorities had not restricted the number of Latter-day Saint missionaries. The British Home Secretary, Edward Shortt, opposed readmission of missionaries to England because he believed Latter-day Saint proselyting would contribute to internal disorder. Even the well educated had been influenced by fictional portrayals of the Latter-day Saints.

The new British and European Mission president, Elder George Albert Smith of the Quorum of the Twelve Apostles, appealed to Britons' historic sense of fair play. He pointed out that Utah Latter-day Saints had contributed more than their share of material relief to the British and their soldiers in the war. When his appeal fell on deaf ears, Elder Smith turned to American political leaders for help. Senator Reed Smoot enlisted the aid of the State Department, and in May 1920 the British Home Office finally agreed to grant missionary visas.[9]

The missions on the Continent also struggled at first for want of new missionaries, but by 1920, President George Albert Smith had visited each mission, and new elders began arriving to reinvigorate the European branches. Also that year the Danish-Norwegian Mission was divided, so that in 1920 there were five missions on the Continent: Danish, Swedish, Norwegian, Swiss-German, and Netherlands.

In Germany, hunger was the most acute problem. In 1919 Church president Heber J. Grant arranged through Senator Smoot for the Church

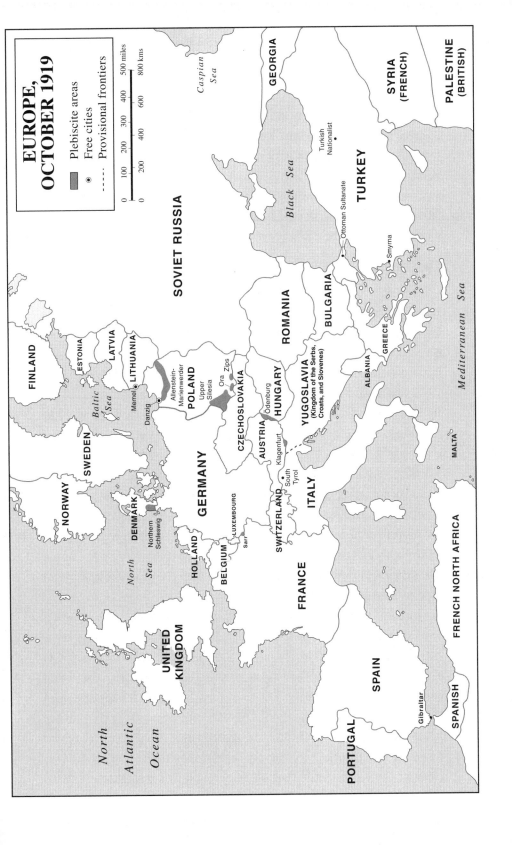

EUROPE,
OCTOBER 1919

Plebiscite areas
Free cities
----- Provisional frontiers

0   100 200 300 400 500 miles
0   200   400   600   800 kms

*North
Atlantic
Ocean*

FINLAND

ESTONIA

LATVIA

LITHUANIA

SWEDEN

*Baltic
Sea*

NORWAY

Memel

Danzig

Allenstein-
Marienwerder

POLAND

Upper
Silesia

Ora Zips

SOVIET RUSSIA

DENMARK

Northern
Schleswig

*North
Sea*

HOLLAND

GERMANY

LUXEMBOURG

Saar

BELGIUM

CZECHOSLOVAKIA

AUSTRIA

Ödenburg

HUNGARY

UNITED
KINGDOM

FRANCE

SWITZERLAND

South
Tyrol

Klagenfurt

ITALY

YUGOSLAVIA
(Kingdom of the Serbs,
Croats, and Slovenes)

ROMANIA

BULGARIA

ALBANIA

GREECE

Black Sea

GEORGIA

Turkish
Nationalist

Ottoman Sultanate

TURKEY

Smyrna

SYRIA
(FRENCH)

PALESTINE
(BRITISH)

*Caspian
Sea*

PORTUGAL

SPAIN

Gibraltar

SPANISH

FRENCH NORTH AFRICA

MALTA

Mediterranean Sea

to buy United States government commodities in France to distribute among the European Saints. Swiss-German Mission president Angus Cannon called sixty German brethren to full-time missions and established a special fund to care for their families. Their efforts produced immediate results, and in 1919 the Swiss-German Mission recorded 595 convert baptisms, mostly in Germany. The next year was even more amazing with 1,155 joining the Church, far more than in any other mission in the Church at the time. With the downfall of the former oppressive government, the Church's future in Germany looked promising.[10]

The Church in Britain between the Wars

The British Mission pressed forward under apostolic leadership from 1920 to 1939, when World War II broke out.[11] In December 1928, the First Presidency established separate heads for the European and British Missions, both still to be located in London. Church membership in Europe, which stood at about 8,000 in 1920, slipped to about 6,500 in 1939, when war began. Baptisms per year were modest, averaging 235 in the 1920s and 202 in the 1930s.[12] This growth was more than offset by the emigration of many Saints to America in hopes of a better life and increased chances for their children to marry in the faith.

Why was Britain no longer a fertile missionary field? In general, the British people were more pleasure seeking and less interested in religion. Many felt disillusioned and disenchanted with religion after witnessing the horrors of the Great War. Science and other forms of learning were more highly esteemed than religious devotion. Furthermore, the Church still suffered in the 1920s from the effects of anti-Mormon novels and an adversarial popular press.

Inflammatory newspaper accounts, lurid novels, and anti-Mormon dramas and films, such as the popular *Trapped by the Mormons*, were still rife through 1924. Missionaries continued to hold street meetings as their primary tool for creating interest in the Church, sometimes provoking extreme antagonism. President Ezra Taft Benson later described one such event from his mission: "The next Sunday evening we held our street meeting down near the railway station as scheduled. The crowd was large and unruly. . . . When the saloons closed, the rougher, coarser element came out on the streets, many under the influence of liquor.

... Soon an attempt was made to trample us under their feet. ... During the excitement, my companion and I became separated. ...

"When I arrived at the lodge [apartment], I found that my companion was not yet there. I worried and then prayed and waited. I became so concerned about him that I decided to disguise my appearance by putting on an old American cap and taking off my topcoat. Then I went out to try to find him. As I neared the place of the meeting, a man recognized me and asked, 'Have you seen your companion?'

"I said, 'No. Where is he?'

"He responded, 'He's down on the other side of the railway station with one side of his head mashed in.' ... [When we finally found each other] we threw our arms around each other and knelt together in prayer."[13]

During the 1920s, the various British Mission presidents—Elders George Albert Smith, Orson F. Whitney, David O. McKay, and James E. Talmage—countered the anti-Mormonism in the press. Their ardent appeals, especially those of Elder Talmage, a native of England and a member of various learned societies in Britain, succeeded in calming and educating the public. Numerous converts attributed their initial interest in the Church to what they read in the newspapers. Gradually editors and reporters began to defend the Latter-day Saints.

As mission president, Elder David O. McKay introduced two slogans that bolstered the Saints' courage and endurance. These were "Every Member a Missionary" and "Build Zion in Britain." These powerful challenges were introduced to the Church worldwide in the 1950s and 1960s, again with profound results.

The 1920s were tremendously difficult for the British Saints. High unemployment followed Britain's loss of supremacy in world commerce. Especially hard hit was Wales' coal-mining industry. President Talmage encouraged the Saints to weather valiantly through these hard times, and local Relief Societies mobilized to aid the distressed.

The Great Depression, the worldwide aftermath of the 1929 stock market crash in the United States, hindered the work in Britain. Church members in America could afford to send few missionaries.

British unemployment reached its highest level in history. The First Presidency sent a message to the British Saints through the *Millennial*

James E. Talmage

Star to live righteously, avoid extravagance, cultivate habits of thrift, and live within their means. By observing these principles, the British Saints not only survived the 1930s but grew stronger. By 1935 twelve branches had constructed modest facilities.

The 1937 centennial celebration of the Church's first mission in that land was a joyful time in the British Mission. Church president Heber J. Grant and his first counselor, J. Reuben Clark Jr., presided over numerous festivities and conferences. President Grant dedicated several chapels and on 30 July dedicated a plaque in Preston honoring the first baptisms in the River Ribble exactly one hundred years previous to the day.

Other events in the 1930s strengthened the British members and the missionary work. For one thing, the Mutual Improvement Associations for young people began holding missionwide conferences for young people. Of all the Latter-day Saint activities of the decade, those that most changed public perceptions of the Church were organized missionary sports and the missionary Millennial Chorus. The baseball and basketball teams, known as the Rochdale Greys and the Catford Saints, won various national titles and helped interest investigators. The choral group toured Britain and won the praise of many. These activities, which helped banish the "Mormon Menace" image, were promoted by dynamic mission president Hugh B. Brown, later an apostle and a member of the First Presidency. One of President Brown's assistants, young Marvin J. Ashton, later a member of the Council of the Twelve, couldn't sing well enough to be in the Millennial Chorus but redeemed himself by his athletic prowess as a Catford Saint.

During the early era of great success in the British Mission, from 1840 to 1870, the Irish, who were predominantly Roman Catholic, had not been as receptive to the gospel. Only two branches, one in Belfast and one in Dublin, had taken root in the Emerald Isle. In the late nineteenth century, a home-rule movement won widespread support among the Irish. Ireland's drive for independence, postponed by World War I, achieved partial realization in 1922. The twenty-six southern, mainly Catholic, counties became an independent dominion within the British Commonwealth. From that time until 1939, a few missionaries continued to preach in Ireland but with sparse results. Then in September 1939, missionaries were suddenly called home to America when war broke out in Europe.

The Church in Germanic Europe

In the 1919 Treaty of Versailles, the victorious Allied Powers punished Germany for the war, requiring demobilization of troops and navy and unbearable war reparation payments. Internal discord and astronomical inflation rocked Germany, a country trying for the first time in its history to establish a democracy. Into this chaos and the resulting spiritual vacuum came hundreds of ambassadors of The Church of Jesus Christ of Latter-day Saints. The Church's progress in Germany during this decade more than tripled that of any other mission field. The 1920s and early 1930s until Hitler came to power were the golden age of the Church in Germany.[14]

Many factors were involved in this success. The German people were humble, perhaps for the first time in centuries, and the eighty-five German Saints who became missionaries while waiting for the arrival of American elders found their countrymen ready to hear their message. The Church's image in America and Germany had steadily improved, and newspapers freely carried Church announcements under the new government's commitment to religious liberty. Welfare assistance from Church headquarters was readily available. Many Germans, because of their national and cultural traits, were drawn to such Latter-day Saint doctrines and practices as devotion to the family, the role of women in the home, the idea of a chosen people and the house of Israel, the spiritual power of choir and congregational singing, the excitement of doing genealogical research to seek out ancestral roots, and the orderly nature of the Church's hierarchical and priesthood structure.

When President Angus Cannon toured the German branches immediately after World War I ended, he found meetings swelling with dedicated members and hosts of investigators. The next British and European Mission president, George Albert Smith, visited numerous congregations in 1920 and marveled at the loyal Latter-day Saints who had kept the faith during the recent conflict.

During this era the Mutual Improvement Associations began operating for the first time in Germany. In 1928 Scouting was begun for the boys and missionwide youth conferences were inaugurated. The youth held musical contests throughout the mission, and many branch choirs and orchestras were started.

The German part of the Swiss-German Mission contributed about 90 percent of the local missionaries as well as about 90 percent of the progress. The number of baptisms soared to 1,155 in 1920, a total far exceeding any other Church mission over the previous fifty years. The trend continued, reaching a record high of 1,795 in 1924.

In August 1925 Elder James E. Talmage, European Mission president, presided over the dividing of this most successful mission in the Church. The western part of the mission remained the Swiss-German Mission with headquarters in Hamburg, and the eastern part was named the German-Austrian Mission with headquarters in Dresden, later changed to Berlin. In both missions the momentum of conversions continued. Another realignment forming the West German, the East German, and Swiss-Austrian Missions took place in 1938 on the eve of World War II.

The Church was immensely strengthened both in America and Europe during the 1920s and 1930s from the success of missionary work among the German-speaking peoples. Thousands of these Saints emigrated to Utah, developing large pockets of German-speaking Saints,

David O. McKay and Serge F. Ballif with missionaries in Austria, 1922

primarily in Salt Lake City. These new arrivals contributed great spiritual and temporal strength to a Church membership struggling under economic difficulties. The German Saints who remained in their homeland also formed exceptional branches. At no time previously in Church history had congregations outside America achieved such stability and success. A few cities had multiple branches, especially in eastern Germany.

Contributing to this astounding growth was the publication of numerous doctrinal books in German. Among them were *Gospel Doctrine,* by President Joseph F. Smith, *A Rational Theology,* by Elder John A. Widtsoe, *Articles of Faith* and *Jesus the Christ* by James E. Talmage; and *Teachings of the Prophet Joseph Smith.* The translator, Max Zimmer, a member of the Church from Basel, Switzerland, also translated numerous lesson manuals for the auxiliaries and retranslated the Book of Mormon during these years. Later, during World War II, Brother Zimmer presided over many German-speaking Saints.

Though the Church grew by leaps and bounds in Germany after World War I, especially in eastern Germany, the same was not true in Switzerland and Austria. Fewer than a hundred baptisms per year occurred in these countries between the wars.

Other Efforts in Europe

Elsewhere in Europe after World War I, Church leaders strived to strengthen existing branches and plant the gospel in new fields. Once more missionaries were sent to France, where the mission had been closed twice previously. In 1923 European Mission president David O. McKay created a new French Mission, comprising France, Belgium (formerly part of the Netherlands Mission), and the French-speaking areas of Switzerland. The headquarters were in Geneva, Switzerland. Modest success took place over the next fifteen years as American missionaries reached out to the youth by forming basketball teams. Most baptisms were young people. Thirty-three branches in the mission, some with chapels of their own, developed some stability. In 1930 mission headquarters were moved from Geneva to a Paris suburb. Mission membership, still mostly in Switzerland and Belgium, exceeded 1,000 by 1939 when World War II broke out and the missionaries were withdrawn.

The Netherlands Mission progressed slowly during the interwar years. Holland was beset with economic and labor unrest during the entire 20 years. Most investigators and converts came from the ranks of the unemployed. In 1939 Church membership in Holland stood at 2,845.

Similar conditions existed in the three Scandinavian missions. The Church had stabilized in Denmark, Sweden, and Norway, and the Church introduced all the auxiliary organizations into the branches. Yet missionaries in Scandinavia continued to battle anti-Mormon prejudice from government and state church officials. Baptisms remained scarse in the interwar period.

In 1929 European Mission president John A. Widtsoe opened a completely new mission field in Czechoslovakia.[15] This nation was a hybrid democratic country created for the Slavic peoples of central Europe at the end of the Great War by world leaders in Paris. The year before, Elder Thomas Biesinger, then eighty-four years old, had returned to Prague, the city where he had been imprisoned for preaching the gospel forty-five years earlier. When President Widtsoe dedicated the land for the preaching of the gospel on 24 July 1929, only seven Church members, all in one family, resided in the country: the Brodils, who had joined the Church in

John A. Widtsoe

Vienna before World War I and had lived in Czechoslovakia since the war. They welcomed the missionaries with open arms.[16]

President Widtsoe obtained permission from the minister of the interior, the chief of police, and other officials for missionaries to preach in Czechoslovakia. He then chose Arthur Gaeth, a twenty-four-year-old American just completing his service in the German-Austrian Mission, to preside over the new mission. The Czechoslovakian republic was blessed at this time with a combination of religious freedom and a lack of a state church. Latter-day Saint efforts in the community led to some 250 favorable newspaper and journal articles. President Widtsoe arranged to give two radio lectures, which were translated and delivered by a local professor. The citizens of Prague, who were greatly interested in sports, enjoyed the missionary-sponsored baseball and basketball teams, and the Church established close ties with the local YMCA. The missionary elders also became involved with the local Boy Scout program. The hardy Czech people, who admired good health practices, were also attracted to the Word of Wisdom.

On 6 April 1930, the one hundredth anniversary of the organization of the Church, the missionaries in Czechoslovakia held their first conference. Most newspapers printed accounts of the centennial celebration. The mission distributed a songbook of seventy songs in the Czech language, and President Gaeth delivered radio addresses in both German, a language spoken by many of the citizens, and Czech. In 1933 the Book of Mormon was published in Czech, along with a number of new tracts and booklets.

President Gaeth remained mission president until 1935, ten years after he first became a missionary in Germany. Early in his presidency, he had returned briefly to America to marry a Czech-American convert to whom he had been introduced by the Widtsoes. During his presidency President Gaeth visited Hungary, Yugoslavia, Romania, and Russia. He found that insufficient religious freedom in those nations precluded sending missionaries to them. At his mission's end, President Gaeth was replaced by another of the elders originally sent to Czechoslovakia, Wallace F. Toronto.

President Toronto and his small group of missionaries continued to achieve slow but steady growth. A major hindrance to their work was the preoccupation of most Czech people with politics, specifically the very real threat of a takeover by Nazi Germany. In 1937 Church president Heber J. Grant visited Czechoslovakia, and forty articles appeared in the local press, giving the Church much-needed visibility.

The following year, just before Hitler invaded Czechoslovakia in March 1938, most of the missionaries were withdrawn. Yet gospel ties could still transcend political animosities. Historian Kahlile Mehr recorded: "Under the increasing burden of German control, the Prague Branch met to celebrate Mother's Day in May 1939. The service was drawing to a close when the back door opened to reveal a young German naval officer in uniform. Anticipating the worst, the congregation froze. Hesitating but a moment, the officer smiled and walked down the center aisle to meet President Toronto. Then the officer explained to the group that he, too, was a member of the Church and had come to worship. The women expressed their relief in tears; the men nodded in approval. The officer bore his testimony not to the enemies of his country but to the friends of his religion."[17]

In July 1939, German Gestapo (secret police) agents arrested four missionaries. Missionary work had to end for the time being. Four branches totaling approximately 130 Saints composed the fledgling Church of Jesus Christ of Latter-day Saints in Czechoslovakia.

The Church in Europe under National Socialism

Adolf Hitler, German National Socialist (Nazi) party leader, plotted in the early 1920s to establish himself as dictator of a powerful military state in Germany. When he became chancellor in 1933, he brutally seized control of the German government to establish his dictatorship, which he called the Third Reich. Hitler's goals included ridding Europe of what he and his party called the Red menace (Communism), the Jewish menace, and the "treacherous" German leaders who had surrendered to the Allied Powers in 1918. He would preserve the purity of German blood and fulfill the "destiny" of the Germans to expand into eastern Europe and Russia to rule the "inferior" peoples there.

At first the Latter-day Saints fared quite well in the Third Reich.[18] They were not a well-known religious denomination, and as long as they remained quiet, Nazi officials and storm troopers (SS) did not bother them. Germans, including many Latter-day Saints, thought Hitler seemed in the early years (1933–36) of his dictatorship to be helping Germany recover from economic and political disasters. When Latter-day Saint missionaries helped in various ways with the 1936 Olympics in Berlin, some Nazi officials even complimented them. By 1937 the Latter-day Saints numbered approximately 14,000 in Germany, and no major conflicts had arisen between the Church and the Nazi state.

Some Latter-day Saints held pro-Nazi sympathies in the 1930s, and a few members joined the Nazi Party. A handful of Mormon men served with the SA, or the Nazi "brown shirts" military force. But in 1937, Nazi atrocities began to surface. Gestapo agents spied on members and Church services. Two indiscreet American missionaries had their picture taken draped in a Nazi flag. Their action was discovered, but they were transferred out of the country before being arrested. One by one, the Church's freedoms were curtailed. Boy Scouts and the Primary were eliminated so as not to compete with the Young Folks and Hitler Youth movements. Hymns could not be sung or missionary tracts distributed that mentioned "Israel" or "Zion." Elder James E. Talmage's *Articles of*

Faith was banned because it referred to Israel and Zion. Party officials sometimes prohibited street meetings and outlawed tracting. As censorship mounted, a few missionaries spent short stints in jail.

During this time of tremendous fear, a few Church leaders barred some Latter-day Saint Jews and Jewish investigators from church meetings and took care to see that nothing antagonistic toward the government was spoken from the stand or discussed in classes.

Preparations for War

In the summer of 1938, President J. Reuben Clark Jr. of the First Presidency toured the European missions. He delivered President Heber J. Grant's prophetic advice that the European Saints should assume more Church and priesthood responsibilities and depend less on the missionaries. At a mission presidents' conference in Berlin, President Clark instructed each president to formulate a detailed plan for an evacuation should the missionaries be recalled, specifying the neutral nations of Switzerland, the Netherlands, and Denmark as the safest avenues for leaving the Continent.

In September 1938, after Hitler annexed Austria and German troops were poised to attack on the Czech border, the First Presidency ordered the evacuation of all missionaries from Germany and Czechoslovakia. When war was averted at a meeting of European heads of state in Munich, the missionaries returned to their fields of labor. Their practice run proved useful a year later.[19]

By mid 1939 missionary work was virtually impossible. As missionaries witnessed the mobilization of the mighty German war machine and tensions increased, President Clark, formerly the United States Undersecretary of State, used his State Department contacts to keep Church leaders apprised of European developments almost hourly. Finally, on 24 August 1939, the First Presidency again ordered the evacuation of all missionaries from Germany and Czechoslovakia. Elder Joseph Fielding Smith of the Quorum of the Twelve Apostles, who was in Europe to conduct mission meetings, took charge.

Many missionaries had harrowing experiences before passing by fierce German border guards into the safety of neutral countries.[20] When missionaries attempted to cross into the Netherlands, the Dutch

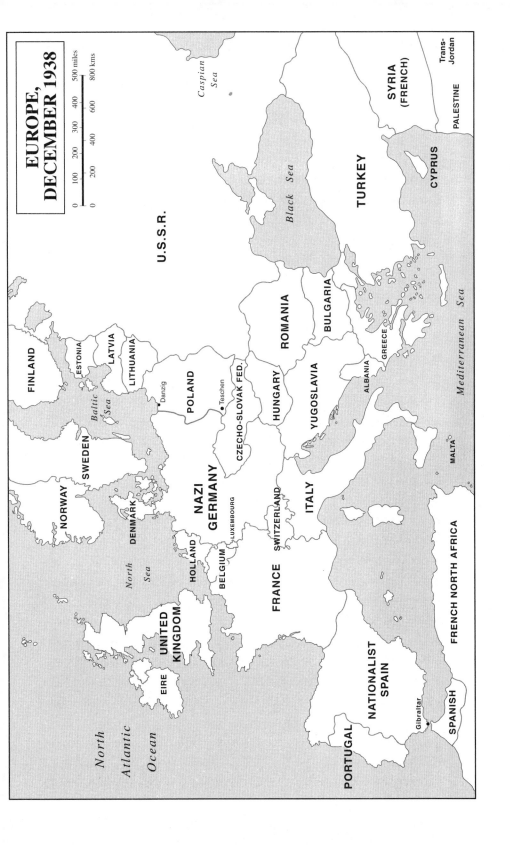

EUROPE,
DECEMBER 1938

0   100   200   300   400   500 miles
0   200   400   600   800 kms

North
Atlantic
Ocean

North
Sea

Baltic
Sea

Caspian
Sea

Black   Sea

Mediterranean   Sea

U.S.S.R.

FINLAND

ESTONIA

LATVIA

LITHUANIA

SWEDEN

NORWAY

DENMARK

Danzig

POLAND

Teschen

CZECHO-SLOVAK FED.

NAZI
GERMANY

HOLLAND

BELGIUM

LUXEMBOURG

SWITZERLAND

FRANCE

UNITED
KINGDOM

EIRE

PORTUGAL

NATIONALIST
SPAIN

Gibraltar

SPANISH

FRENCH NORTH AFRICA

HUNGARY

ROMANIA

BULGARIA

YUGOSLAVIA

ITALY

ALBANIA

GREECE

MALTA

TURKEY

CYPRUS

SYRIA
(FRENCH)

PALESTINE

Trans-
Jordan

authorities at the border rescinded their promise to allow the elders in. Thus, with very little money, these missionaries had to find their way north to the Danish border instead.

The Lord's hand guided many in the evacuation. For example, in the West German Mission, the mission president assigned Elder George Seibold, a burly former football player, to search prayerfully in various German towns for thirty-one elders, many of them worried and without sufficient funds, and escort them to safety. At the Rhine city of Köln, Elder Seibold got off the train at a large station filled with thousands of people. By whistling the missionary song "Do What Is Right, Let the Consequence Follow," he located eight missionaries. Through inspiration, he found all the others, usually in places other than their apartments, including one in a restaurant in an obscure village.

At the same time in Czechoslovakia, President Toronto was seeking the release of the four missionaries who had been imprisoned by the Gestapo. On the evening of 31 August, he finally obtained the last elder's release. He set apart twenty-one-year-old Josef Roubicek to preside in his absence, and then President Toronto and the four missionaries boarded the last train to leave Czechoslovakia. They passed through Berlin early the next day and that afternoon boarded the last ferry to cross from Germany to Denmark.

Every missionary was safe. Day after day in the Copenhagen chapel, evacuated missionaries from the continental European missions met with Elder Joseph Fielding Smith, awaiting instructions from Salt Lake. Elder Smith pronounced a blessing on the nation of Denmark for its generosity in receiving all the missionaries, promising that when war came the nation would be spared great devastation.

In Salt Lake City, the First Presidency soon ordered the evacuation of all missionaries from Europe. Most crossed the Atlantic on cargo ships with makeshift accommodations for several hundred passengers each. President J. Reuben Clark regarded the evacuation as miraculous: "The entire group was evacuated from Europe in three months, at a time when tens of thousands of Americans were besieging the ticket offices of the great steamship companies for passage, and the Elders had no reservations. Every time a group was ready to embark there was available the necessary space, even though efforts to reserve space a few hours before had failed. . . . Truly the blessings of the Lord attended this great enterprise."[21]

The Church in Britain During World War II

British Mission president Hugh B. Brown quickly evacuated his elders and sister missionaries after receiving the telegram from the First Presidency.[22] He had already reserved one hundred spaces on the United States Lines. President Brown was visibly distraught when Britain declared war on 3 September. He had fought in the First World War as a Canadian officer and knew full well the horrors to follow. He stayed in London a few weeks longer to transfer mission leadership to local members. Placed in charge of the British Mission was Andre K. Anastasiou, a native Russian who had come to England during World War I at age nineteen. President Brown's departure in January 1940 marked the first time in the 103-year history of the mission that Britain was completely without American missionaries. Some members felt deserted; a few stopped attending church. Under difficult circumstances the mission president and his counselors kept publishing the *Millennial Star* throughout the war.

In person President Anastasiou successfully petitioned the British Ministry of Labour and National Service to exempt district and branch presidents from military service. Almost all other British Latter-day Saint adults entered some form of war service. In some cases, one priesthood leader served two congregations, conducting services in one on Sunday morning and in the other on Sunday afternoon. With the approval of the First Presidency, President Anastasiou called men with health or disability deferments and a few women to full-time missions. Hundreds of other members served a few hours per week as part-time home missionaries to continue to share the gospel in Britain.

The war meant tight times. When Sister Lucy Ripley was asked if she were willing to serve a full-time mission, she replied that she had no money for books or clothing. But the branch president assured her that she would be provided for. In what to Lucy was a miracle, relatives supplied necessary books and scriptures, and she procured clothing just before rationing went into effect. Throughout Sister Ripley's mission, loving members provided her and her companions with enough money and food to keep them in the field.[23]

World War II brought many changes to the British Saints in their everyday routines and in church activities. Wartime congregations were mostly women and children with a few priesthood holders to conduct the meeting, bless and pass the sacrament, and be the principal speaker. Canadian and American members met with the British Saints wherever allied armed forces were stationed in Britain to await being shipped off to battlefronts in North Africa and on the Continent.

Parts of Britain were bombed heavily by the German Luftwaffe in the months-long Battle of Britain. Nevertheless, war fatalities among British Saints were remarkably low: only twenty-three among both civilians and servicemen. President Anastasiou testified, "Every month we had more than one report of bombings among the members, but no casualties, and we were always grateful for the Lord's protection of His saints."[24]

President Hugh B. Brown returned to the British Mission in May 1944. He praised President Anastasiou and his colleagues for their remarkable accomplishments. During those four and a half years, the number of branches had increased from sixty-eight to seventy-five, and the mission had collected more than eighty thousand dollars worth of tithes and offerings. At the suggestion of President Brown, Brother Anastasiou emigrated with his family to Utah, where he accepted a mission call to France and later translated many items of Church literature into his native Russian.

In addition to superintending the mission, President Brown served as field coordinator for Latter-day Saint servicemen throughout Europe. He labored indefatigably throughout Britain to strengthen Church members who had lost their way in the stress and chaos of war. At war's end, some 6,000 British members were on the rolls and could still be traced by Church leaders.

The Church on the Continent During World War II

The only European countries that managed to remain neutral throughout the war were Switzerland and Sweden. All other nations were swept into the conflict by the mighty German war machine.

Church members on the Continent suffered immensely. Elder Thomas E. McKay, the last American mission president of the East German Mission before the war, directed Church affairs on the Continent from Salt Lake City as best he could. Eventually all communications were cut off to countries affected by the war.

At the beginning of the war, a few German Latter-day Saints opposed the Nazi Party. One member, Heinrich Worbs from Hamburg, was arrested after he unwittingly remarked to an informer that a newly erected Nazi monument was honoring just another "butcher." When Brother Worbs returned from a concentration camp six months later, he privately and in terrible fear reported having endured numerous torturings. He died shortly thereafter.

Perhaps the best-known case of opposition to the Nazis by Latter-day Saints involved three sixteen- and seventeen-year-olds who dared to speak out. The leader of these Hamburg teens was Helmuth Hübener; his friends were Rudolf Wobbe and Karl-Heinz Schnibbe.[25] In 1941 young Helmuth, a gifted student with an aptitude for history, geography, politics, and music, concluded with his friends that they must oppose Nazi tyranny. Helmuth's resolve was strengthened after his brother, who was serving as a German soldier in France, sent him a shortwave radio. Secretly Helmuth and his friends listened late at night to BBC (British Broadcasting Corporation) broadcasts from England—strictly forbidden by the Nazi government—that told the German people of Nazi atrocities and warmongering. The Nazis controlled the press, and few Germans had an accurate idea of events at that time. "When I spoke with Helmuth," related Karl-Heinz, "I suddenly realized that Nazism was not merely a lot of minor annoyances and isolated infringements upon certain peoples' rights, but a thoroughgoing system of murderous, lying evil."[26]

Helmuth took notes of the BBC broadcasts, typed handbills on the typewriter he used as branch clerk, and duplicated them on the branch's mimeograph machine. The young men distributed the handbills in mailboxes and phone booths and posted some on bulletin boards. Over the ensuing eight months, Helmuth wrote pamphlets, twenty-seven different titles in all, on a wide variety of issues.

In February 1942, the Gestapo arrested Helmuth after he tried to

Rudi Wobbe, Helmuth Hübener, and Karl-Heinz Schnibbe

recruit others at the government office where he worked. Through tor-
turing Helmuth, the secret police learned about Karl-Heinz and Rudi and
their connection with the Church. All three young men were tried before
the Reich's feared Blood Tribunal in Berlin and convicted of conspiracy
to commit high treason. Helmuth was sentenced to death and his friends
to hard labor in a prison camp. Shortly before he was beheaded by guil-
lotine on 27 October 1942, Helmuth wrote to loved ones: "I am very
thankful to my Heavenly Father this agonizing life is coming to an end
this evening. I could not stand it any longer anyway! My Father in
Heaven knows that I have done nothing wrong. . . . I know that God lives
and He will be the proper judge of this matter. Until our happy reunion
in that better world."[27]

Helmuth left the judgment of his case to God because he had already
been judged by his Hamburg branch president, a Nazi sympathizer, who
had excommunicated him. Perhaps the branch president had meant to
protect the Church and its members from Nazi reprisals. He had denied
entrance to meetings to Solomon Schwarz, a Latter-day Saint Jew,

Berlin prison, Plîtzensee, where Helmuth Hübener was beheaded in October 1942

reproved members for listening to anti-Nazi propaganda, and prayed for Hitler and the Nazis in church meetings. Brother Schwarz wept outside the chapel when he was forbidden entrance. The Nazis later executed him at the death camp at Auschwitz.

Gestapo agents attended branch meetings after the arrest of Helmuth and his friends, and many members feared for their lives. District president Otto Berndt was taken into Gestapo headquarters for questioning because Nazi officials suspected adult collaboration in young Hübener's sophisticated anti-Nazi work. Relying upon the Lord for inspiration, President Berndt kept the Church out of the Hübener case and was released. Before he left, however, a Nazi official warned him, "Make no mistake about it, Berndt. When we have this war behind us, when we have time to devote to it and after we have eliminated the Jews, you Mormons are next!"[28]

The nearly 14,000 German Saints were the largest group of Church members in Europe at the beginning of the war. Countless stories of faith and endurance continue to be told of those Saints. One of them, Herbert Klopfer, a presiding elder in Berlin, was called as president of the East German Mission after the American missionaries were evacuated.

In 1940 he was drafted but remained stationed in Berlin, where he was able to conduct mission business from his military office. Three years later he was ordered to the western front. He left mission affairs and the care of his family in the hands of his two counselors. He spent a short time in Denmark, where he attended services as he could among the Saints. The Danes at first feared him because of his German uniform, but they grew to trust him as he bore witness of his brotherhood and of the truthfulness of the gospel. Then he was transferred to the eastern front. In July 1944, President Klopfer was listed as missing in action. After the war, his family learned that he had died in March 1945 in a Russian hospital.[29]

Another young Latter-day Saint, Hermann Mössner from Stuttgart, had a very different experience as a German soldier. He was captured by the British while fighting in western Europe and was transported to a prisoner-of-war camp in England. With little else to do, Hermann began sharing the gospel with fellow prisoners. When four men accepted his message and requested baptism, Brother Mössner wrote to Church headquarters in London for advice. Soon Elder Hugh B. Brown visited the camp and authorized Hermann to baptize the converts. Years later Brother Mössner was called to serve as the first president of the Stuttgart Stake.[30]

German Saints suffered on the home front even more when the American and British bombing raids began. Most meetinghouses and members' dwellings in the cities were eventually destroyed. One Sunday a Hamburg branch president felt impressed to close the service abruptly and direct his congregation to the nearest bomb shelter. They reached safety just before the bombs hit.[31] With their meeting places destroyed, the Saints held services in their homes. They stockpiled food, clothing, and household supplies for emergencies as best they could, aiding and encouraging one another.

The long-suffering and faith of the Latter-day Saints was evident in other places in Europe as well. In France, which was occupied by the Nazis in 1940, Léon Fargier bravely worked to sustain Church members. "Whether on foot or bicycle, whether in the occupied zone or the free zone, he traveled to members' homes on often-secret visits," wrote his biographer, Alain Marie. "With authority granted him by his priesthood leaders, he blessed, baptized, confirmed, ordained to the priesthood, held meetings, and many times risked his life in an effort to sustain his fellow Church members." The Gestapo ordered Brother Fargier to desist and even arrested him on occasion. But at the peril of his life he continued. "He was a pioneer [of the Church in France] in the truest sense, serving with humility, reverence, and quiet dedication under extraordinary circumstances. The consequences of his courage and faith will be felt for generations."[32]

The Danish Mission was presided over during the war by local elder Orson B. West. Denmark suffered during the war, although not as desperately as other occupied countries, in fulfillment of Elder Joseph Fielding Smith's prophecy. The Nazis restricted regular church services, but occasionally members were allowed to meet together. Despite economic and political turmoil, the Danes' tithes and fast offerings increased. At a conference in Copenhagen in June 1944, the Saints' spirits rose when they placed a plaque dedicated to Joseph Smith at the entrance to their chapel. In brief news articles, approximately eighty newspapers commented favorably on the conference and the Church.[33]

Norway also suffered under Nazi occupation for five long years. When the mission president left, he charged Bergen Branch president Erling Magnesen to feed the Lord's Norwegian sheep. President Magnesen promised the Bergen Saints that the Lord would protect them from harm through the grim times ahead if they would live the gospel of Jesus Christ to the best of their ability. Though these members suffered many trials and narrow escapes from death, every one was spared. One survivor later commented, "To me, the legacy of the account of the LDS members of the Bergen Branch parallels the legacy of the account of Helaman's 2,000 warriors of the Book of Mormon."[34]

In neutral Switzerland, Elder Thomas E. McKay, before leaving for America in 1940, appointed local member and prolific translator Max Zimmer to preside. President Zimmer trained priesthood and auxiliary leaders and distributed Church literature to the Saints. He called Swiss member missionaries who spent two evenings per week teaching and baptizing new converts. In 1944 he obtained permission from Nazi officials to visit Latter-day Saint soldiers in prisoner-of-war camps inside Germany. After the war, President Zimmer discovered documents at the

German Embassy in Bern revealing that the Nazis had planned to invade Switzerland, set up concentration camps there, and incarcerate enemies of the regime, including many specifically named Latter-day Saint leaders.[35]

Sweden was also neutral during the war, but the Swedes were nearer the war's devastations. Two bombs fell on Swedish soil, and at times church meetings were interrupted by air-raid alarms. When seventy American missionaries were evacuated in 1939, Fritz Johansson, a married missionary and a relatively new convert, became acting mission president. After the war he reported: "The Swedish Saints pulled together marvelously. They increased their tithes and fast offerings—many by three to five hundred percent—and stepped up their support in all areas of Church activity. Everyone was needed, and the Spirit of the Lord attended us in abundance during these trying times. The gift of healing was often manifest. Love and unity prevailed."[36]

Of all the Nazi-occupied countries, the Netherlands, occupied in 1940, suffered the worst. The invading army confiscated most Church property as "war booty" that they claimed was American. Yet despite many dangers, the local missionaries continued teaching the gospel, baptized 275 during the war, and succeeded in maintaining contact with all branches.

The city of Rotterdam was bombed mercilessly for eight days, causing the two branches in the city to consolidate. Branch president Henry A. Hekking lived with his family in the remaining Rotterdam chapel to forestall its confiscation by the Nazis. President Hekking, arrested many times, was always released on a technicality, evidence to the members of the Lord's hand in protecting their leader. Toward the end of the war, the Germans rounded up all able-bodied Dutch men for transport to Germany as slave labor. On the way, President Hekking jumped out a train window. He disguised himself and for more than three weeks waded marshes, swam rivers, and with God's help evaded arrest to return to his branch and his family.[37]

In 1942 Pieter Vlam, second counselor in the acting mission presidency in Rotterdam, was arrested by the Nazis as a war criminal and sent to a concentration camp in Poland. As a prisoner, he conducted "MIA meetings," organized a choir, preached the gospel to any interested parties, and eventually baptized seven individuals. One of his converts, J. Paul Jongkees, later became a stalwart leader in the Church in the Netherlands and the first president of the Holland Stake.[38]

Meanwhile, general authorities in America counseled Church members worldwide regarding their attitudes toward the conflict. In a formal statement, the First Presidency taught that "hate can have no place in the souls of the righteous" and explained that the Saints in all combative countries were "under obligation to come to the defense of their country when a call to arms was made." They stated that if Latter-day Saint soldiers took the lives of their nation's enemies, they would not be considered murderers. They further declared that "this Church is a worldwide Church. Its devoted members are in both camps." The First Presidency promised those servicemen who lived clean lives, kept the commandments, and prayed continually that the Lord would be with them and nothing would happen to them that would not be to the honor and glory of God and to their salvation and exaltation.[39]

Worldwide, some 45 million people had lost their lives in the war. In Europe the death toll exceeded even that of the fourteenth-century bubonic plague. Was there any chance that order would come out of the chaos? What hope was there for the members of The Church of Jesus Christ of Latter-day Saints in Europe? These were the questions that faithful Saints often asked in 1945 as the bombing in Germany reached its ugly zenith.

NOTES

1 An excellent source on Britain during this period is Louis B. Cardon, "The First World War and the Great Depression 1914–39" in V. Ben Bloxham et al., eds., *Truth Will Prevail: The Rise of the Church of Jesus Christ of Latter-day Saints in the British Isles 1837–1987* (West Midlands: Corporation of the President of The Church of Jesus Christ of Latter-day Saints, 1987), 335–60.

2 *Millennial Star* 76 (15 October 1914): 612–14; 664–65; 79 (3 May 1917): 274–75.

3 *Millennial Star* 76 (29 October 1914): 693; 76 (5 November 1914): 714–16; 78 (27 April 1916): 264–66; 79 (19 April 1917): 248–49.

4 Gilbert W. Scharffs, *Mormonism in Germany* (Salt Lake City: Deseret Book, 1970), 54–59.

5 Keith C. Warner, "History of the Netherlands Mission of The Church of Jesus Christ of Latter-day Saints, 1861–1966," master's thesis, Brigham Young University, 1967, 63–67.

6 Andrew Jenson, *History of the Scandinavian Mission* (Salt Lake City: Deseret News Press, 1927), 434–42, 462–65, 533.

7 Joseph F. Smith, in Conference Report, April 1917, 2–23.

8 *Der Stern* 52 (1 December 1920): 361.

9 Cardon, "The First World War and the Great Depression," 340–43.

10 Scharffs, *Mormonism in Germany,* 58–60.

11 An excellent source for this period is Cardon, "The First World War and the Great Depression 1914–39," 341–60.

12 Richard L. Evans, *A Century of "Mormonism" in Great Britain* (Salt Lake City: Deseret News Press, 1937), 244.

13 Ezra Taft Benson, in Conference Report, April 1985, 48–49.

14 Scharffs, *Mormonism in Germany,* 59–65, 79–86.

15 Some excellent sources on Czechoslovakia are Kahlile Mehr, "Enduring Believers: Czechoslovakia and the LDS Church, 1884–1990," *Journal of Mormon History* 18 (Fall 1992): 111–54; Kahlile Mehr, "Czech Saints: A Brighter Day," *Ensign* 24 (August 1994): 46–52.

16 Ruth McOmber Pratt and Ann South Niendorf, "Her Mission was Czechoslovakia," *Ensign* 24 (August 1994): 53.

17 Mehr, "Czech Saints: A Brighter Day," 49.

18 An excellent source on this subject is Joseph M. Dixon, "Mormons in the Third Reich: 1933–1945," *Dialogue* 7 (Spring 1972): 70–78. I also gained information from an interview with John K. Fetzer, 21 June 1994. Fetzer was a missionary in Nazi Germany from 1935 to 1937.

19 David F. Boone, "The Worldwide Evacuation of Latter-day Saint Missionaries at the Beginning of World War II," master's thesis, Brigham Young University, 1981, 1–15.

20 Ibid., 16–61.

21 J. Reuben Clark Jr., in Conference Report, April 1940, 20.

22 An excellent source for this period is Louis B. Cardon, "War and Recovery, 1939–1950," in Bloxham et al., *Truth Will Prevail,* 361–93.

23 Lucy Ripley Bradbury, "No Money, No Books, Nothing," *Ensign* 23 (October 1993): 43–44.

24 Cardon, "War and Recovery," 377.

25 The best sources for this story are Blair R. Holmes and Alan F. Keele, *When Truth Was Treason: German Youth Against Hitler* (Urbana, Ill.: University of Illinois Press, 1995); Karl-Heinz Schnibbe with Alan F. Keele and Douglas F. Tobler, *The Price: The True Story of a Mormon Who Defied Hitler* (Salt Lake City:

Bookcraft, 1984); Rudi Wobbe and Jerry Borrowman, *Before the Blood Tribunal* (Salt Lake City: Covenant Communications, 1992).

26 Schnibbe, *The Price*, 35.

27 Holmes and Keele, *When Truth Was Treason*, 240.

28 Ibid., 291 n. 18.

29 W. Herbert Klopfer, "Enemy Soldier at the Pulpit," *Ensign* 20 (June 1990): 59–60.

30 *Church History in the Fulness of Times* (Salt Lake City: The Church of Jesus Christ of Latter-day Saints, 1989), 528.

31 Scharffs, *Mormonism in Germany*, 104–5.

32 Alain Marie, "Léon Fargier: His Faith Wouldn't Go Underground," *Ensign* 21 (September 1991): 29–31.

33 Marius A. Christensen, *History of the Danish Mission of The Church of Jesus Christ of Latter-day Saints* (Provo, Ut.: Brigham Young University Press, 1966), 154–66.

34 John Floisand, "Inner Peace Can Come in Time of War," *Church News*, 26 February 1994, 7.

35 Dale Z. Kirby, "History of The Church of Jesus Christ of Latter-day Saints in Switzerland," master's thesis, Brigham Young University, 1971, 103–8.

36 C. Fritz Johansson, "Wartime Mission in Sweden," *Ensign* 11 (April 1981): 44.

37 A Hekking family history entitled "The Church in the Netherlands" is in my possession.

38 Warner, "History of the Netherlands Mission," 69–73; Melvin Leavitt, "Captive Missionary," *New Era* 7 (April 1977): 18–19.

39 Conference Report, April 1942, 90, 92–95.

CHAPTER 8

Postwar Western Europe

1945 WORLD WAR II ENDS IN EUROPE; GERMANY DIVIDED INTO FOUR ZONES OF OCCUPATION

1946 ELDER EZRA TAFT BENSON CONDUCTS MISSION OF MERCY IN WAR-TORN EUROPE

1949 NATO IS ESTABLISHED; GOVERNMENTS OF WEST GERMANY AND EAST GERMANY ARE FORMED

1951 DAVID O. MCKAY BECOMES NINTH PRESIDENT OF THE CHURCH

1952 PRESIDENT MCKAY MAKES FIRST OF SEVEN VISITS TO EUROPE

1955 SWISS TEMPLE IS DEDICATED

1958 LONDON TEMPLE IS DEDICATED

1966 ITALIAN MISSION IS OPENED

1970 SPAIN MISSION IS OPENED

1971 FIRST AREA GENERAL CONFERENCE IS CONVENED IN MANCHESTER, ENGLAND

1973 AREA GENERAL CONFERENCE IS CONVENED IN MUNICH, WEST GERMANY

1974 AREA GENERAL CONFERENCE IS CONVENED IN STOCKHOLM, SWEDEN

he horrors of the European war ended in May 1945 when the Nazis surrendered to Allied troops that had closed in on Berlin from both east and west. Church president Heber J. Grant died a week later, leaving his successor, George Albert Smith, to lead the Church during the crucial era of rebuilding. In an article addressed to the Saints around the world President Smith set the example: "I do not have an enemy that I know of. . . . All men and all women are my Father's children, and I have sought during my life to observe the wise direction of the Redeemer of mankind—to love my neighbor as myself."[1]

One of the high priorities of the Church in late 1945 was reestablishing contact with the Saints in war-devastated Europe. Communication had been cut off for up to six years, and hundreds of Saints had been left homeless when cities were destroyed. The destruction throughout Germany was almost beyond belief. Everywhere lay the rubble of bombed-out buildings and abandoned cars, buses, tanks, and weapons. Rivers were filled with garbage, sewage, and dead bodies. An acute shortage of food greatly compounded the suffering. By day families scoured through garbage heaps and war-gutted fields for morsels to eat. And in a few months, with the coming of cold weather, the lack of fuel jeopardized the health of most German families. Citizens of the Netherlands, where bombing and looting had also been rife, were suffering similar shortages. Germany itself was divided into four zones occupied and administered by armies of the victorious powers: Britain, the United States, France, and the Soviet Union.

By fall 1945, the Church was mailing relief supplies to Europe in small, regulation-size packages. The cost soon became prohibitive, and President George Albert Smith and Elder John A. Widtsoe traveled to Washington, D.C., with a request. The brethren were granted a twenty-minute interview with President Harry S Truman. "I have just come to ascertain from you, Mr. President, what your attitude will be if the Latter-day Saints are prepared to ship food and clothing and bedding to Europe," President Smith said. Truman replied with a smile, "Well, what do you want to ship it over there for? Their money isn't any good." President Smith explained that the Church wasn't interested in selling these goods. "They are our brothers and sisters and are in distress. God has blessed us with a surplus, and we will be glad to send it if we can have the co-operation of the government." President Truman was impressed and pledged government support in the Church's enterprise.[2]

Meanwhile, Latter-day Saint American servicemen, who just weeks before had been the hated enemy of the Germans, sought out their brothers and sisters in distress. The Americans shared their rations with their fellow Saints and embarked on rebuilding projects during their off hours. With the aid of these generous Saints from the occupying forces, the Church in the western part of Germany was rebuilt comparatively quickly.

The First Presidency at first planned to send to Europe Elder John A. Widtsoe, a member of the Twelve and former European Mission president. Elder Thomas E. McKay, an assistant to the Twelve and the most recent European Mission president would accompany him. At a meeting of the First Presidency and the Quorum of the Twelve on 22 December

1945, however, President Smith announced that upon learning of the dire conditions in Germany, he and his counselors had changed their minds. They would send a younger man than Elder Widtsoe to Europe. Elder Harold B. Lee remembered, "I began quickly to look around the table, speculating as to who would be called. One of the first men I eliminated was Elder [Ezra Taft] Benson, who had the largest family as well as the youngest. I'd not quite made my survey around the table when President Smith announced that they had decided to call Elder Benson to go to Europe." The brethren asked Elder Benson, then forty-six, what his wife would say. "I assured the Brethren that I could always count on my wife's full support in any call from the Church," Elder Benson wrote in his journal.[3] His vigor and vast experience in both agricultural economics and working with government officials were tremendous assets in this difficult undertaking. He chose as companion and translator Frederick W. Babbel, an army chaplain who had served as a missionary in Germany before the outbreak of the war. Elder Benson's assignment as European Mission president was to do "everything possible to alleviate the suffering of the members of the Church," to reorganize each European mission that existed before the war, and to "make available to all the benefits and blessings of the Gospel."[4]

Elder Benson's Mission to War-Torn Europe

President Ezra Taft Benson and Brother Babbel departed Salt Lake City on 29 January 1946 and did not return until just before Christmas. They traveled more than sixty thousand miles and visited fourteen countries during their ten-month mission. They frequently referred to the scriptural promise: "And they shall go forth and none shall stay them, for I the Lord have commanded them" (D&C 1:5). Elder Benson later reported in general conference: "Barriers have melted away. Problems that seemed impossible to solve have been solved, and the work . . . accomplished through the blessings of the Lord."[5]

President Benson first visited President Hugh B. Brown and the Saints in Britain, who also were suffering from lack of food and fuel, although not as severely as those on the Continent. From England President Benson flew to Paris and then traveled by train, jeep, and boat

Elder Ezra Taft Benson supervised the delivery of welfare supplies to war-torn Europe in 1946

to Belgium, Holland, Denmark, Sweden, and Norway. In each place, acting mission leaders informed him of the spiritual and temporal condition of the Saints. President Benson distributed food and clothing to members who had suffered five years of Nazi occupation. They were overjoyed to see an apostle from Zion, and President Benson could not hold back the tears at witnessing their continuing devotion. He called many brethren and a few married couples on missions. He was pleased to learn that Swedish members, who had not been attacked during the war, had sent food and clothing to their Scandinavian and Finnish brothers and sisters.

Finally in March President Benson and Brother Babbel obtained permission from military authorities to enter occupied Germany, the first American civilians to do so. Their first stop was to visit a conference of Saints in Karlsruhe on the Rhine River. Brother Babbel recounted the scene: "Parking our car near massive heaps of twisted steel and concrete, we climbed over several large piles of rubble and threaded our way between the naked blasted walls in the general direction which had been pointed out to us. As we viewed the desolation on all sides of us, our task seemed hopeless. Then we heard the distant strains of 'Come, Come Ye Saints' being sung in German. . . . We hurried in the direction of the sound of the singing and arrived at a badly scarred building which still had several usable rooms. In one of the rooms we found 260 joyous saints still in conference, although it was already long past their dismissal time. . . . With tears of gratitude streaming down our cheeks, we went as quickly as possible to the improvised stand. Never have I seen President Benson so deeply and visibly moved."[6]

President Benson later spoke of that event: "They realized that at last, after six or seven long years, representatives from Zion, as they put it, had finally come back to them. Then as the meeting closed, prolonged at their request, they insisted we go to the door and shake hands with each one of them as he left the bombed-out building. And we noted that [many] of them, after they had passed through the line went back and came through the second and third time, so happy were they to grasp our hands. As I looked into their upturned faces, pale, thin, many of these Saints dressed in rags, some of them barefooted, I could see the light of faith in their eyes as they bore testimony to the divinity of this great latter-day work, and expressed their gratitude for the blessings of the Lord."[7]

President Benson soon learned of critical food and clothing shortages among the German Saints, particularly those in the Russian sector of East Prussia and East Berlin. He arranged with the International Red Cross in Geneva, Switzerland, to deliver Church donations and other purchased supplies to Germany and then, miraculously, gained audience with American general Joseph T. McNarney in Frankfurt to arrange distribution. The general granted special written authorization to sidestep military channels to deliver relief supplies to the stricken Frankfurt Saints.

President Benson's miraculous journeys continued into the other occupied zones, even into the areas of East Prussia and Silesia that after the war had become part of Poland. Military and other European officials were amazed at how quickly shipments were arriving from a church in America. European Church leaders openly wept for joy and gratitude as they examined clothing and sacks of grain at the storehouses where the welfare goods arrived. In all, ninety-three railroad carloads of supplies arrived in Germany.

President Benson learned that local German brethren, both single and married, were accepting mission calls and bringing many new converts into the Church. At this time in 1946, the Saints knew of 184 Church members who had been killed in battle and of 120 more who had died of bombings, disease, and starvation. A far greater number of members—1,728—were still unaccounted for.[8] One somewhat predictable phenomenon in the missionary work occurred: some investigators, "inspired" by the arriving food supplies, joined the Church. They came to be known as "Büchse Mormonen" or "Tin-can Mormons."

In March, President Benson visited Czechoslovakia. He was delighted to see the work of Josef Roubicek and to discover that the members had initiated missionary work on their own. He conducted a stirring testimony meeting of 28 members. In June 1946 Wallace Toronto, who had not been released as mission president, returned to the country along with two American elders.

In July President Benson visited Finland to dedicate the country for the preaching of the gospel. When he returned to America, the First Presidency assigned him to find a mission president who could speak Finnish. He made this a matter of prayer. In 1947 at a conference of the Chicago Stake, he met Henry A. Matis, a counselor in the stake presidency and a convert who had Finnish roots and language ability. "It always amazed Ezra," he later mused, "how the Lord intervened to move the Church forward." That year Brother Matis was called as the first Finnish Mission president.[9]

By the time President Benson completed his European mission, he had placed mission presidents in Britain, France, Holland, Switzerland, West Germany, East Germany, Czechoslovakia, Denmark, Sweden, and Norway. Some of them had served in the same posts before the war. In late 1946, Elder Alma Sonne, an assistant to the Twelve, succeeded Elder Benson as European Mission president.

President Benson's work in Europe sparked another miracle of compassion between 1946 and 1948, this time in Holland. At the beginning of World War II, the German army had inflicted horrible physical damage upon the Dutch, destroying more than 400,000 homes and 8,000 farms. Nazi occupation was especially brutal. The German government systematically robbed Holland's foodstuffs, fuel, and clothing, leaving Dutch civilians destitute during the winter of 1944–45. Bitterness ran deep among the Dutch; even the Saints were not immune.

President Cornelius Zappey of the Netherlands Mission directs the loading of welfare potatoes on their way to fellow Saints in Germany

The stricken Dutch Saints were among the first recipients of Church supplies after President Benson's 1946 visit. Soon afterwards mission president Cornelius Zappey began emphasizing a new theme: "Love One Another." Because potatoes were Holland's best crop, President Zappey proposed to priesthood leaders that where they had land they start branch or quorum potato projects. Where they didn't, they were to start sewing projects. Before this immense welfare project had been completed in 1948, the Dutch Saints had sent to Germany tons of food and clothing. "When President David O. McKay learned what the Dutch Saints were doing, he called it 'one of the greatest acts of true Christian conduct ever brought to my attention,'" recorded historian William G. Hartley. The Dutch Saints' generosity testified to the deeper success of the Church's relief mission to Europe. "The healing of souls was as important as the nourishing of bodies."[10]

A New Order in Europe

Gradually through 1949, conditions in Europe returned to some semblance of normalcy. More and more missionaries were allowed to return to the mission fields. The exceptions were in Soviet-controlled East Germany and Czechoslovakia, where oppressive Communist governments gradually restricted Church privileges.

World War II reconfigured world politics. By 1949 Europe had divided into two spheres—the western democracies and the eastern-bloc states under Soviet Union hegemony. Under American leadership, the western allies formed the North Atlantic Treaty Organization (NATO) to defend against further Soviet encroachment. The American-, British-, and French-occupied zones of Germany and later West Berlin united in a democratic state called the Federal Republic of Germany. The Soviets countered by creating a Communist puppet-state in East Germany called the German Democratic Republic. The Cold War between east and west, well underway, dominated events on the world stage for the next forty years.

Circumstances for the Church were also vastly different. Encouraged by the United States, most western European nations adopted or enhanced democratic principles of government that included freedom of religion. Missionaries no longer had to battle local and national governments, the press, and the clergy for the right to preach. But in Soviet-dominated eastern Europe, the Church had to wait for the end of the Cold War to preach the gospel of Jesus Christ.

Western Europe recovered rapidly, in large part because of the Marshall Plan proposed by United States Secretary of State George Marshall and endorsed by President Truman and the Congress. The Marshall Plan provided seed money for industry in European countries allied to the United States. The resulting "economic miracle," as history books now acclaim it, restored war-ravaged western Europe to its former international status and standard of living by 1970.

Building Zion in Europe

In 1947 Church population worldwide had reached one million members. By 1950 membership in Europe had declined from its previous twentieth-century peak of about 31,000 in 1939 to less than 29,000 in 1950 because of war casualties, loss of contact with members during the war, and postwar emigration to the United States. The drop in membership

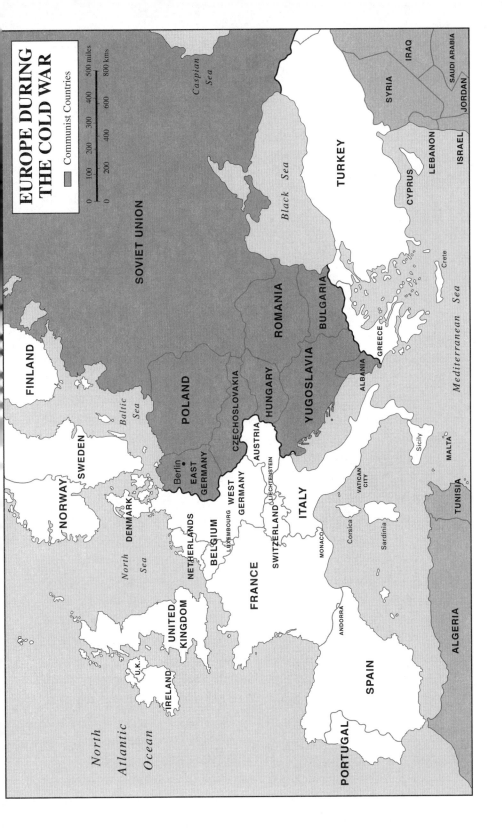

EUROPE DURING THE COLD WAR

■ Communist Countries

| 0 | 100 | 200 | 300 | 400 | 500 miles |
| 0 | 200 | 400 | 600 | 800 kms |

SOVIET UNION

FINLAND

NORWAY

SWEDEN

Baltic Sea

DENMARK

POLAND

EAST GERMANY

Berlin

CZECHOSLOVAKIA

AUSTRIA

HUNGARY

ROMANIA

YUGOSLAVIA

BULGARIA

ALBANIA

GREECE

Black Sea

Caspian Sea

TURKEY

CYPRUS

SYRIA

LEBANON

ISRAEL

JORDAN

IRAQ

SAUDI ARABIA

North Sea

United KINGDOM

U.K.

IRELAND

NETHERLANDS

BELGIUM

LUXEMBOURG

WEST GERMANY

LIECHTENSTEIN

SWITZERLAND

FRANCE

MONACO

ITALY

VATICAN CITY

Corsica

Sardinia

Sicily

MALTA

ANDORRA

SPAIN

PORTUGAL

ALGERIA

TUNISIA

Mediterranean Sea

Crete

North Atlantic Ocean

of only 2,000 reflected numerous conversions in most European missions since the war. Approximately 6,000 members resided in the British Isles; 6,000 in West Germany; 6,000 in East Germany; 3,500 in the Netherlands; 1,600 in Sweden; 1,600 in Denmark; 1,700 in Norway; 1,000 in Switzerland; 500 in Belgium; 600 in Austria; 300 in France; and 100 in Czechoslovakia.

Church President George Albert Smith continued to emphasize the brotherhood of all mankind. Known as the greatest builder of good will for the Church in his day, President Smith with his counselors J. Reuben Clark Jr. and David O. McKay set the stage in the aftermath of World War II for unprecedented world growth, especially for the Church in Europe.

Although comparatively fewer Saints had emigrated to Zion during the first half of the twentieth century, no sense of permanence had developed in Europe until in the 1950s when the general authorities actively took to Europe all aspects of Zion: strong local leadership, larger meetinghouses, improved missionary methods, better communication with Church headquarters, frequent visits from Church leaders, and, above all, temples.

In April 1951 David O. McKay became the ninth president of the Church. President McKay began in 1952 a series of visits to Europe over the next eight years. Under his innovative leadership, the Church in western Europe developed new solidarity and permanence. Mission presidents in Europe were directed to discourage emigration to America as much as possible. A 1953 letter from the First Presidency stated: "It is the present intention of the Church to . . . provide temples throughout the world that the members may remain in the areas and yet have opportunity to receive the blessings of the temple ordinance, all to the end that . . . spreading the Gospel to all nations, tongues and people might be consummated in the shortest possible time."[11]

Between 1950 and 1953, the Church experienced a net drop in missionaries because of the Korean War. But when a truce was achieved, more missionaries than ever entered the force, doubling and tripling in number throughout the decade. Transporting missionaries also became easier with the introduction of jet travel from America to Europe.

In 1955 President McKay dedicated the Swiss Temple, broke ground for a temple in England, and arranged for the Tabernacle Choir to visit several European countries. Local leadership increased, congregations became more solid, and the rate of conversions grew. President McKay directed the construction of many new meetinghouses and the translation of vast stores of material into western European languages. President McKay's work in Europe mirrored Church developments worldwide throughout the 1950s.

Postwar United Kingdom

The massive devastations of World War II naturally hindered missionary work in Britain after the war. Shortages of food, housing, transport, and other necessities slowed the British government's granting of visas to American missionaries. At first mission president Selvoy Boyer spent most of his energies reorganizing branches and repairing meetinghouses that had fallen into disrepair or been damaged by bombing. Before leaving in 1946, Elder Ezra Taft Benson had remarked, "Never has there been so much favorable sentiment towards the Church and such opportunities to interest people in our message. It would help so much to have suitable places in which to meet."[12]

By 1947 more than a hundred missionaries had arrived in Britain. British newspapers interviewed with favor many idealistic young American elders, and numerous investigators started attending meetings. The Millennial Chorus and the LDS sports teams were reconstituted and proved as successful as before the war. Elders rented stalls on Britain's traditional market day to display literature in town squares. Posters in London's underground subway system also attracted interest. By 1949 the British Mission had a full complement of missionaries. Convert baptism totals shot upward from 36 in 1949 (the highest total since before World War I) to 593 in 1950.

The Church at mid century in Britain stood at a threshold. Interest in Mormonism was at its highest point in the twentieth century. Yet hundreds of British Saints were still emigrating each year to America to seek a better life, and the Church needed a more stable base to truly flourish in the British Isles. Derek A. Cuthbert, a Nottingham convert who later became a general authority, outlined five specific needs: a harvest of converts who would stay; better communication, both with Church headquarters and the British media; development of local leadership and financial strength; provision of adequate physical facilities; and ultimately, a house of the Lord, a holy temple.[13]

President David O. McKay, a descendant of British converts from both Scotland and Wales, brought to his office considerable British experience. In 1897, as a young elder, he had served in the British Mission. As an apostle in 1921, he visited the mission as part of his world tour and a year later returned as mission president. He knew the British Isles well and possessed an innovative vision of how to make the work flourish in his ancestral home.

President McKay had long believed that the emigration of faithful Saints must be halted. As prophet he undertook an extensive nine-week visit to Britain and Europe in 1952. David Lawrence McKay, who accompanied his father as a personal secretary, reported, "He understood intuitively that his visit was the experience of a lifetime for the Saints and willingly stood in line, shaking hands for hours with entire congregations after nearly every conference."[14]

Meanwhile, during the early 1950s, the Church in Britain made rapid strides in missionary work. When numbers of American missionaries were temporarily reduced during the Korean War from 1950–53, mission president A. Hamer Reiser called hosts of local members to serve as district missionaries. These member-missionaries considered themselves pioneers in their own land and substantially increased mission success.

Plans for a temple in Britain developed rapidly. The search for a site began with President McKay's visit in 1952, and when he visited again a year later, he announced that the London Temple would be constructed in Newchapel, some twenty miles southeast of the metropolis. In 1955 President McKay broke ground at the site.

The year 1955 stands out for other reasons as well. The Salt Lake Mormon Tabernacle Choir accompanied President McKay to the groundbreaking. Their earlier public concerts in Glasgow, Manchester, and London stirred large audiences. At each concert, Elder Richard L. Evans of the Quorum of the Twelve asked all choir members who had British ancestry to stand, and when virtually the entire choir arose, the applause was deafening.

The London Temple, dedicated in 1958

Later in the year, Elder Spencer W. Kimball of the Twelve toured the mission for a month, traveling 2,200 miles and speaking in twenty meetings. He stressed the need for the Saints to remain in Britain, assume leadership roles in business and society, and prepare for stakehood. For the first time, British Melchizedek Priesthood holders were organized into elders quorums. Fourteen districts produced five quorums. Local priesthood holders were thereby provided training and greater fellowship and leadership opportunities.

As temple preparations increased, so did genealogical research. The technique of microfilming had been invented in 1938, but World War II postponed data collection in Britain. By the early 1950s, ten camera operators were microfilming British civil and church parish records. Nearly every branch established a genealogical organization that received guidance from the British Mission Genealogical Department headquartered at the temple site.

The British Mission was thriving. As congregations absorbed new converts, brought the less active to full participation, developed new leadership, and gathered records of their kindred dead, the British Saints joyfully anticipated their promised temple. This period of excitement has been called the great awakening in British Mission history.[15]

Postwar Scandinavia

The announcement of the Nazi surrender in May 1945 brought joy to all Scandinavian Church members. In Denmark and Norway, which had been occupied by Germany and where widespread poverty prevailed, the Saints anticipated returning to their meetinghouses in peace and enjoying the comforts of electricity and warmth. The recreation hall in the Copenhagen chapel had been used during the war as an air raid shelter and could now be returned to its former uses. Members looked forward to the return of mission presidents and elders.

On his relief mission to Europe, President Ezra Taft Benson visited each Scandinavian country in February and March 1946. Radio stations and newspapers interviewed the apostle and commented favorably on the Church's mission of mercy to Europe. The Saints gladly received his stirring call to reestablish the work of the Lord among their countrymen, and the Danish and Norwegian members gratefully accepted the thousands of clothing packages from their brothers and sisters in America.

The first missionaries began to arrive in May 1946. Recent liberation from the Nazis made Americans popular in Denmark and Norway, and missionaries were allowed into many areas where the Church had not been for decades. Almost immediately new converts came into the Church. By 1948 the Scandinavian missions were baptizing two and three times more converts than in the years between the wars.

At the same time, however, scores of members, including many leaders, chose to emigrate to America to obtain the full benefits of Zion. After President McKay's 1952 visit, mission presidents more strongly encouraged the members to stay. Emigration decreased and, after the dedication of the Swiss Temple in 1955, dropped to a trickle. Elder Spencer W. Kimball of the Twelve visited the Scandinavian missions in 1955 and directed that local members fill branch leadership positions to allow them to develop leadership abilities and to give missionaries many more hours to find and teach investigators. As a result, membership in

Denmark, Norway, and Sweden increased dramatically to about 3,000 in each nation by 1960.

Until 1950 members and missionaries in Norway had used the Danish translation of the Book of Mormon, but in that year the Norwegian Saints received their own translation. Norwegian translations of the Doctrine and Covenants and the Pearl of Great Price followed in 1954 and 1955, respectively.

Postwar Finland

Finland, a nation that stretches more than seven hundred miles from the Arctic Circle to the Baltic Sea, lies between Scandinavia to the west and Russia to the east. Over the centuries it has been a field of battle many times. In this century it endured retreating Nazi armies and two invasions from the Soviet Union. The Finns prize their freedom and proudly point to their throwing off political subjection of any kind. They have a word that describes their national character: *sisu,* meaning, "don't give in; stick to it."

A sizable Swedish-speaking minority inhabits Finland's south and west coastal cities, and the first missionaries to Finland spoke Swedish. There were 129 Church members in that nation when the Finnish Mission was opened in 1947. During the seven years that Henry A. Matis served as mission president, the Church gained legal status, began micro- filming state Lutheran Church records, translated the Book of Mormon into Finnish, and published it in 1954. Missionaries, in addition to teach- ing the gospel, taught English, played and coached basketball, and did everything they could to raise the Church's profile. By the late 1950s, membership reached its first thousand in Finland, presaging even greater growth during the 1960s.

Many Finnish Saints, although grateful to be members themselves, were nonetheless shy about sharing the gospel with their friends or even telling their acquaintances that they had joined the Church. It was and is a national trait not to share personal feelings with many people. The member-missionary program was thus more difficult to incorporate.[16]

Postwar Netherlands

World War II devasted the Netherlands. Nazi officials had destroyed thousands of buildings and farms and robbed Dutch households of their valuables. Hunger stalked the people; some members starved to death at the end of the war. For the Church another distressing concern in Holland was the introduction into Latter-day Saint worship services of such sectarian practices as lighted candles on the sacrament table. Four years with no communication from Church leaders had allowed various schisms to develop.[17]

The arrival of Elder Ezra Taft Benson and new mission president Cornelius Zappey in early 1946 helped the Saints recover from these maladies. Carloads of food, clothing, and fuel from American Saints miraculously changed the Dutch Saints from beggars to seeming millionaires in those times of scarcity. Dutch government officials were delighted when an additional Church shipload of supplies was sent for general distribution to the Netherlands Red Cross. In acknowledgment, the Minister of Foreign Affairs officially decorated President Zappey with the Medal of Gratefulness. The Church finally gained a positive public image in Holland.

The visit of Church president David O. McKay to Holland in 1952 further improved the Church's public standing. The prophet met and spoke with Queen Juliana. Church members were pleased to receive more public notice and to listen to their beloved leader. On this occasion and throughout the 1950s, President McKay urged the development of local leadership in the branches and districts.

The Church turned another corner in Holland in 1955 when the national government granted official recognition. Before that the Church could not hold property or construct buildings. Also that year the Mormon Tabernacle Choir performed two sold-out concerts in Amsterdam and received wide acclaim from the press, radio, and television. Missionaries, motivated by President McKay's visit, worked harder and more effectively. Holland, which had been one of the least productive European missions, became one of the highest baptizing missions in the second half of the decade.

In 1956 a miraculous healing, recorded in the mission history, paved the way to even greater Church service for one Dutch family. Sister Jongkees of Rotterdam was operated on for an intestinal obstruction, and after the operation an embolism brought her dangerously near death for several days. Members and missionaries fasted and prayed many days in her behalf. At Christmas she was totally blind. On the morning after Christmas, Brother and Sister Jongkees knelt together in prayer. He said later that he had never offered a prayer of greater fervency, inspired by trust in his wife's faith. "No sooner had they completed their prayer than Sister Jongkees turned to her husband and said excitedly, 'I can see your face—I can see. I can see, I can see!' President Rulon J. Sperry and Sister Sperry visited her on December 30, and she told them the color of their clothing and said she could see the tears in their eyes. Miracles through faith have not ended."[18] When the first Dutch stake was created in 1961, Brother Arie Jongkees was called as the patriarch and the Jongkees' son Paul was called as the stake president.

Postwar Germany

Germany had played an important role on the world stage since its unification as one country in 1871. From the 1870s to 1945, the German military was legendary in its discipline, methods, leadership, and size. German culture and music became world renowned. Even Germany's potent industrial base was only temporarily disabled after World War II. But humbled into unconditional surrender in 1945 and divided into four zones of military occupation, Germany suffered an ignominy brought on by deceitful totalitarian leaders. And when Germans began governing themselves in 1949, Germany was no longer united but split into the Federal Republic of Germany (West Germany), allied to the United States and western European countries, and the German Democratic Republic (East Germany), part of the Soviet Eastern Bloc. (The story of the Church in East Germany is told in Chapter 9.)

The Church in West Germany was a scene of constant shifting for fifteen years after the war. Beginning in 1950, hundreds of German Latter-day Saints each year took advantage of American refugee laws and emigrated to America at a much higher rate than members leaving either Britain or Scandinavia. The mission presidents attempted to quell the zeal to leave for America, but a false rumor that the Church planned a mass emigration of the Saints to "Zion" worked against their counsel. Before 1953 many Saints from the Russian Zone (East Germany) fled to the West before the fierce clamping down by the Communist regime. Though some East German Saints continued on to the United States, more than half took up residence in West German communities, forming branches in some of the towns. These former East German Saints provided a solid base of leadership for the Church in West Germany.

Church leaders in Salt Lake City hoped that Germany might again lead out in missionary growth as it had between the two world wars, but missionary work proved difficult in West Germany through 1960. Though grateful for the heavy infusion of American money provided under the 1948 Marshall Plan and generally tolerant of the hundreds of thousands of American military personnel on West German soil, the German people stopped short of approval of this "American sect," as the LDS Church was generally regarded. Official recognition of the Church in 1953 stopped overt difficulties with the government, but the people as a whole clung to their long-standing religious traditions.

Other circumstances thwarted the growth of the Church in West Germany. The German people were caught up in their postwar economic miracle, and keeping up with rapid changes in society, earning a living, and acquiring possessions took precedence over interest in religion. Religious devotion further declined as many Germans, soured by Nazi propaganda and the ugly realities of World War II, determined to trust only their own industry to better their lives. Social customs were also a challenge. The German traditions of beer drinking and coffee drinking were exceedingly hard for investigators to overcome. And German religious tradition persisted. The two state churches—the Evangelical (Lutheran) and the Roman Catholic—did not allow other denominations to gain a foothold easily. Since the late seventeenth century, when religious fratricide had finally given way to peace, a German was either Evangelical Protestant (generally in north or east Germany) or Catholic (generally in the south). To break from either of those strong traditions was a major social change.

The missionaries attempted to break down barriers in a number of ways. In the 1960s, for example, mission president John K. Fetzer used

Rotary International, an important club of businessmen worldwide, to bolster the Church's credibility. Elder Richard L. Evans of the Quorum of the Twelve, elected president of Rotary International for 1965–66, traveled widely and spoke at many Rotarian functions abroad, including an important dinner in Munich as part of his tour that year. Always he was introduced as an important official in the LDS Church as well. President Fetzer, a Salt Lake City businessman and Rotarian before his call, used Elder Evans's prominence as current president to be invited to speak at Rotary clubs throughout Bavaria and Baden-Würtemburg. President Fetzer allayed much prejudice against the Church through these speeches to prominent and influential men. Perhaps the most important was the bishop of 2.6 million members of the German Evangelical Lutheran Church in the Stuttgart area, who desired to gain a correct understanding of the LDS Church. Through this connection, the missionaries were able to place press releases about the Church in numerous local papers.[19]

The Church gradually became stronger in West Germany. The completion of the Swiss Temple in 1955 helped build solidarity among the Saints. With the influx of many new missionaries, the Church grew in West Germany from about 6,000 in 1950 to about 20,000 in 1960. The First Presidency increased the number of missions to six by 1962: the North German, West German, Central German, South German, Bavarian, and Berlin Missions.

In the North German Mission, Elsa Duckwitz of the Celle Branch is an example of the struggle and faith of many German Saints. Elsa was reared as a Latter-day Saint. During the war "she lost her home and fled with her two small sons. They lived for three and a half years in different camps, and in one of them her youngest son died in her arms." With her surviving son, Norbert, she lived in a small room with people full of lust and hate. "The only thing to which I could hold was prayer to a living God, which gave me strength to keep on going," Sister Duckwitz related. "After those difficult years, light came into my life, and we were again able to attend church. I had to walk from 16 to 20 kilometers [approximately 10 to 12 1/2 miles], but we were happy to be home again. Our family was again intact. The Lord gave us a small daughter, and we were able to go to the house of the Lord to be sealed for all eternity."[20] As a young man Norbert Duckwitz attended Brigham Young University and later became a professor there.

Postwar Austria

Austria, annexed by Nazi Germany in 1938, sustained severe destruction and, at war's end, was also divided into four military districts. In 1955 Austria once again became independent but politically neutral, emerging as an advocate of peaceful solutions to world problems. Its capital, Vienna, became one of the world's most important international cities, a crossroads of east and west, and the third official United Nations city, along with New York and Geneva.

In 1946 Elder Ezra Taft Benson reestablished the Austrian District of the Swiss-Austrian Mission with branches in Vienna, Salzburg, Linz, and Haag. Missionary production remained low in the first decade after the war, in part because Austria was staunchly Roman Catholic. Then, in the mid to late 1950s, eighteen new Austrian cities were opened to missionaries, resulting in more baptisms and bringing Austria to about 1,800 members by 1960. In that year, the First Presidency divided the Swiss-Austrian Mission, and Austria was given its own mission, headquartered in Vienna.

Graz, a city of some 300,000 about a hundred miles south of Vienna, yields an example of the pioneering Church effort. An Austrian soldier, Engelbert Schauperl, learned about the Church while stationed in Salzburg and was baptized in 1942. After the war, Engelbert went back to his home in Graz and introduced the gospel to his family. No one else in Graz belonged to the Church, so Brother Schauperl held Sunday School in his home. Years later an elder, Josef Cziep from Vienna, moved with his family to Graz, and with the Schauperls formed a small branch that met in a restaurant pub, closed to business on Sundays. Finally missionaries were assigned to Graz in 1953. The branch grew steadily and by 1960 had over 300 members.[21] When the Vienna Stake was created in 1980, Graz had one of the wards.

Immo Luschin, a highly respected businessman, and his family joined the Church in Graz in 1960 after several years of searching for a faith that taught eternal marriage and would protect his children from worldly attitudes. Brother Luschin wrote: "Compared with what we saw around us, ours was a singularly happy union. Before we were married, Helmi and I had agreed that there would be no divorce in our life. Moreover, we seemed to be a little different from our friends in that we were probing and questioning as to what the purpose of life should be. Many of our friends seemed to have the attitude that life was given in order that we get out of it what we could—namely, 'eat, drink, and be merry, for tomorrow we die.' . . . Problems, they believe, should be covered rather than solved, especially if the solving implied self-restraint. The most desirable thing was not to eliminate transgression, but not to *get caught* at it."[22]

Early in 1960, Immo sought the Lord in prayer, longing for truth and private peace, and was answered by a visit from Latter-day Saint missionaries. Immo's only knowledge about the Church was its association with plural marriage and Joseph Smith's supernatural visitations, both of which he ridiculed. At first he shunned the inexperienced missionaries, but his admiration for their fortitude convinced him to meet them in his office. The elders insisted that they pray each time, which impressed Immo. Repeatedly he probed with such questions as, "If a child were born, and, without even a chance of being baptized, died, why should it be condemned to go to the kind of hell my church has devised for it?" Sometimes he touched on topics nearer his experience. "During our marriage, my wife and I have both felt that we should also be together in heaven, even though we fail to see at the moment how this is possible." The missionaries gladly discussed these topics, referring to the scriptures. Their answers made sense. Because Immo spoke and read English fluently, he asked to read the Book of Mormon in that language, a feat he accomplished in one night. He quit his long-time smoking habit with the Lord's help, and in late August he was baptized. His family soon followed. European Mission president Alvin R. Dyer called Brother Luschin within a few weeks to be the Church's translator of German in Europe, a job he filled for the next six years. Within a year he was called as the first Austrian branch president in Graz. In 1966 he and his family moved to European Mission headquarters to supervise other translators in addition to his own translation work. Eventually Brother Luschin translated all the latter-day scriptures and the temple endowment into German. He also translated for the prophets and general authorities when they visited German-speaking Europe. From 1972 to 1977, he served as president of the Swiss Temple.[23]

Postwar Switzerland

Switzerland, with its long history of courage, freedom, and political neutrality, provided a base for Church activities in continental Europe following World War II. Because of Swiss neutrality, channels of communication were open between Switzerland and other nations. Elder Ezra Taft Benson took advantage of that open communication when he visited Switzerland in early 1946 and stored Church welfare supplies in the International Red Cross warehouses in Geneva.

President Benson reestablished the Swiss-Austrian Mission in 1946 with headquarters in Zürich; American missionaries immediately returned and renewed proselyting. In the ensuing years, many Swiss members chose to emigrate to the United States. This loss of members hampered growth, as did open opposition from the Reformed and Catholic churches. Although the Swiss government tolerated other religions, more so than any other continental European government, it still officially recognized only two religions.

When David O. McKay became Church president in 1951, he and his counselors decided to establish the first European temple near the Swiss capital of Bern, in part to help convince European members to stay in their home countries. Switzerland with its greater religious tolerance was the natural choice for a house of the Lord, and its location in central Europe gave it close rail connections to all other countries. In addition, most Swiss speak at least two languages and often as many as five—an important factor because the Swiss Temple was to serve the Saints in France, Belgium, Germany, Austria, Sweden, Finland, Norway, Denmark, and the Netherlands, as well as American servicemen and their families stationed in Europe. Thousands of war refugees had sought asylum in Switzerland, and Church leaders urged converts among them to seek employment in the Bern area where the temple was projected to be built.

President McKay visited numerous possible temple sites near Bern

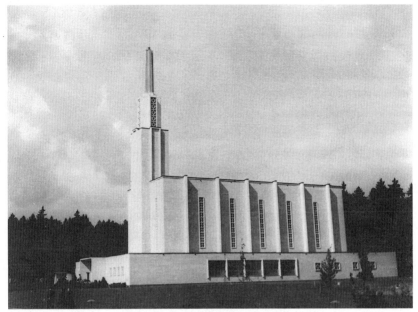

The Swiss Temple, dedicated in 1955

in 1952 as did Samuel E. Bringhurst, mission president in Switzerland, who enlisted the fasting and prayers of European members and missionaries. Acknowledging the help of the Lord, Church officials obtained a beautiful piece of property next to a national forest in Zollikofen, a suburb of Bern. Construction began, but in August 1955, just a month before the scheduled dedication, it seemed that the temple might not be finished in time. In the last week, workmen willingly labored night and day to complete the beautiful structure.

President McKay presided over the dedication ceremonies, a holy event attended by members from many European nations and conducted in seven different languages. The Mormon Tabernacle Choir sang. Reflecting upon the recent war, President McKay indicated that the temple would elevate people to a more Christlike way of living. "I think I have never felt in all my life the veil quite so thin," mused Elder Ezra Taft Benson after the dedication. "The action taken by the First Presidency in extending temples into Europe had the benediction and approval of our Heavenly Father. I shall never forget that glorious event! To me it was the most important event that has transpired in Europe in 118 years since the gospel was first taken to those shores."[24]

Immediately after the dedicatory services, temple president Samuel E. Bringhurst conducted ordinance sessions. Language difficulties were overcome in a spirit of loving cooperation. The Swiss Temple originated a new practice: no longer would the patrons go through several ordinance rooms during the endowment ceremony. Instead they all sat in one ordinance room to view a film giving instructions in their own language. Church employee Gordon B. Hinckley had supervised the preparation of the film and the dubbed-in voices of European immigrants and returned missionaries in different languages. And he had carefully shepherded copies of the film and voice tapes through customs. Thus Saints traveling to the temple from various European countries could receive the blessings of the temple in their own language and in a relatively short time.

The Swiss Temple brought new life to the Church in Switzerland and other parts of Europe. Many members became reactivated. Tithes and offerings increased. New missionary enthusiasm followed, and baptismal rates grew. Neighbors of the temple in Zollikofen pointed with pride to "our temple" and willingly rented rooms to temple visitors. At the time of the temple dedication in 1955, about 2,200 members resided in Switzerland. The number had swelled to about 3,600 in 1960.

Postwar France and French-Speaking Switzerland and Belgium

France is a nation rich in history and tradition. Since about 1700, the French took pride less in religion than in strong intellectual traditions—their language and literature, monuments, art, music, food, beautiful cities, and historical achievements. With Germany no longer unified after World War II, France was also the largest and most populous western European country.

The Church of Jesus Christ of Latter-day Saints struggled to gain a foothold in France. Before World War II, the French Mission experienced a series of stops and starts. Then the scourge of Nazi occupation humbled the French people, and liberation by allied forces fostered gratitude toward Americans. With this new attitude in France, the Church built a firmer base in the late 1940s and 1950s than at any previous time in history. Even so, few families were converted, and many stable members chose to emigrate to the United States.

The French Mission included Belgium and the French-speaking Swiss cantons near Geneva where six times as many members lived than in all of France. Every year Switzerland and Belgium surpassed France in the number of baptisms. Success in France, where the Church was regarded as no more than a "sect," was still the lowest in all of western Europe.

Among the early members who remained in France were Louis and Marie Gaston of Nice. In 1950, Louis attended all the local churches looking for Christ's true church. Marie learned of the Latter-day Saints from a friend at the market. The name, The Church of Jesus Christ, sounded right to them, and when the Gastons attended a meeting, held in a small room, they felt from the members the spirit of testimony of the Savior. The whole family was baptized at Christmastime in the Turkish Baths of Nice. Within a year, Louis was ordained an elder and called as branch president. The Gastons led the branch in service and sharing the gospel with friends and with customers at their shop. Within two years, the Nice Branch had more than a hundred people attending each Sunday.[25]

Unfortunately, apostasy among missionaries led to a tragedy in the French Mission in 1958. A missionary known for his charisma, Elder William Tucker, experienced unparalleled success. His intensity, determination, and enthusiasm won converts, and he was called as counselor in the mission presidency to travel throughout the mission tracting with other missionaries and teaching them successful proselyting methods. Historian Kahlile Mehr reported: "Ironically, while trying to convert others, Tucker continued to sway from his own conversion. Even prior to his mission, he had concluded that the Church had erred in abolishing polygamy. At some point he developed aberrant views regarding priesthood authority, the guidance of the Spirit, the temple garment, and the Word of Wisdom." Elder Tucker swayed other missionaries to his "visionary" thinking. When Tucker learned of the apostate teachings of the polygamous LeBaron family, founders of the Church of the Firstborn headquartered in Mexico, he began promulgating them among his adherents. The apostasy was discovered, and visiting apostles, who were in Europe for the London Temple dedication, held a church tribunal to investigate. Nine missionaries were excommunicated. The mission was in temporary disarray.[26]

In the ensuing two years, the remaining missionaries, shaken, redirected the French Mission toward a more permanent rejuvenation. Henry D. Moyle of the First Presidency visited the mission in December 1959. He asked the missionaries what goals they would set for themselves for the new year. They consulted and returned with a baptismal goal of 400 for 1960, a total four times the average of any of the previous ten years. President Moyle laughed and said, "I love to see men with more faith than I have!" Then somberly he prophesied: "Brethren, you can have those 400 by the 4th of July." By 4 July 1960, 404 new converts had been baptized, and the total stood at 942 by year's end. "It was an exceptional year in which the mission broke from the statistical mire of its past and was regenerated with an influx of new members."[27]

In 1961 the French East Mission was created, and the following year the first French meetinghouse was dedicated in Nantes. As the decade of the 1960s unfolded, a sizable number of converts came from French refugees who had fled from Algeria when that former colony won its independence in a revolution.

The Church Matures in Britain

In 1958 the London Temple was completed, and more than 76,000 attended open house tours. In September President David O. McKay presided at dedicatory services, an event that symbolized more than anything else that the Church had finally reached maturity in Britain. Derek Cuthbert described the occasion as "the crowning experience of my life." Elder Hugh B. Brown of the Council of the Twelve and a former British missionary and mission president welcomed visitors as they entered. Brother Cuthbert thought how gratifying it must be for Elder Brown to witness "the results of his and others' labours in the British Mission. As we sat there I knew that all of the former missionaries to Great Britain back to Elder Heber C. Kimball himself were rejoicing with us."[28]

The British Saints basked in the warmth of frequent visits and communication from Church headquarters. President McKay visited Britain four years in a row, which was unprecedented for a prophet. In 1955 Elder

Spencer W. Kimball toured England, Scotland, Ireland, and Wales for twenty-three days. Elder Adam S. Bennion of the Twelve toured the mission a year later and continued the emphasis on developing leadership. Regularly each year thereafter, members of the Twelve visited the British Mission. A concerted building program gathered steam. Throughout the 1950s, every branch was charged to establish a building fund and prepare to construct a chapel; many were completed during the decade. Mission youth conferences and district Relief Society presidents conferences in 1958 and 1959 strengthened the auxiliaries.

Late in the 1950s, President McKay declared: "This is a New Era in the British Mission."[29] The number of convert baptisms doubled and then tripled in a year. By 1960 membership in the British Mission reached 14,000, more than double the number a decade earlier.

Two significant goals of the New Era were dividing the British Mission and establishing British stakes of Zion. In March 1960, Elder Harold B. Lee of the Quorum of the Twelve joined President McKay to create the North British Mission, headquartered in Manchester. Later in the year, the First Presidency announced two more missions: the Scottish-Irish Mission and the Central British Mission. Hundreds of missionaries flocked into the United Kingdom, began using a simpler teaching plan, and worked harder than ever before. District missionaries continued to emphasize the member-missionary theme.

Also in March 1960, Elder Lee organized the eagerly awaited Manchester Stake, the first stake in all of Europe. British Saints now felt that the Church had been firmly established in their native land. The next year three more British stakes were created, and by 1970 there were eight.

The 1960s was a period of unprecedented growth in Great Britain. From an annual growth rate per year of about 10 percent in the 1950s, the rate rose to almost 40 percent in the early 1960s. Warning bells began to ring for Church leaders. Derek Cuthbert, first counselor in the mission presidency at the time, explained: "The three main challenges that were thrust upon us were, firstly, the need to integrate new members, whose influx became almost a deluge, considering the small base from which the Church was starting. Secondly, the need [for new facilities] to accommodate these new Saints. . . . Thirdly, there developed a desperate need for supplies and curriculum materials. In the days before the New Era we could 'get by' with simple fellowshipping, converted houses, and a few manuals, often recycled year to year."[30]

Mission and stake leaders combined to find solutions. Newly baptized men became part of the Senior Aaronic Priesthood program and prepared for ordination to the Melchizedek Priesthood. New sisters were introduced to Relief Society with its evening meetings, bazaars, and charitable service activities. But a greater challenge was the huge influx of youth. These young converts, later dubbed "baseball baptisms" because missionaries often met them while organizing baseball teams, were numerous. Local leaders charged all Aaronic Priesthood, MIA, and Primary officers and teachers to become acquainted with the new young members and involve them in various activities. Unfortunately, however, most fell away because they had not been properly taught by the missionaries and their parents had not been sought out and taught also.[31]

From the massive number of youth baptisms a pool of young men remained from which building missionaries were called in the 1960s. Fifty church buildings were constructed through this program in just five years, and a new Church office complex and a general distribution center in London provided Church curriculum materials. All necessary supplies were now at the fingertips of the British Saints.

In 1962 the European Mission, which supervised the various individual missions, was divided into the West European and the European Missions. The West European Mission (for the British Isles) was organized with headquarters in the handsome Hyde Park Chapel in London. Elder N. Eldon Tanner of the Twelve was first to preside, and he was followed by other general authorities later in the decade.

Also in 1962, a separate Irish Mission was organized, covering both the Republic of Ireland and Northern Ireland. Northern Ireland, also known as Ulster, was part of the United Kingdom. The Church remained sensitive to the divisions in Ireland and tried to avoid becoming embroiled in conflicts. Religious strife between Catholics and Protestants continued to be a serious problem, especially in Ulster. Terrorist bombings at times jeopardized Church activities and meeting places.

An important innovation with long-range consequences took place in 1968. The Church, under the leadership of John M. Madsen of the England Southwest Mission, started a home-study seminary program in four stakes in Britain. This program soon spread, for it proved of inestimable value in preparing young people to fill missions and marry in the temple.

The 1960s ended with an astounding total of 57,000 baptized in the British Isles during the decade; during the previous ninety years, less than half that number had joined the Church. Furthermore, emigration of Saints to America dropped to almost nothing. The Church was truly coming of age in Great Britain. When the First Presidency decided in 1970 to hold area general conferences in various parts of the world, they chose Manchester, England, as the first location.

The conference, attended by some 12,000 enthusiastic Saints, was a spiritual capstone to Church stability in Britain and a key to expanding the Church worldwide. President Joseph Fielding Smith, who had labored some seventy years earlier as a missionary in England, presided at the 1971 conference and blessed the Saints. Numerous other general authorities, many of whom had also been British missionaries, spoke. A highlight of the conference was the singing of "This Is Our Place," a hymn written especially for the occasion:

> In Britain's chosen countryside,
> Mid England's dales and Scottish hills,
> Welsh mountains green, and Irish lakes;
> Here we live, and here we will serve.

> This is our place, here we will stay,
> To build, to strengthen ward and stake.
> Until the Lord supreme shall reign;
> This is our place, here we will serve.[32]

The Church on the Continent through the Mid 1970s

The Church established the headquarters of the European Mission in Frankfurt, West Germany, in 1960, renewing enthusiasm among Church members on the Continent. Eventually a large office complex was developed, with departments for temporal affairs and for distributing and translating Church materials. Alvin R. Dyer, an assistant to the Twelve, was the first president. He announced that new meetinghouses would be constructed and new stakes established when enough districts were ready. During the 1950s, poor facilities had embarrassed members trying to interest their friends in the Church. Local members gladly contributed both funds and building skills to the new chapels. Soon labor missionaries participated on a large scale, and President Dyer encouraged setting higher goals for baptisms. The first stakes on the Continent were created in 1961: the Dutch Stake, in Holland; the Swiss Stake, in Zürich; and the West Berlin, Stuttgart, and Hamburg Stakes in West Germany.

Dishearteningly, most converts of the early 1960s fell away, and toward the end of the decade the number of baptisms slumped as well. Elder Ezra Taft Benson, beloved by the European Saints because of his 1946 mission of mercy, returned in 1964 to preside over the European Mission. Elder Benson directed a more deliberate approach to baptisms, requiring, for example, that converts live the Word of Wisdom a full month before being baptized.

Elder Benson dedicated scores of chapels during his tenure and organized separate congregations for the American servicemen and their families stationed in West Germany. Since World War II, the American members had often met with the German Saints and contributed generously to local building funds. But when a huge NATO contingent began massing to counterweight the burgeoning Soviet military presence in eastern Europe, many American Latter-day Saint servicemen were sent to Germany, enough to justify both English- and German-speaking congregations. Nonetheless, the two groups often participated in joint activities because, in every case, they shared meetinghouses. Eventually four "servicemen" stakes were created in West Germany, each with its own missionaries, and a high proportion of convert baptisms came from American military personnel. The biggest challenge in the American units of the Church was the constant turnover due to the reassignment of the young enlisted personnel; the biggest asset was the officers, who were almost all experienced in Church procedures.

Another achievement of President Benson's service in Europe during this time was the creation of annual youth conferences, first in Germany, then in Scandinavia, and gradually in most other nations on the

Continent. The great challenge remaining to European members who stayed in their home countries was to marry within their own faith. Frequent youth conferences provided opportunities for members to meet one another and then to marry in the Swiss Temple. More than anything else these conferences brought solidarity and growth to the Church in the 1960s, and they became a staple of the Church in Europe. Then in the late 1960s and early 1970s, the Church Educational System established seminaries and institutes of religion in western European countries, which helped more and more European young people to qualify to serve full-time missions and to marry in the temple.

In 1961 Henry D. Moyle of the First Presidency established Switzerland's first stake in Zürich. As a young missionary, Elder Moyle had started his labors in that city and had wondered if he would ever see a stake created there. The first stake president, Wilhelm F. Lauener, had emigrated to America after the war, gained professional expertise and Church experience, but then, after fasting and prayer, returned to his native land. President Lauener testified often to the Saints "that the Lord led us to America to learn to serve Him better and now we are back here because He wants us here."[33] President Lauener's second counselor was Hans B. Ringger, who years later was called to the Church's First Quorum of the Seventy.

Baptism statistics leveled off in Germany, Switzerland, Austria, and the Scandinavian countries, but new stakes were nevertheless created and plans laid for still others. Asmund H. Hernes, whose grandparents had joined the Church in Norway in the early 1900s, expressed the pervasive optimism of western European Saints: "I learned the gospel at [my mother's] knee," he related, "and though the auxiliaries weren't functioning fully at that time and Narvik was the northernmost branch of the Church, a few faithful members met regularly, eager to tell all they met that the Lord had spoken again. Now we have seen the dawning of a new day. Not only the standard works, but lesson manuals and other materials are available in Norwegian. Tent camps and youth conferences are held every year. . . . I have seen beautiful modern chapels built in Trondheim (where I served as branch president), Bergen, Drammen, and Oslo, and two temples have been built to accommodate the Saints in Europe. The gospel is spreading rapidly."[34]

In France the work prospered. Over the decade from 1960 to 1970 membership grew from 1,509 to 8,606. "Most significant was the conviction that it was now possible to do missionary work among the Catholics of western Europe in the same way, and with as encouraging results, as among Protestants," observed historian Douglas Tobler.[35]

Simultaneously Catholicism was undergoing a major transformation, ignited by the Vatican II decisions of the 1960s and early 1970s. This transformation made it possible for the gospel to be introduced into Italy and Spain and eventually into Portugal.

A New Start in Italy

Italy, seat of the Roman Catholic Church, was long without the opportunity to receive the saving principles and ordinances of the gospel. But once missionary work resumed in earnest in 1965, Italy became one of the stronger countries of the Church in Europe.

A few American Latter-day Saints were stationed in Italy after World War II. In the early 1960s, they and their families and a few native Italians were organized into branches and groups under the Swiss Mission.

One of those native Italian members was Vincenzo Di Francesca. This brother was converted to the gospel by reading a discarded copy of the Book of Mormon that he had found in a trash can in New York City in 1910. He didn't learn the real name of the book and its association with the Church until 1930. Various war-related events kept him from joining the Church until 1951, when he was baptized and confirmed in his native Sicily by President Samuel E. Bringhurst of the Swiss-Austrian Mission. He was endowed in the Swiss Temple in 1956. When missionaries returned to Italy in 1965, Brother Di Francesca was waiting for them. He died in November 1966, active and devoted to the end. His story was told in the *Church News*, the *Improvement Era*, and finally in the Church's award-winning film *How Rare a Possession—The Book of Mormon*.[36]

With the publication of the Book of Mormon in Italian in 1964, a few missionaries in Switzerland and Germany began teaching *Gastarbeiter*, or guest workers—Italians who had left Italy to find more lucrative

A portable baptismal font used in the late 1960s in the Italian Mission

employment. These missionaries learned Italian, and in 1965 Ezra Taft Benson, president of the European Mission, transferred them to labor in northern Italy, forming an Italian zone within the Swiss Mission. On 10 November 1966, at approximately the same spot on Mount Brigham where Elder Lorenzo Snow had dedicated Italy for missionary work 116 years earlier, Elder Benson rededicated the land for the preaching of the gospel. In the dedication prayer, he prophesied that thousands of Italians would be brought into the Church. The first convert in the new Italian Mission was Leopoldo Larcher, who later served as the first native Italian mission president.

The Church grew rapidly in Italy in the late 1960s and early 1970s, especially in the northern provinces, which were going through a period of industrialization and social transformation. Moving into new homes and new lifestyles, many people felt freer to explore the gospel. The Church was also introduced into Rome, southern Italy, and Sicily—strongholds of Catholicism.

Sister Maria Nappi related in 1973: "Before we joined the Church my husband liked to go hunting on the weekends. He also liked to play cards. He rarely if ever visited his parents, and he usually came home quite late at night. The change since we joined the Church is a big one. There's love in the home now. We're together almost every evening. It's beautiful to see the cooperation in our home now."[37]

Beginnings in Spain

Spain, along with smaller Portugal, occupies the Iberian Peninsula. Throughout the centuries, Spain has remained a land apart, geographically, religiously, and culturally. Spanish rulers embraced the Roman Catholic faith and values, promoted doctrinal and spiritual loyalty through the Inquisition, and established Roman Catholicism in its vast colonial empire. Spain certainly remained untouched by Protestantism. Proud of its history as a bulwark of Catholicism, Spain remained for many years relatively untouched by the Restoration as well.

Francisco Franco emerged from the bloody 1936–39 Spanish Civil War as the ruler of his country. An intensely nationalistic and pro-Catholic dictator, Franco nonetheless gradually warmed up to the United States and in 1953 allowed an American military base to be built on Spanish soil. That meant the arrival in Spain of some Latter-day Saint military personnel. Some were married and took their families with them. A few others married Spanish wives and brought them into the Church. Others shared the gospel with Spanish friends. One of the first converts, in 1967, was Jose Oliveira, an attorney and moviemaker who years later became the first stake president in Spain.

Under political pressure, Franco gave the Cortes (parliament) more power in 1967. One of the first enactments of the Cortes was the Religious Liberty Law, which permitted recognition of any church if its meetings included a certain number of native Spanish citizens. The Church qualified because of the Spanish converts and some investigators. On 22 October 1968, after unceasing efforts by the Madrid Servicemen's Branch, the Spanish Minister of Justice granted the Church official recognition. The newly separate Spanish-speaking branch in Madrid operated under the direction of the French Mission.

On 19 May 1969, Elder Marion G. Romney of the Twelve, who had learned Spanish while growing up in the Mormon Colonies in Mexico, dedicated Spain for the preaching of the gospel. The apostle Paul had visited Spain, Elder Romney recalled, and Nephi had prophesied of Columbus, whose discoveries in America hastened the restoration of the gospel. Brother Oliveira was present at the dedicatory serves and heard Elder Romney's petition: "Bless the native people, that they may be leaders of their own people, that Zion may grow and increase in this land."[38]

A month later, the first four full-time missionaries arrived, transferred from other Spanish-speaking missions. Soon more arrived, and in 1970 the Spanish Mission was established with headquarters in Madrid.

Progress in Spain was slow at first because most people were unwilling to break from their strong traditions. Some missionaries were even jailed for preaching. But a few investigators joined the Church. One was Gloria Cejudo of Sevilla. She "had been active in her own church; but overwhelmed by the burden of raising a family alone and disenchanted by manifold injustices, she began to lose faith. From the depths of her despair she cried out, 'Oh, God, show me if you exist!' Two young elders had knocked at every door on the Cejudos' street during that November of 1969, but later, while crossing through the area, they felt impressed to knock on just one door. Gloria Cejudo's heartfelt plea had been answered. She was the second person baptized in Sevilla, and served as Relief Society president almost from that time." During those critical beginning years, many American Saints were transferred to Madrid for business or military reasons, and they, too, gave their experience and support to the work. By June 1974, 691 Spanish members were living in seventeen branches, and there were 300 American members in the Spanish Mission.[39]

Area Conferences in Western Europe

The Church established a milestone in continental Europe by convening an area general conference in Munich, West Germany, in August 1973. All members from West Germany, Austria, Switzerland, France, Italy, Spain, Belgium, the Netherlands, and the American servicemen stationed on the Continent and in the Middle East were invited to attend. The members in these countries totaled some 55,000, as follows: West Germany 25,000; Austria 2,600; Switzerland 4,500; France 7,600; Italy 4,800; Spain 800; Belgium 2,700; and the Netherlands 7,000.

Some 14,000 Saints attended this conference held in the Olympic Hall in Munich. Miraculously, 100 East German Saints gained permission from their Communist government to attend. The *Ensign* reported: "It was an experiment in love and brotherhood. They came from nations that had been enemies, that had engaged each other in deadly combat. There were great language barriers. By train they came, by bus, by car. Those from outside the host country carefully husbanded their passports or their papers. (A few had been turned back at the border because their papers were not in order.) Some stayed in public campgrounds; some in dormitories (such as schoolhouses); some in small guest houses and hostels that are so popular in Europe. The 700 members of the two Munich branches took care of some 700 visiting Saints in their homes."[40]

President Harold B. Lee, the Church's eleventh prophet, conducted the general sessions. He quoted Galatians 3:26–29 and then interpreted the passage in modern terms: "We are neither English nor German, nor French, nor Dutch, nor Spanish, nor Italian, but we are all one as baptized members of The Church of Jesus Christ of Latter-day Saints, and also we are Abraham's seed as the apostle Paul declared and therefore heirs according to the promise."[41] The conference included numbers by the Mormon Tabernacle Choir, choirs from each of the nations represented, and cultural programs featuring roadshows, folk singing, and folk dancing.

Elder Gordon B. Hinckley of the Quorum of the Twelve spoke to the members' hearts: "I have seen many beautiful sights in Europe, but I think I have never seen a more beautiful picture, a more inspiring sight, than this congregation of Latter-day Saints gathered from many nations of Europe. Your faces radiate the spirit of the gospel. In your presence one feels the strength of personal testimony. You feel the warmth of one another's faith, the strength of one another's companionship.

"But it was not always so. Most of you are converts to the Church who pass through the difficult struggle of conversion. You have known loneliness and heartache. When you leave this afternoon and return to your homes . . . to the association of those who do not see as you see and do not think as you think and who are prone to ridicule, you may feel again that loneliness.

"But as members of the Church, you have come as a city set upon a hill which cannot be hid. To those about you, you are different, just as the true gospel is different from the philosophies of the world."[42]

A year later, a similar area general conference convened in Stockholm, Sweden, for the Scandinavian and Finnish Saints. This time the twelfth prophet, President Spencer W. Kimball, presided. The membership by 1974 had reached 4,100 in Denmark; 4,300 in Norway; 5,100 in Sweden; and 2,100 in Finland for a total of 15,600 members in that northern European area.

President Kimball spoke at length on personal worthiness through keeping the commandments—"all the commandments"—and reviewed many of them, from personal prayer to morality, from attendance at meetings to holding family home evenings, from paying tithing to living the Word of Wisdom. "These things are basic," he declared. "Let no man nor woman rationalize or justify with loose interpretation of the world these important standards." He preached also of missionary work and the building up of branches within nations by encouraging isolated Saints to gravitate to the larger Church centers within the nation, so that both they and the branches might bless each other. He spent considerable time, in this area of the Church where there was only one stake (Copenhagen Denmark Stake, created two months before the conference), raising the sights of the people to the establishment of more stakes and setting the goal of "dotting the countryside" with stakes, preparing the way for "a temple in each of your lands!"[43]

These two area general conferences held in Munich and Stockholm combined with the 1971 area general conference in Manchester, England, in presaging permanence and growth for the Church in Europe. Two aspects of the Church's history—frequent persecution and mass emigration to an American Zion—had become a distant memory.

NOTES

1 George Albert Smith, "After Eighty Years," *Improvement Era*, April 1950, 263.

2 George Albert Smith, in Conference Report, October 1947, 5–6; "President Smith in East on Mission of Mercy," *Church News*,

10 November 1945, 1; "President Smith Returns from Successful Trip to Capital," *Church News,* 17 November 1945, 1, 7.

3 *A Labor of Love: The 1946 European Mission of Ezra Taft Benson* (Salt Lake City: Deseret Book, 1989), 6–7.

4 *Millennial Star* 108 (March 1946): 80–81.

5 Ezra Taft Benson, in Conference Report, April 1947, 153.

6 Frederick W. Babbel, *On Wings of Faith* (Salt Lake City: Bookcraft, 1972), 36.

7 Benson, in Conference Report, April 1947, 154.

8 *Labor of Love,* 63.

9 Sheri L. Dew, *Ezra Taft Benson: A Biography* (Salt Lake City: Deseret Book, 1987), 231.

10 William G. Hartley, "War and Peace and Dutch Potatoes," *Ensign* 8 (July 1978): 18–23.

11 Keith C. Warner, "History of the Netherlands Mission of The Church of Jesus Christ of Latter-day Saints 1861–1966," master's thesis, Brigham Young University, 1967, 146.

12 Louis B. Cardon, "War and Recovery, 1939–1950," in V. Ben Bloxham et al., eds., *Truth Will Prevail: The Rise of The Church of Jesus Christ of Latter-day Saints in the British Isles, 1837–1987* (West Midlands: Corporation of the President of The Church of Jesus Christ of Latter-day Saints, 1987), 389.

13 Derek A. Cuthbert, *The Second Century: Latter-day Saints in Great Britain, Volume I, 1937–1987* (Cambridge, England: Cambridge University Press, 1987), 7.

14 David Lawrence McKay, *My Father, David O. McKay* (Salt Lake City: Deseret Book, 1989), 221.

15 James R. Moss, "The Great Awakening," in Bloxham, *Truth Will Prevail,* 394–402.

16 Auli Rämö, "The LDS Church in Finland," unpublished paper, Brigham Young University, 7 March 1994.

17 Warner, "History of the Netherlands Mission," 76–105.

18 Warner, "History of the Netherlands Mission," 164.

19 As a missionary I participated in this project by soliciting speaking appointments for President Fetzer among Rotarians.

20 "To Be a Woman in the Church," *Ensign* 3 (August 1973): 36–38.

21 *Die Geschichte der Mormonen in Österreich* (Vienna: Austrian Mission of The Church of Jesus Christ of Latter-day Saints, 1965), 39–40.

22 "Thank God for the Missionaries," in Hartman Rector and Connie Rector, *No More Strangers* (Salt Lake City: Bookcraft, 1971), 48–49.

23 Information on Brother Luschin comes from ibid., 47–55, interview with Immo Luschin von Ebengreuth by James R. Christianson, The James Moyle Oral History Program, in LDS Church Historical Archives.

24 Ezra Taft Benson, in Conference Report, October 1955, 107.

25 LaRene Porter Gaunt, "A Blooming in France," *Ensign* 25 (March 1995): 43.

26 Kahlile Mehr, "The Trial of the French Mission," *Dialogue* 21 (Fall 1988): 27–45.

27 Ibid., 42.

28 Cuthbert, *The Second Century*, 33.

29 Ibid., 35.

30 Ibid., 51.

31 Ibid., 52–53.

32 Ibid., 110.

33 Kirby, "History of The Church of Jesus Christ of Latter-day Saints in Switzerland," 156.

34 Asmund H. Hernes, "My Grandfather's Courage," *Ensign* 4 (July 1974): 45.

35 Douglas F. Tobler, "The Church in Europe," *Encyclopedia of Mormonism*, 5 vols. (New York: Macmillan Publishing Company, 1991), 2:473.

36 Jay M. Todd, "The Saga of the Di Francesca Story," *Ensign* 19 (September 1989): 73.

37 "To Be a Woman in the Church," 38.

38 Betty Ventura, "The Saints in Spain," *Ensign* 5 (April 1975): 8–9.

39 Ibid.

40 Doyle L. Green, "Meeting in Munich: An Experience in Love and Brotherhood," *Ensign* 3 (November 1973): 71.

41 Ibid., 76.

42 Ibid., 79.

43 Jay M. Todd, "Konferens," *Ensign* 4 (October 1974): 78–79.

CHAPTER 9

Behind the Iron Curtain

1945 WORLD WAR II ENDS AND MOST OF EASTERN EUROPE FALLS UNDER CONTROL OF THE SOVIET UNION

1949 GOVERNMENTS OF WEST GERMANY AND EAST GERMANY ARE CREATED; COLD WAR BEGINS IN EARNEST

1961 BERLIN WALL IS BUILT BY THE COMMUNISTS

1968 ELDER THOMAS S. MONSON VISITS GERMAN DEMOCRATIC REPUBLIC (EAST GERMANY); CZECHOSLOVAKIA IS INVADED BY SOVIET TROOPS

1969 DRESDEN MISSION IS CREATED

1975 ELDER MONSON DEDICATES EAST GERMANY FOR THE PREACHING OF THE GOSPEL

1977 PRESIDENT SPENCER W. KIMBALL VISITS POLAND AND EAST GERMANY

1982 FIRST STAKE IN EAST GERMANY IS CREATED IN FREIBERG

1985 DEDICATION OF TEMPLE IN FREIBERG, EAST GERMANY

MARCH 1989 FIRST MISSIONARIES ENTER EAST GERMANY; FIRST EAST GERMAN MISSIONARIES ARE SENT ABROAD

1989 FALL OF THE BERLIN WALL

1990 GERMANY IS REUNITED

The Church of Jesus Christ of Latter-day Saints experienced little success in central and eastern Europe (except for eastern Germany) before World War I, mainly because of government and religious restrictions. In the nineteenth and early twentieth centuries, governments in this part of Europe were closely aligned with such state religions as the Russian Orthodox and Roman Catholic Churches. Between the two world wars, only eastern Germany and the hybrid democratic nation of Czechoslovakia were open to the Church.

Farther east, in Russia, the Bolsheviks gained control of the country during the 1917 October Revolution, created the Soviet Union, and installed Communist Party headquarters in Moscow. Bent on worldwide revolution, the Communists absolutely forbade religious freedoms, thus preventing teaching opportunities for the Church in the Soviet Union until the revolution of 1989.

After World War II, the Soviet Union wrested control of satellite states in central and eastern Europe as a buffer region between Russia and Germany. Much of what had been eastern Germany became part of either Poland or the Soviet Union. By 1949 the political divisions between Communist eastern Europe and American-influenced western Europe were clearly defined. The four zones of occupied Germany were restored to German governance. The Allied powers—United States, Britain, and France—agreed to the formation of the democratic Federal Republic of Germany (West Germany). The Russian-occupied sector of Germany became the Communist-controlled German Democratic Republic (East Germany). Most western European nations combined with the United States and Canada to form the North Atlantic Treaty Organization (NATO) as a military deterrent to Soviet aggression. The Soviet Union countered with an east European military alliance of its own, the Warsaw Pact, consisting of the USSR, Poland, Hungary, Czechoslovakia, East Germany, Romania, and Bulgaria.

From 1949 to the 1980s, both east and west conducted an escalating arms race. The armies, navies, air forces, and nuclear weapons of both east and west were braced for battle the entire time. Europe was caught in the middle of this Cold War, which extended worldwide to engage nearly every country.

An Iron Curtain of barbed wire and land mines separated east and west Europe, and the Berlin Wall, built in 1961, divided East and West Berlin. For many, the Iron Curtain and the Berlin Wall symbolized the Cold War and the nuclear standoff.

Postwar East Germany

Allied bombing raids early in 1945 devastated many east German cities, especially Berlin and Dresden. During 1945 meetings in Yalta and Potsdam, the Allies permitted the Soviet Union to gain first military and then political control over the east European countries the Russians had liberated from the Nazis. The full fury of Soviet soldiers anxious to avenge barbarities inflicted on them, their families, and their country during the war was let loose on the eastern German people during the savage occupation of Germany's Russian Zone.

Before World War II, there were approximately 14,000 Latter-day Saints in Germany. About 8,000 were in eastern German locations taken over at the end of the war by the Soviet military. When the Potsdam Accords gave parts of eastern Germany to Poland or the USSR, most Germans in these areas, including Latter-day Saints, fled to East Germany. According to best estimates, taking into account war deaths and the mobility of the members, approximately 6,000 Saints resided in East Germany in early 1946. Between 1946 and 1952, when some mobility was still possible, more than 1,500 Church members went either to West Germany or on to the United States, leaving fewer than 4,500 members in the German Democratic Republic. Because of Communist government restrictions, the Saints could not fully practice their religion. The heroic struggles and faith of the East German Saints after World War II and during the Cold War are among the most touching stories in Church history.[1]

Immediately after the war, the primary struggle of all Germans, including the Saints, was for food. Edith Krause, a teenager at the time, remembered: "We had to walk two kilometers to get water. . . . After three days a truck came with bread. . . . We were permitted to dig the canned goods out of the rubble [of a cannery]. . . . The young people organized service projects to get food to the older people." Yet the Church went on. "We visited the members of the Branch in their homes and held devotionals and firesides. We sat in our meetings in our coats and wrapped in blankets," said Edith. "We were thankful and full of hope, because we knew the Lord would not forget his people."[2] Acting East German Mission president Richard Ranglack and other leaders did everything they could to keep the Church members alive and together. Members who had fled former German provinces taken over by the Soviet Union and Poland were cared for in temporary Latter-day Saint refugee camps.[3]

Late in 1945, some LDS German soldiers returned to their homes in eastern Germany. More than four hundred had been killed or imprisoned by the Russians. President Ranglack called the worthy returning soldiers, whether married or single, to serve missions in order to provide adequate

Walter Krause (center) attends conference with other Church members in Leipzig in the 1950s

priesthood leadership in each branch and rekindle proselyting that had ended abruptly in 1939. Walter Krause, twenty-eight years old, responded to the call by saying, "If the Lord needs me I will go." Brother Krause, who in 1973 was the first native patriarch ordained in East Germany, remembered the beginning of his mission: "On December 1, 1945 I set out with 20 Marks in my pocket, a piece of dry bread, and a bottle of herb tea. One Brother had given me a winter coat that had belonged to his son who did not return from the war. Another Brother who was a shoemaker gave me a pair of shoes."[4] These thirty-one young and not-so-young missionaries provided necessary leadership for the stricken German Saints.

Paul Langheinrich of the mission presidency launched a genealogy-gathering program. One young missionary, Rudolf Poecker, who had learned Russian during the war, negotiated with Soviet military officials for permission to obtain genealogical records, mostly of Jews, hidden in salt mines from the Nazis. Elder Poecker and Elder Walter Kindt labored together in Halberstadt for eleven months, developed an eternal friendship during their labors and Book of Mormon studies together, strengthened the branch, and baptized twenty converts. Later both men served in turn as president of the Germany Düsseldorf Mission. Elder Poecker and his wife, Elfriede, developed a slogan during his missions: "We are separated for a short time so we can be together forever."[5]

When Ezra Taft Benson of the Quorum of the Twelve Apostles and also European Mission president arrived in the Russian sector of Berlin in March 1946, his soul revolted at what he saw: "The wreckage to lovely government buildings, universities, monuments, museums, parks, and business blocks cannot possibly be understood unless seen. . . . My heart is heavy as I reflect on these awful, never-to-be-forgotten scenes. Truly war is hell in all its fury."[6] President Benson consoled the Saints in their temporal distress and was in turn inspired by their faith and activity. Comparing the members to other Germans who were still in deep depression, many having committed suicide, President Benson noted: "Our Saints, on the other hand, are full of hope, courage, and faith, and everywhere they look cheerfully forward with expressions of deepest faith. . . . It was one of the greatest demonstrations we have ever seen of the real fruits of the gospel in the lives of men and women."[7] The apostle counseled the Saints in eastern Germany to "put away your hatred and bitterness and help build up the work of the Lord."[8]

Conditions gradually brightened for the Saints in the Russian Zone as the branches grew stronger and new members came into the Church. Russian occupation authorities were at first generous with the Church, its members, and their requests. Nearly 12,000 Saints convened for a mission conference in Leipzig in June 1946. Later in the year, Elder Alma Sonne, an assistant to the Twelve, replaced Elder Benson as European Mission president; Walter Stover, a German Saint who had emigrated to America, took over as the East German Mission president until 1951. President Stover was a gentle and generous man who had arranged for his own car to be shipped overseas so he could visit the members in the eight districts. But driving an American car in the Russian sector caused problems. His biographer, Melvin Leavitt, wrote: "There was some danger in these travels. He was arrested several times, and once he was taken at gunpoint to be tried by a Russian military court as an American spy. . . . He had been promised by President George Albert Smith that the adversary would have no power over him as long as he was doing his duty, and this promise was honored many times."[9]

Members of the Dresden Branch pose outside their meetinghouse in 1950

President Stover's scrapes with the government typify what happened throughout the entire eastern zone. Russian authorities restricted the Latter-day Saints' privileges as they came to perceive the Church as an American organization and its missionaries as American spies. Some elders, even though they were German citizens, were imprisoned. After the 1948 Berlin Airlift and the formation of the German Democratic Republic (GDR) in 1949, the Church suffered increasing hardships. No property could be purchased. No missionaries of any kind could serve. Members of the East German secret police (the infamous *Stasi*) attended meetings and harassed members. The *Stasi* attempted to solicit damaging information on the Church from the members. Finally, it became impossible for members to leave the country, even on visits. Throughout the 1950s, leaders of the North German Mission, headquartered in Hamburg, visited the East German Saints and gave them instruction and encouragement.

East Germany's Darkest Days

In 1961 the Cold War deepened into a freeze when Soviet leader Nikita Krushchev and East German Communist leaders brought on the Berlin crisis by severely restricting traffic between West and East Berlin

President David O. McKay visits Berlin in 1952

and constructing, almost overnight, the Berlin Wall between the two sectors. Both NATO and the Warsaw Pact braced for war.

From 1961 on, official Church visits to East Germany came almost to a standstill. Occasionally the Berlin Mission president and a few others obtained permits to visit Leipzig during the city's renowned fair. Members always thronged to these annual fairs, hoping to meet with one another and visiting Church authorities.[10]

During such rare visits, leaders carried with them lesson manuals and other Church literature. East German Saints then typed the information, making carbon copies for each branch. From time to time in the 1960s Communist authorities banned even these makeshift items of literature. The East German secret police required branch presidents to apply to hold each meeting, report who would speak, and list the topics.

The 1960s were perhaps the darkest days for the East German Saints as they plodded on under strict government supervision. Yet today these same members look back on this period "with great fondness—even joy," wrote Gerald and Norma Davis. "The more they were driven together

Henry Burkhart directs a meeting of district and branch leaders in Dresden, 1955

from outside pressures, the closer they grew to one another, to the Church, and to the Lord. Attendance at meetings was high; home teaching and visiting teaching assignments were carried out with devotion and sincerity; members looked out for one another and helped one another; tithes and offerings were donated faithfully."[11] Considerable intermarriage among East German Saints at this time made of the Church "a large, extended family or clan" on a literal as well as the usual spiritual level.

Some local Church leaders had held positions since the 1940s and continued to hold them into the 1970s and 1980s. Henry Burkhart, who had served as a counselor to President Stover, became the presiding officer when President Stover returned to America. According to historian Douglas Tobler, Brother Burkhart "literally lived his life in service to his fellow East German Saints and the Church, meeting and interceding with government authorities, answering questions, pleading the Church's case, and accounting to government interrogators both for the leaders abroad and the Saints at home."[12] President Burkhart was aided by two equally noble counselors: Walter Krause and Gottfried Richter.

In 1968 the ministry of Elder Thomas S. Monson began in eastern Europe. Then the youngest member of the Council of the Twelve, the forty-three-year-old Elder Monson was vigorous enough to endure the rigors of forty-eight-hour visits behind the Iron Curtain. Elder Monson, who had grown up among German immigrants and then presided over them as a young bishop, loved the German Saints with all his heart. Elder Monson recalled feeling apprehensive on his first visit, knowing Americans were being incarcerated on false charges: "It was a little bit frightening to go through Checkpoint Charley and see the machine guns and the shepherd dogs, the Doberman pinscher dogs waiting for a false move on your part. . . . And so you simply had to realize that your objective was higher than any earthly authority and, with trust, in you went."[13]

On one such visit, Elder Monson spoke in 1968 to the Saints in Görlitz near the Polish border. "As I stood to speak . . . I felt the inspiration and I followed it. . . . I said, 'I promise you in the name of the Lord that every blessing that accrues to a Latter-day Saint who is faithful in any other nation of the world will be yours.' After that promise I began to realize what I said. They had no patriarchs, a wall prevented them from going to the temple, they had no missionaries, and they couldn't print church materials. I offered the most sincere and humble prayer of my life asking my Heavenly Father to honor that promise and he did every whit."[14]

In 1969 Elder Monson organized the Dresden Mission to care for the members in East Germany, then numbering about 3,700 in four districts. A few elderly couples were called as part-time district missionaries. Percy K. Fetzer, former Berlin Mission president and son of German immigrants to Salt Lake City, was called as patriarch to the eastern European Saints, most of whom were in East Germany. Brother Fetzer made numerous short trips into the Communist countries to give patriarchal blessings and help Elder Monson provide leadership training. In 1973 Walter Krause was granted permission to visit Salt Lake City for general conference. President Harold B. Lee called this faithful elderly man to be the first local patriarch to his people and prophesied that he would give more than one thousand blessings. Brother Krause, although he felt he would soon die because of ill health, accepted this responsibility. His health improved, and in 1996 he was still giving patriarchal blessings, having given approximately seventeen hundred.[15]

On 27 April 1975, Elder Monson and a small group of Saints ascended a hill near the Elbe River in Dresden to plead for the Church in East Germany. That remarkable dedicatory prayer indicates its profound importance to the Church in eastern Europe: "Thou knowest, Heavenly Father, the faith of the people of this land, the many tens of thousands who have embraced thy gospel, and have served to build up the Church wherever they have been. . . . Thou knowest, Heavenly Father, the sufferings of this people, and thou hast been near to them in time of trouble and in times of joy. . . . Heavenly Father, wilt thou intervene in the governmental affairs? Cause that thy Holy Spirit may dwell with those who preside that their hearts may be touched and that they may make those decisions which would help in the advancement of thy word."[16]

As Elder Monson prayed, a church bell chimed in the valley below. "At the conclusion of the prayer, I gazed heavenward," Elder Monson reported. "I noted a ray of sunshine which streamed from an opening in the heavy clouds, a ray which engulfed the spot where our small group stood. From that moment I knew divine help was at hand."[17]

In August 1977, Church president Spencer W. Kimball, after a historic visit to Poland, visited the Saints in the Dresden chapel, which had once been an officers' casino. The prophet added his testimony that the faithful East German Saints would one day do temple work and that the youth in the audience would go on missions.

Miraculous Events in East Germany

In the late 1970s and early 1980s, Henry Burkhart, president of the Dresden Mission, met frequently with East German officials, seeking permission for members to travel to the temple in Switzerland to do sacred ordinance work. Finally in 1982, tired of his appeals but still unwilling to permit whole families to leave the country, officials asked President Burkhart, "Why in the world don't you build a temple here?" Other factors motivating these officials were a desire to display their purported new openness toward the West and to draw money into East Germany.[18] Their actions signalled the end of the government ban on the Church owning property. Church officials quickly evaluated the unexpected invitation and decided to construct a temple in Freiberg, near Dresden.

Church buildings in Freiberg, German Democratic Republic: the temple (left), a family history center (center), and a stake center (right)

In August 1982, soon after the temple in Freiberg was announced, the Freiberg Stake was created. In 1983 ground was broken for both the temple and a stake center, and in 1984 the Leipzig Stake was organized. All East German Saints were now within the bounds of a stake of Zion. At the same time, the government gave permission to build chapels in Dresden, Leipzig, Zwickau, and Karl-Marx-Stadt.

The Freiberg Temple was completed in 1985, and an astounding 90,000 visitors toured the new edifice. What drew them was not the chance to see a large church—Germany is renowned for its magnificent cathedrals—but the uniqueness of a relatively unknown religion gaining permission to build a sacred sanctuary. Thousands of German people testified of the Spirit they felt when they visited the temple. President Gordon B. Hinckley dedicated the temple on 28 June 1985, and Henry Burkhart was set apart as its first president. Immediately the Saints attended with marvelous dedication. President Monson observed: "For its size, this temple is one of the busiest temples in the Church. It is the only temple where one makes an appointment to participate in an endowment session. It is the only temple I know of where stake presidents say, 'What can we do? Our home teaching is somewhat down because everyone is in the temple!' When I heard that comment, I thought, 'Not bad—not bad at all!'"[19]

Still, without missionaries, the Church in East Germany was not growing and, in fact, had dropped from almost 6,000 in 1946 to fewer than 3,500 in 1985. To grow would require missionaries—trained, full-time missionaries. Mission presidents from West Germany obtained permission to go to East Germany to train stake missionaries. This effort produced several new baptisms each year from 1986 through 1988.

The First Presidency decided to petition the Communist government to allow missionaries into the German Democratic Republic and for East German young men to leave their country as missionaries to other lands. In October 1988, President Thomas S. Monson and others, including the two East German stake presidents and the temple president, met with high government officials in Berlin. Kurt Löffler, state secretary for religious affairs, responded: "We want to be helpful to you. We've observed you and your people for twenty years. We know you are what you profess to be: honest men and women."[20]

This tribute was echoed at a subsequent meeting in Berlin with Erich Honecker, East German chief of state. Herr Honecker said to President Monson: "We know you. We trust you. We have had experience with you. Your missionary request is approved."[21]

"My spirit literally soared out of the room," President Monson later related. "The faith and devotion of our members in that nation have not gone unnoticed by God. . . . The long period of preparation is past. The future of the Church unfolds. Thanks be to God."[22]

East German Saints were overjoyed to greet the forty-four full-time missionaries from outside, all handpicked from other German-speaking missions by the European area presidency. One elder recalled his arrival in the German Democratic Republic Dresden Mission: "As my companion . . . and I entered the chapel for the first time, the Relief Society broke into a song of welcome. . . . The faces of the sisters reflected the fulfillment of many, many years of prayers."[23] The mission president was a West German, Wolfgang Paul, who had been serving as the Germany Hamburg Mission president.

Members had already fellowshipped investigators in many wards and

This meetinghouse in Dresden, German Democratic Republic, served as the mission office when the mission opened in March 1989

branches, so when the missionaries arrived in 1988 they soon had many baptisms: 569 by the year's end.

Latter-day Saints participated in the 1989 autumn revolution, including the courageous demonstrations in the "hero city" of Leipzig on 9 October. The fall of the Berlin Wall on 9 November rapidly changed the political climate in East Germany. Government authorities granted permission for more missionaries to enter the country, and President Ed J. Pinegar of the Missionary Training Center in Provo, Utah, rerouted numerous elders and sisters assigned to other German-speaking missions to the German Democratic Republic Dresden Mission.

The year 1990 saw even more changes. West German politicians pushed for unification as the Communist government in the GDR weakened. Free elections in March established a democratic government in East Germany. Then the two German nations, the United States, the Soviet Union, Britain, and France agreed to a consolidation of German currencies in July and finally to unification on 3 October. On both sides of the former Iron Curtain people rejoiced throughout the year, even though everyone knew that unification would not be easy.

The former German Democratic Republic rapidly westernized, but missionaries noted that many former East Germans remained more humble and teachable than the average citizen in Germany's secularized west. An advertisement of the Book of Mormon in a popular magazine produced more than 13,000 referrals. "The people of [the Dresden Mission], so long hidden from the beauties of knowing the Savior, are responding to the message of the gospel. They hunger for truth and accept the missionaries quite well," explained President Paul.[24]

One convert was a Dresden airport officer responsible for passport control. He had dealt closely with LDS missionaries each time they arrived or departed. One day missionaries struck up an extended conversation with him. "As we talked," President Paul related, "we made an appointment for the missionaries to teach him. He and his family were baptized. He is a fine missionary for us. He is sharing the gospel with others."[25]

Most baptisms in the Dresden Mission were of Germans, but missionaries also taught and baptized more than 200 African men from the Marxist state of Mozambique who were in East Germany as guest workers. Before they left Germany in late 1990 and early 1991, the Europe Area presidency prepared them to lead the Church in their native land.

In October 1990, soon after German reunification, President Thomas S. Monson presided over a large regional conference in Berlin and consolidated the Berlin Stake members from former East and West Berlin, and its suburbs, plus branches of the northern part of eastern Germany.

In July 1991, the Germany Berlin Mission was divided from the Germany Dresden Mission. The number of missionaries in the two missions in eastern Germany soon nearly doubled, thus enabling the Church to send missionaries into cities with no existing branches and in some cases to cities where no LDS missionaries had ever been. Both missions experienced steady growth, although the initial surge of baptisms leveled off. East German missionaries sent to England, the United States, Canada, Argentina, and Chile began returning home from their missions, providing valuable leadership. In 1994 the Dresden Mission headquarters were moved to Leipzig, and the northern branches of the Berlin Stake were formed into a separate district headquartered in Neubrandenburg.

The East German Saints continued to supply numerous examples of missionary miracles to Church members worldwide.

Czechoslovakia

In 1939 when Hitler invaded Czechoslovakia, missionary work and supervision among hundreds of members came to a sudden halt in that land. Though the devastation of war was not as drastic in Czechoslovakia as in eastern Germany, Church members still suffered, particularly from famine. Young Josef Roubicek valiantly kept the Church afloat during the war, published a mission letter, and even baptized several new converts. But a strong membership base had not been developed before the war, as it had been in Germany, and in 1946 the Church found fewer than a hundred members still faithful.[26]

Wallace Toronto, called in the late 1930s as Czechoslovak Mission president, had never been released. He served in Czechoslovakia again from 1946 to 1950. During that time, he presided over thirty-six elders and sisters, who furthered the growth in many branches, even after February 1948, when the Communists took full control of the government in Prague. For a time the Church continued to function in Communist Czechoslovakia, but in 1949 two missionaries were accused of spying and jailed. The government began to expel missionaries from the country. Looking to the future, President Toronto inaugurated a rigorous course of training and study for Czech priesthood holders and prepared priesthood and auxiliary courses of study. By 1950 all missionaries had departed to complete their calling elsewhere in Europe. Finally the Czech government abolished the mission on 6 April of that year, denouncing the Church as a subversive American organization. Approximately 200 Church members were living in Czechoslovakia at this time.

"For the Mormons of Czechoslovakia, the years from 1950 to 1989 were a time of chill, warmed only by an inner flame of faith," observed chronicler Vaughn Roche.[27] In the United States President Toronto and the returned American missionaries who had served from 1929 to 1939 and 1946 to 1950 in Czechoslovakia became "patron saints" to the Czech members. Through the years, this group shipped money, clothing, medicine, and Church publications to the members. They even provided a car for the district president to travel to the small branches and raised funds to print the Book of Mormon in Czech.

The Czech members suffered their greatest isolation in the 1950s and 1960s. Meetings were illegal, and members secretly visited each other in their homes. "None were imprisoned, none executed. But the threat existed, and because it did, there could be no communication with LDS church headquarters in Salt Lake City. Church members in Czechoslovakia were on their own. In fact, it was considered risky to make mention of religion in letters between members."[28]

A few times, Czech members were allowed to attend conferences in Dresden, East Germany. Their first contact with Church leaders from America took place in 1964 when the Swiss Mission president, John Russon, visited with them for a few days. Other visits to Czechoslovakia by various American Saints, including Wallace Toronto, followed in the next few years.

The "Prague Spring" of 1968 raised hopes for democracy and freedom in 1968, when progressive Alexander Dubcek became head of the Czechoslovakian Communist Party. But hope died quickly. The Soviet Union invaded with tanks, and the secret police made life almost unbearable for the Saints. It was a crime even to speak of God. "One of our members was reported for having Church books," reported a missionary in Czechoslovakia in 1991. "The police came to her home and stood in front of her and tore up every piece of her Church literature. That was the way life was."[29]

In the early 1970s, President Henry Burkhart of the Dresden Mission was given responsibility for the Czech Saints. In 1972 he called forty-year-old Jiři Šnederfler, who had remained faithful since his baptism in 1949, to identify and visit every member throughout Czechoslovakia.

In 1975, after the Helsinki Accords guaranteed more human rights to eastern Europeans, Czech members in six branches began meeting in private homes. The government ignored the thirty-five to forty in attendance as long as they did not make any disturbance. The members removed their shoes, closed the shades, and sang the hymns softly. But the Spirit in these meetings was powerful, and the members were strengthened by unannounced yearly visits from former missionaries.[30]

Starting in 1981, Edwin Morrell, one of the previously expelled missionaries and now president of the Austria Vienna Mission, began making quarterly visits. He formally established the Czechoslovakia District in 1982 with Brother Šnederfler as president. "Gradually the members found quiet ways to share the gospel and each year held a number of private baptisms," explained President Morrell. "Surely this has been the prime example in the Church of member-missionary work."[31]

Otakar Vojkůvka, one of those member-missionaries, served as branch president in Brno during the 1940s and 1950s. One way Brother Vojkůvka maintained his Christian ideals in an atheistic country was to become a teacher of yoga, a Hindu philosophical system that emphasized meditation, self-control, spiritual insight, and physical exercises. One of his students was Olga Kovářová, a young university student. "A schoolmate who knew I was interested in yoga told me one day, 'Olga, I traveled last Sunday to my parents and I met on the train a wonderful man. He is about seventy-five, and he is an expert in yoga.' She had taken his address, so I visited this man. He appeared to me seventy-five in his age but in his heart nearer eighteen and full of joy. This was so unusual in Czechoslovakia at that time of cynicism. We started to speak of life, and I saw that he was not only educated but knew how to live joyfully. I became very good friends with him and with his whole family. . . . We had many discussions over many months." In time Brother Vojkůvka revealed to Olga that his ideas were based on the teachings of the LDS Church. Brother Vojkůvka and his son Gád, the new branch president, lent Olga a copy of the Book of Mormon in Czech and taught her gospel principles. In 1983 under cover of darkness, Olga was baptized in a reservoir near Brno.

Sister Kovářová continued her studies and became a professor at the local university, a trusted position she would never have secured if her Church membership had been known. She was required to teach Communist ethics, but she devised ingenious ways to teach principles of righteous and joyous living. Meanwhile she and other Church members began teaching yoga classes. Gradually a few converts came into the Church through these unusual contacts. After the Freiberg Temple was dedicated in 1985, the baptismal rate in Czechoslovakia jumped from a handful to about twenty each year. Olga remembered Church meetings in the Vojkůvka home: "At first we were only seven; by 1989, we were about sixty in this one room. We had only one Book of Mormon among us; it was forty years old, from before the time of Communism. The neighbors, noticing the many visitors, wondered why their elderly neighbor Mr. Vojkůvka had so many young friends. One neighbor asked him, 'Mr. Vojkůvka, what do you celebrate each Sunday? So many young people are coming to your house.' He answered simply, 'We learn to be happy.' After the revolution, this neighbor returned to say, 'I think that I too need your school of life.'"[32]

Hungary

As part of the Austro-Hungarian Empire, Hungary had been a small outpost for the Church from the late nineteenth century through 1914. From 1914 until the mid 1980s, however, the Church had no presence in that country except for Janos Denndörfer, a Hungarian of Germanic descent who lived in Hungary virtually isolated from the Church from 1915 until his death in 1974.

Janos Denndörfer had joined the Church before World War I on a working visit to western Germany. Becoming strong in the faith and ordained to the Aaronic Priesthood, he then returned to Hungary. Janos faithfully read his scriptures and Church books, reared his children according to Christian principles, and recorded his tithing in a bank book that he hoped one day to pay. In 1955, a Church representative was able to visit and ordain him to the Melchizedek Priesthood. In 1967 a neighbor reported him to the government for proselyting. He was accused of being an American spy, and officials confiscated his treasured Church books. In 1973 Walter Krause visited from East Germany to give Janos a patriarchal blessing. In it was the promise that he would go to the temple before he died. Finally, in 1975, at age eighty-one, Brother Denndörfer received a passport, went to the Swiss Temple, received his endowment, and performed temple work for 785 of his ancestors. According to Brother Denndörfer's biographer, Douglas Tobler, "this modern pioneer had maintained a vibrant faith even when the full array of Church organization was not available. In his exemplary life, we discover that any limitation upon our own 'imitation of Christ' is primarily from within ourselves, that even where freedom and social contact with the Saints are circumscribed, no one is ever really alone when God is with him."[33]

During the 1970s, a few Hungarian Saints living in other countries began to contact their relatives and friends in Hungary to share their faith. An attempt was even made to establish a branch in Budapest, but fear of government reprisals aborted the effort. In 1978 the First Presidency asked Joseph T. Bentley, a retired Brigham Young University administrator, to reside in Budapest with his wife for eighteen months, make friends, and lay the groundwork for regular missionary work. Elder Bentley and David M. Kennedy, the First Presidency's special representative to foreign governments, made some initial contacts with government and university officials that later bore fruit.[34]

Poland

Throughout the Cold War, a few Saints—mostly ethnic Germans—continued to live in western Poland, which was once part of Germany. Some of these members had joined the Church while visiting western Europe or the United States. In 1975 Elder David M. Kennedy started the process of obtaining recognition for the Church from the Polish Communist government. He developed close relationships with various officials, including Kazimierz Kakol, minister of religion. Because of his careful negotiations, in early 1977 the government granted the Church legal recognition, the first for an eastern European country. Regional representative Percy K. Fetzer gathered eight Polish members from throughout Poland to represent the Church at the official signing of papers in Warsaw. Among the signers was an ethnic Pole Fryderyk Cherwinski, designated official head of the Church in Poland. The Church could now own property, conduct worship services, and explain principles of the gospel to people who voluntarily asked for information. (No other means of proselyting was permitted at this time.)[35]

In August 1977, President Spencer W. Kimball visited Warsaw and the few members who lived there. The prophet dedicated the land for the preaching of the gospel and invoked a blessing upon the people: "We pray that thou will bless these fathers and mothers in this nation, that they may bring up their children in righteousness, . . . and bless the children that they may grow up to be honorable, peaceful, loving parents themselves, so that the generations may bring to Thee, their Lord, great satisfaction in the development of the souls of men." A series of missionary couples, some of them native to Poland, staffed a modest visitors center in Warsaw as the Church's official representatives.[36]

Another representative of the Church in Poland was Dennis B. Neuenschwander of the Church Genealogical Department. Since 1968 he had negotiated with the Polish government and religious officials for rights to microfilm priceless Catholic Church records. By 1986 Brother Neuenschwander had established microfilming contacts through all of eastern Europe, including the Soviet Union.

Through 1980 and 1981, Polish workers united in the Solidarity Labor Union and demanded recognition of more rights. Poland's Communist government, backed by the Soviets, crushed the emerging freedom fight, outlawed the Solidarity Union, and declared martial law. Despite these setbacks and the imprisonment of union leader Lech Walesa, the Solidarity Union continued to operate underground throughout the 1980s. Church members were forbidden to meet in public until the mid 1980s.

Yugoslavia

Yugoslavia, which means "south Slavic state" was a hybrid nation created from several Balkan countries after World War I. Beginning in the early 1970s, Church representatives made various contacts, but the powerful Communist government of Marshall Tito and later daunting instability and civil war prevented the Church from being established in that nation. Actually, there is no such thing as a Yugoslavian people or language. The nation, before its breakup in 1991 and 1992, consisted of six semiautonomous republics that possessed different languages, ethnic groups, religions, and nationalistic impulses: Slovenia, Croatia, Bosnia-Herzegovina, Serbia, Montenegro, and Macedonia.

The Church established a foothold in Yugoslavia after basketball legend Krešimir Cosic returned to his native land. "Kresh," as he was known affectionately, was recruited by Brigham Young University basketball coach Stan Watts at the Mexico City Olympic games in 1968. His gregarious personality endeared him to BYU followers, and his unique style of play impressed American basketball fans. While at BYU, Kresh joined the Church, baptized by noted religion professor Hugh Nibley. Although Brother Cosic was offered a job by several National Basketball Association teams, he decided instead to return to his native land, where he coached and starred on the Yugoslav Olympic team in 1972. Before he left Utah, however, the Church called him to be the presiding elder in Yugoslavia. Throughout the 1970s and early 1980s, Brother Cosic converted numerous friends, paved the way for a few missionaries to enter Yugoslavia, served as the district president, and translated the Book of Mormon and other important literature into Serbo-Croatian. In 1992 Brother Cosic was named deputy ambassador from Croatia to the United States. In an interview, he said that living the gospel helped him personally to overcome hate, an attribute that unfortunately is too common in the fratricidal civil war raging in his homeland. "It is the permanent relationship with the Spirit that teaches you—not just when the hard times come, when you are facing a war, but every day. I try to live the best I can to maintain this relationship."[37] Krešimir Cosic labored indefatigably for the kingdom of God until his untimely death from cancer in 1995 at the age of forty-six.

Some of the earliest missionaries to Yugoslavia in 1972 went to Zadar, Krešimir Cosic's home, from the North Italian Mission because Zadar is a city of many Italian-speaking people. Legal problems prematurely ended their stay, however. In 1977 Church representatives reentered Yugoslavia in Brother Cosic's province of Croatia. They were not allowed to proselyte and could only make friends. Gradually membership reached about 200 by 1989 and spread into the major cities of Croatia, Serbia, and Slovenia.

Throughout the Cold War, Church leaders and members prayerfully considered the plight of the Saints whose heroic faith was all that sustained them in very restrictive circumstances. Those prayers were answered as new opportunities arose for the Church behind the Iron Curtain in the early 1980s—opportunities the faithful Saints attributed to the hand of God. Likewise, many Church members see the hand of God behind the revolutions that began in eastern Europe in 1989.

NOTES

1 See Douglas F. Tobler, "Before the Wall Fell: Mormons in the German Democratic Republic, 1945–89," *Dialogue* 25 (Winter 1992): 11–30; Garold and Norma Davis, "Behind the Wall: The Church in Eastern Germany," *Ensign* 21 (April 1991): 22–27.

2 Davis and Davis, "Behind the Wall," 22.

3 Another good source on events in immediate postwar East Germany is Arthur Gaeth, "Our Members in the Russian Zone, 1946," MS 5805, in the LDS Church Historical Archives.

4 Davis and Davis, "Behind the Wall," 22–23.

5 Bruce A. Van Orden, "'What Will You Lay on the Altar for Christ?': The Discipleship of Rudolf and Elfriede Poecker," unpublished paper; Kahlile Mehr, "The Langheinrich Legacy: Record-Gathering in Post-War Germany," *Ensign* 11 (June 1981): 22–25; *A Labor of Love: The 1946 European Mission of Ezra Taft Benson* (Salt Lake City: Deseret Book, 1989), 61–63.

6 *A Labor of Love,* 60.

7 Ibid., 65.

8 Tobler, "Mormons in the German Democratic Republic," 16.

9 Melvin Leavitt, "Freely Given: Walter Stover, A Legend of Generosity," *Tambuli,* October 1987, 30.

10 Davis and Davis, "Behind the Wall," 25.

11 Ibid., 26.

12 Tobler, "Mormons in the German Democratic Republic," 21–22.

13 B. William Silcock, Excerpts from the Field Interviews for the KBYU Documentary *Fortress of Faith,* March 1990, 9–10.

14 Silcock, *Fortress of Faith,* KBYU Productions, May 1990.

15 Matthew Heiss and Gerry Avant, "Faith, Courage Sustain German Couple," *Church News,* 11 July 1992, 4–5.

16 A copy of Elder Thomas S. Monson's dedicatory prayer is in my possession.

17 Thomas S. Monson, in Conference Report, April 1989, 67.

18 Ibid.; Phillip J. Bryson, "Background on the Temple in the German Democratic Republic: An Eyewitness Account," address delivered 3 July 1985, Brigham Young University, Provo, Utah.

19 Monson, in Conference Report, April 1989, 68.

20 Ibid.

21 Ibid, 69.

22 Ibid.

23 Davis and Davis, "The Wall Comes Down," 32.

24 J Malan Heslop and Fae Heslop, "Gospel Work Begun before Berlin Wall Fell Is Accelerating," *Church News,* 20 April 1991, 11.

25 Ibid.

26 Good sources on the Church in Czechoslovakia are Kahlile Mehr, "Enduring Believers: Czechoslovakia and the LDS Church, 1884–1990," *Journal of Mormon History* 18 (Fall 1992): 111–54; Kahlile Mehr, "Czech Saints: A Brighter Day," *Ensign* 24 (August 1994): 46–52.

27 Vaughn Roche, "A Faithful Resistance," *This People,* Holiday 1993, 15.

28 Ibid., 16–17.

29 J Malan Heslop and Fae Heslop, "Change of Pace and Place Taken in Stride and with a Smile," *Church News,* 30 March 1991, 10.

30 Lecture by Spencer J. Condie to Brigham Young University Religious Education faculty, 4 December 1988; lecture by Edwin Morrell in Brigham Young University Kennedy Center, 9 October 1990.

31 Edwin Morrell, "Openings for Missionaries to Work in Central Europe," *Daily Universe,* 15 March 1990, 4.

32 Olga Kovářová Campora, "Fruits of Faithfulness: The Saints of Czechoslovakia," *Women Steadfast in Christ,* ed. Dawn Hall Anderson and Marie Cornwall (Salt Lake City: Deseret Book, 1992), 134–47; Carri P. Jenkins, "After the Revolutions: The Reemergence of Values," *BYU Today* 45 (March 1991): 30–34.

33 Douglas F. Tobler, "Alone with God: One Mormon's Life in Twentieth-century Hungary," *Ensign* 23 (April 1993): 50–52.

34 Information for this section was drawn from Kahlile Mehr, "The Gospel in Hungary—Then and Now," *Ensign* 20 (June 1990): 8–14; Kahlile Mehr, "The Eastern Edge: LDS Missionary Work in Hungarian Lands," *Dialogue* 24 (Summer 1991): 21–45.

35 Martin B. Hickman, *David Matthew Kennedy: Banker, Statesman, Churchman* (Salt Lake City: Deseret Book, 1987), 350–53; "Kosciol Jezusa Chrystusa Swietych w Dniach Ostatnich Warszawaw" [also available in English as "The Church of Jesus Christ of Latter-day Saints in Warsaw"], a pamphlet available at the Church History Library in Salt Lake City, Utah; interview with John K. Fetzer, 19 July 1994.

36 Hickman, *David Matthew Kennedy,* 353–56.

37 Carri P. Jenkins, "He Seeks Winning Game Plan for Peace," *Church News,* 9 January 1993, 7.

CHAPTER 10

Modern Western Europe

1974   **PORTUGAL LISBON MISSION IS OPENED**

1985   **STOCKHOLM SWEDEN TEMPLE IS DEDICATED**

1987   **FRANKFURT GERMANY TEMPLE IS DEDICATED**

1990   **GREECE ATHENS MISSION IS OPENED**

1995   **PRESIDENT THOMAS S. MONSON HOSTS KING AND QUEEN OF SWEDEN AT STOCKHOLM SWEDEN TEMPLE GROUNDS**

 he Church of Jesus Christ of Latter-day Saints continued to mature in western Europe in the early 1970s after the area general conferences held in England, West Germany, and Sweden. The Church established permanent administrative, distribution, temporal affairs, and translation centers in Solihull, near Birmingham, England, and in Frankfurt, West Germany, in the 1970s. Country by country, Church president Spencer W. Kimball conducted other area general conferences in the late 1970s, which inspired the Saints to greater unity within their own countries and with members all around the globe. In the 1980s, regional conferences became the norm.

The Church Educational System established seminary and institute of religion programs, adding incalculable support to the Church's growth and maturity. Church members, nurtured in the gospel from their infancy, grew up, went on missions, married in the temple, and began rearing children of their own in their native lands. These second-, third-, and even fourth-generation Latter-day Saints did more to build the Church in Europe than any single program or effort.

When a branch becomes a ward and a district becomes a stake, these ecclesiastical units are considered self-sustaining and are no longer under the nurturing wing of the mission. In the 1970s and 1980s, more stakes and missions were organized in western Europe. Missionary work opened in Portugal in 1974 and prospered, surpassing any other place in western Europe. Limited missionary work began in Greece in the late 1980s.

Several native Europeans were called as general authorities to help govern the Church.

By the late 1970s and early 1980s, the designation of European Mission president had been dropped and resident general authorities directed Church affairs in Europe. Beginning in 1984, three members of the Seventy resided in Frankfurt as an area presidency to administer European Church affairs, one member being specifically assigned to the British Isles. Later a separate area presidency was headquartered in England. As of 1996, three administrative areas were organized in Europe: the *Europe North Area*, headquartered in Solihull, England, for the United Kingdom, Ireland, Scandinavia, and Finland; the *Europe Area*, headquartered in Frankfurt, Germany, for Germany, the Netherlands, Belgium, Switzerland, Austria, France, Slovenia, Spain, Portugal, Italy, Malta, Greece, Cyprus, and all Middle Eastern countries where Church members resided; and the *Europe East Area*, also headquartered in Frankfurt, for the Czech Republic, Slovakia, Poland, Hungary, Romania, Bulgaria, Croatia, Serbia, Albania, Estonia, Latvia, Lithuania, Ukraine, Belarus, Armenia, Russia, and all other eastern European countries with missions.

Essentially, the Europe Area had countries with stakes; the Europe East Area, the countries emerging in the gospel with no stakes. Thus the Europe East Area presidency could focus on rapid development.

In the modern era Church members have been blessed with additional temples in Europe. Following are the operating temples and their dedication dates, plus two other temples announced but not yet dedicated as of 1996:

1. Swiss (1955; rededicated 1992). Located in Zollikofen, Switzerland, near Bern

2. London (1958; rededicated 1992). Located in a rural area of England southeast of London

3. Freiberg Germany (1985). Located in eastern Germany

4. Stockholm Sweden (1985). Located in the Stockholm suburb of Västerhaninge

5. Frankfurt Germany (1987). Located in the Frankfurt suburb of Friedrichsdorf

6. Preston England. Located in the village of Chorley, near Preston

7. Madrid Spain

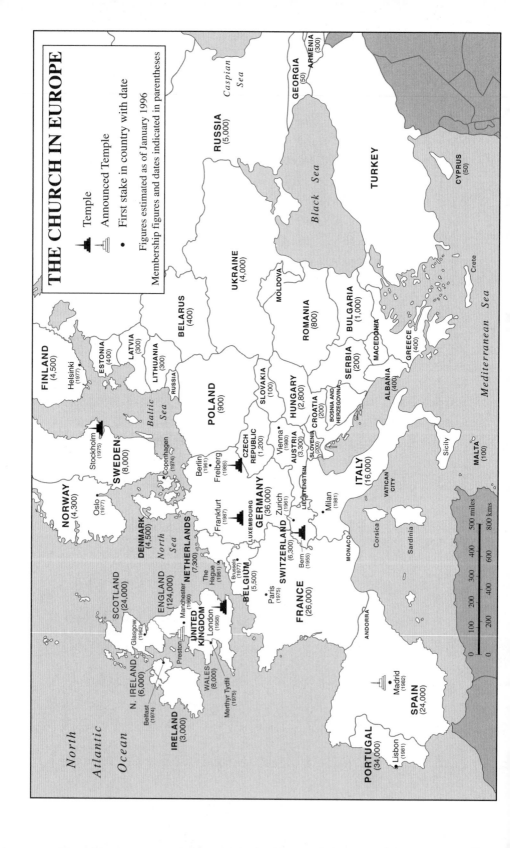

THE CHURCH IN EUROPE

- 🏛️ Temple
- ⛪ Announced Temple
- • First stake in country with date

Figures estimated as of January 1996
Membership figures and dates indicated in parentheses

North Atlantic Ocean

IRELAND (3,000)

SCOTLAND (24,000)
Glasgow (1982)

N. IRELAND (6,000)
Belfast (1974)

ENGLAND (124,000)
Manchester (1960)
Preston
London (1958)
UNITED KINGDOM

WALES (8,000)
Merthyr Tydfil (1975)

NORWAY (4,300)
Oslo (1977)

SWEDEN (8,000)
Stockholm (1975)

FINLAND (4,500)
Helsinki (1977)

DENMARK (4,500)
Copenhagen (1974)

NETHERLANDS (7,300)
The Hague (1961)

BELGIUM (5,500)
Brussels (1977)

GERMANY (36,000)
Frankfurt (1987)
Berlin (1961)
Freiberg (1985)

LUXEMBOURG

FRANCE (26,000)
Paris (1975)

SWITZERLAND (6,300)
Zurich (1961)
Bern (1955)
LIECHTENSTEIN

SPAIN (24,000)
Madrid (1982)

PORTUGAL (34,000)
Lisbon (1981)

ANDORRA

MONACO

ITALY (16,000)
Milan (1981)
VATICAN CITY

CORSICA
SARDINIA
SICILY
MALTA (100)

ESTONIA (400)
LATVIA (300)
LITHUANIA (300)

POLAND (900)

CZECH REPUBLIC (1,200)

SLOVAKIA (100)

AUSTRIA (3,300)
Vienna (1980)

SLOVENIA (200)

CROATIA (200)

HUNGARY (2,800)

BOSNIA AND HERZEGOVINA

SERBIA (200)

ALBANIA (400)

MACEDONIA

BELARUS (400)

RUSSIA

UKRAINE (4,000)

MOLDOVA

ROMANIA (800)

BULGARIA (1,000)

GREECE (400)

RUSSIA (5,000)

GEORGIA (50)

ARMENIA (300)

TURKEY

CYPRUS (50)

CRETE

Baltic Sea
North Sea
Caspian Sea
Black Sea
Mediterranean Sea

| 0 | 100 | 200 | 300 | 400 | 500 miles |
| 0 | 200 | 400 | 600 | 800 kms |

During the 1960s western Europe lost out to parts of Latin America, the Pacific, and Asia as the most productive area of Church growth. Europe, more than any other world region, had become secularized, essentially stripped of its vital religious orientation and traditions. Most western European nations, with West Germany leading the way, enjoyed immense economic growth, which led to more affluent lifestyles. Prosperity and materialism diminished people's interest in religion. The state churches themselves had become secularized, and most Europeans rarely attended worship services. Family life became less and less important to most citizens. Many openly turned from God to economic pursuits and pleasure-seeking, if not outright hedonism. Yet, despite all these conditions, the Church continued to grow and in some places to prosper.

In the 1980s, most western European nations formed an economic common market, called the European Community, to build a more united and prosperous western Europe. In the 1990s, the European community ran into difficult economic and political problems, changed its name to the European Union, and added three more western European nations, making a total of fifteen member states. This arrangement has proved beneficial to Latter-day Saint missionaries and Church officials because of the elimination of passport and visa requirements within the European Union for citizens of member countries.

Western European countries also reluctantly began to allow political and economic refugees into their boundaries. Missionaries, struggling to find interested parties in settled European society, found many more willing listeners among the foreign guest workers, refugees, asylum seekers, and immigrants. Approximately 60 percent of baptisms in western European missions since 1985 have been of individuals from Africa, Asia, eastern Europe, and Latin America, and of United States military personnel stationed abroad.

The United Kingdom

In the 1970s and 1980s, as the Church in Britain consolidated and steadily grew, a new attitude toward the Church evolved among both members and British citizens at large. President Michael R. Otteson, the Liverpool Stake president in the 1970s, stated, "Today, it is by no means

Country	Estimated Church Membership 1996	Approximate Total Population
United Kingdom	162,000	58,140,000
Ireland	2,500	3,600,000
Denmark	4,500	5,200,000
Iceland	300	264,000
Norway	4,300	4,320,000
Sweden	8,300	8,800,000
Finland	4,500	5,070,000
Netherlands	7,300	15,370,000
Belgium	5,500	10,100,000
Luxembourg	200	402,000
France	26,000	57,900,000
Germany	37,000	81,100,000
Switzerland	6,700	7,045,000
Austria	3,300	8,000,000
Italy	16,000	58,200,000
Spain	24,000	40,060,000
Portugal	34,000	10,600,000
Greece	400	10,600,000
Others	200	
West Europe Area Total	347,000	384,771,000

uncommon to hear the words 'I'm proud to be a Mormon.' While the traditionally British reserve still curbs this outward expression to friends and neighbours, the pride is still there and it is growing. It is not difficult to see why. Mass communications, hand-in-hand with growing membership, have eradicated much of the old-fashioned prejudice and superstition about the Church. . . . Today people write letters to newspapers commenting on the manners of our missionaries, the work ethic of our members, and the morals of our teenagers."[1]

In 1990 Terry Rooney, elders quorum president in Bradford, England, was elected a member of Parliament in Great Britain, the first Latter-day Saint ever so honored. A member of the Labour Party with considerable

Two British teens at a 1992 youth conference

local political service, Brother Rooney was elected with the seat's largest-ever majority. Brother Rooney joined the Church in 1985.[2]

Seminaries and institutes have played a profound role in developing strong members and leadership in Britain. Many wards held early-morning seminary. "How we looked forward to seminary," exclaimed Yana Ivanov of southern England. "It was a chance to discuss with other people our own age the problems one encounters at school as the only member of the Church. We told each other of things that had happened that week, of temptations we had avoided, of the good and bad. We had real friendships that have lasted to this day."[3]

In common with all youth, young British Latter-day Saints have struggled to maintain their standards. They frequently have joined in youth conferences and seminary and institute classes and activities to strengthen one another. Melinda-Jane Davis, age fifteen, of Merthyr Tydfil, Wales, reported in 1992, "I went to a party last week. It was a little bit out of control so I rang my father and went home. I was so scared when I went to school the next morning, but about six of my friends came after me and said they were proud I stood up for myself."[4]

New stakes were created in the 1970s and 1980s as mission districts matured and existing stakes were divided. By 1983, forty stakes covered the entire United Kingdom, and no mission districts remained. By 1996 there were forty-two stakes, the last of which was created in Canterbury, England, by the prophet, Gordon B. Hinckley, during his visit to the United Kingdom and Ireland in 1995. New British missions also came into existence. In 1993 English missions were headquartered in Bristol, Coventry, Leeds, Manchester, and there were two in London. The mission in Scotland was headquartered in Edinburgh.

Two Britons were called as general authorities: Derek A. Cuthbert of Nottingham in 1978 and Kenneth Johnson of Norwich in 1990. Elder Cuthbert had served as a counselor in the British Mission presidency, the director of the London Distribution Centre, stake president, and president of the Scottish Mission. Before his death in 1991, Elder Cuthbert, then a member of the First Quorum of the Seventy, had served in many parts of the world. Elder Johnson, who was baptized in 1959 and later served as a stake president, was called to the Second Quorum of the Seventy in 1990. Three years later he was called to the First Quorum of the Seventy and asked to serve as president of the Europe North Area, headquartered in Britain. In 1995 he was transferred to the area presidency in the Philippines.

The Church has microfilmed huge stores of genealogical records in Great Britain. From 1969 to 1985, three microfilmers worked full time; as more permissions were received, the work expanded. The Church established scores of family history centers in the British Isles. In 1991 area president Jeffrey R. Holland presented to the Federation of Family History Societies microfiche containing the 1881 British Isles census, later put on computer by Church members.

In 1975 President Spencer W. Kimball called for more indigenous missionaries and 157 British young people responded. In 1983 some 400 were called, and the numbers have continued to rise. Missionaries from the United Kingdom have served all over the world. In 1985 the Church's eighth missionary training center (MTC) was established near the London Temple, preparing 450 elders and sisters annually. Forty percent of the missionaries trained there came from the British Isles and the remainder from non-English-speaking European countries, including eastern Europe and the former Soviet Union.[5]

One of the missionaries trained in the London MTC in 1992, Elder Jan Tuček from Czechoslovakia, had been called to serve in London. He left his medical studies with only one year remaining before becoming a doctor. "I wasn't sure I should go," he explained. "Then I saw the video *Called to Serve,* and it answered my prayers." Medical school officials promised to hold a place for him. "But the hard part was explaining to my parents. They felt I could help people more by being a doctor. But I have more important work now for two years. Then I can work my whole life as a doctor."[6]

In the late 1980s, the Church in Britain, particularly in London, numbered most of its converts from Africa, mostly Nigeria and Ghana, and the West Indies. (Many citizens of the former British Empire are annually allowed into Britain for university studies.) These people, living only temporarily in Britain, were humble and receptive to the gospel. Often they approached missionaries when they saw "Jesus Christ" on the name tags and asked to speak about religion. In the 1990s, a number of these African converts were called to positions of leadership in wards and stakes. Fellowshipping new converts by holding African cultural and activity nights, the Church in parts of Britain rapidly gained an African flavor.[7]

During this period, the progress of the Church in Scotland, the northernmost country in the United Kingdom, resembled that in England. Many Scottish members faced frustrations because of the pervasive joblessness endemic to Scotland, but there was a closeness among the Scots that carried over to a general zest and willingness to sacrifice for missionary work, yielding many splits with the missionaries, gospel conversations with friends, and excellent friendshipping of new members. In 1990 Elder Neal A. Maxwell of the Twelve offered a blessing of renewal to Elder Orson Pratt's 1840 dedication of Scotland from Arthur's Seat, a hill that overlooks the Scottish capital, Edinburgh. When missionaries arrived in Scotland, they traditionally climbed Arthur's Seat and dedicated their hearts to serving the Lord.[8]

In September 1992, President Gordon B. Hinckley dedicated the remodeled London Temple, and the number of recommend holders in the temple district increased by 33 percent.[9]

President Hinckley announced at the temple rededication plans to construct another temple in the United Kingdom, this one to be located in Preston, the first British city to receive Latter-day Saint missionaries. On 12 June 1994, an emotional President Hinckley presided at the groundbreaking at the site in Chorley, a suburb of Preston. More than 10,000 Church members from the length and breadth of the British Isles gathered to witness this milestone in their native land. President Hinckley charged all adult members to become worthy of a temple recommend as soon as possible.[10]

In 1996 more than 162,000 Church members resided in the United Kingdom. Missionary productivity had declined through the 1980s, as it had in western Europe generally. Britain was still a class-oriented country with clear distinctions between the upper class, middle class, and working class. Missionaries encountered increasing resistance to their message from the upper two classes. More than half the baptisms in Britain were of converts from third-world countries. Proselyting statistics aside, the Church had become a mature and stable organization in the United Kingdom. The excellent relationship between the Church and Britain was symbolized by the 1996 visit to Utah by former prime minister Margaret Thatcher, now Lady Thatcher, who received an honorary doctorate from Brigham Young University.

Ireland

Ireland became independent from Great Britain in 1949. In 1962 a separate Irish Mission was formed, responsible for the Republic of Ireland and Northern Ireland (Ulster). A stake headquartered in Belfast was created in Northern Ireland in 1974. In 1986 the Newry Branch was organized to include members from both Ulster and the Republic of Ireland—the first branch to span the border. "Some members regarded this as an omen of a bright and more peaceful future for Ireland as a whole."[11]

The Church has not grown as rapidly in Ireland as in other parts of the British Isles.[12] Political and religious strife are major obstacles. Many Irish still resent what they regard as religious persecution by the British over many decades, and outsiders who talk about religion are not well received. Ireland is also less urban than the rest of Europe, and religious and family traditions are still strong.

Inactivity among Latter-day Saints in Northern Ireland has been a challenge. Most converts there have been from among the Protestants, whose culture allows changing religious affiliation. Many Latter-day Saint youth in Northern Ireland, however, have had to steadfastly defend their beliefs to their peers in a country of many "walls, fences, and barriers."[13] Unfortunately, the Saints in Northern Ireland have often distinguished among themselves as "Catholic Mormons" or "Protestant Mormons." Some walls remain.

In 1985 the First Presidency sent Elder Neal A. Maxwell of the Quorum of the Twelve to dedicate Ireland, apart from Britain. His prayer recalled "the first baptism on this island in this very place by one who became a latter-day prophet, John Taylor" and addressed the problem of Ireland's religious strife: "We acknowledge, Father, that we are mere mortals, and so we see nations and we see borders; however, Thou seest but one flock—all of thy children. We plead with Thee to look with fresh favor upon all of Ireland to the end that this Emerald Isle will know further greening through the fullness of the restored gospel. . . . Where there has been strife, may there be peace, and if not full peace, enough peace for Thy cause to move forward as never before. May Thy soothing Spirit, Father, encourage reconciliation through the Restoration."[14]

Negotiations between contending factions in Ulster and between the United Kingdom and the Republic of Ireland seemed fruitful in late 1994. Fighting ceased temporarily, and progress was made toward closer ties between the two Irelands. Reconciliation was still some distance away, however, for terrorist activities were resumed in 1996.

In 1995 approximately 2,500 members resided in the Republic of Ireland. In March, after many years of preparation, the Dublin Ireland Stake came into being. The members rejoiced that Elder Maxwell's prophecy about Ireland uttered a decade earlier was coming to pass.

Denmark

In the nineteenth century, Denmark was economically one of the poorest European nations but at the same time one of the most gospel-rich of all mission fields. By the late twentieth century, commerce had made Denmark one of the wealthiest countries in the world but had also brought in its wake increased secularism and cynicism. The state

Lutheran Church provided little spiritual strength to a country where most inhabitants ignore God in their daily pursuits. Rarely has the Denmark Copenhagen Mission garnered more than 150 baptisms per year in the twentieth century, but the Danish Saints have developed a solid organization.

"The Church's biggest challenge in Denmark today is that we are an ungodly country," sighed President Richardt Andersen of the Copenhagen Denmark Stake in 1992. "One positive thing I can think of about the national state of things in Denmark is that the bad is so blatant that it is obviously wrong to moral people. To our youth, for example, it's like black and white." President Andersen explained why Denmark passed permissive laws in the 1960s. "Suddenly our country was affluent and wanted to show the world that our wealth gave us sophistication and understanding. So we passed laws allowing pornography, nudity on beaches, abortion on demand, marriage of homosexuals. Moral barriers fell all around us."[15]

Despite the decadent moral environment, Danish Saints have attended the temple faithfully. Hundreds traveled to the Swiss Temple after its 1955 dedication. Since 1985 most faithful members make twice-yearly trips to Stockholm, Sweden—a lengthy journey by car and ferry.

Hans and Lissi Dige, baptized in 1986, served a temple mission in Sweden in 1990 and 1991. Before his baptism, Brother Dige fought alcoholism and severe depression. "When we went through the gate of baptism, newborn, we began walking a road that could lead to life and salvation," he said. "In our striving to obey the commandments of God, we have been very blessed. . . . We can still make mistakes in the service of the Lord, but the biggest of them all is to do nothing."[16]

Second- and third-generation Danish Latter-day Saints are finding that fortification against worldly doctrines comes through covenant-making and service. Inge Kreiberg, like most Danish women, felt that "two kids and a job were enough." She was finished with having children. "Then one evening as I prepared to teach an institute class on women's role in giving birth, I stopped cold. I knew I wasn't practicing what the lesson taught."[17] With the birth of their third child, Caroline, the Kreibergs went against the norms of a society that dismissed Inge's primary role as a mother in Zion.

In 1993 the nineteen-year-old basketball star and Church member David Meilsoe created goodwill for the Church when his team won the national championship. "David's attitude toward playing on Sunday is well-known off the court. 'Never on Sunday,' he declares. 'On Sunday I devote myself completely to the Church and the spiritual side of life in order to make it through the coming week. It is a time to ponder life and its important aspects. I'm not perfect; my religion is.'"[18] After his mission, David became a member of the Danish National Team.

In 1996 Denmark had approximately 4,500 members and two stakes. The Copenhagen Stake was created in 1974 and the Aarhus Stake in 1978.

Iceland

Iceland, the island nation in the North Atlantic lying between Greenland and Scandinavia, boasts the northernmost capital city in the world, Reykjavik. Iceland's population is only about 264,000. Inhabitants of that country see little sunlight in the winter and little darkness in the summer. Their language is Icelandic, the modern language closest to original Norse. Most citizens of Iceland are descendants of Vikings who sailed to the island in the 800s seeking new lands and beginning a tradition of freedom and individuality. Iceland became an independent republic in 1944, breaking all government ties with Denmark.

Missionaries were withdrawn from Iceland in 1914 at the outbreak of World War I and did not return until 1975, under the auspices of the Denmark Copenhagen Mission. Efforts in the modern period were built on the work of Latter-day Saint servicemen stationed in Iceland. Mission officials established a branch on the Keflavik military base with 130 servicemen and their families.

Byron and Melva Geslison were among the nearly 10,000 descendants of nineteenth-century Icelandic Saints who had emigrated to Utah, most of them settling in Spanish Fork. In 1975 President Spencer W. Kimball asked the Geslisons to reopen missionary work in Iceland. Their twin sons, both serving missions in Korea, were transferred to Iceland to help. During those first two years, the Geslisons, joined by other missionaries, succeeded in building up a branch in Reykjavik. Since that time, the Geslisons have served two more missions in Iceland. In 1993

Brother Geslison was awarded that nation's highest honor—The Order of the Falcon—by Iceland's ambassador to the United States for strengthening ties between the two countries.[19]

In September 1977, Elder Joseph B. Wirthlin dedicated Iceland for missionary work. He prayed: "Dear Father, we are grateful to thee for the faith of this people and especially for those who embraced the gospel 125 years ago and made the long journey to the Rocky Mountains. The descendants of those noble pioneers are now returning to this land to preach the gospel of Jesus Christ."[20]

Attending this dedication was Sister Sveinbjorg Gudmundsdottir, the first native Icelander to be baptized in the modern era. Her conversion story began when, recently widowed, she sought the Lord in prayer to know his will. Missionaries soon arrived, taught her gospel principles, and baptized her four months later. Her home with two young adult sons became a gathering spot to learn about Mormonism. As many as sixty young people attended meetings at a time in her home. Around this nucleus, Church membership in Iceland has drawn largely young people.[21]

Missionary work in Iceland has proceeded slowly and remains under the direction of the Danish Mission, though missionaries who serve in Iceland learn the more difficult Icelandic tongue and remain in the small island nation their entire missions. The Book of Mormon was published in Icelandic in 1980, followed later by other basic Church literature. Icelandic members have been family history specialists because excellent records date back to the original settlers of Iceland. In 1996 membership was slightly more than 300 in three branches and one district on the island.

Norway

Being a faithful Latter-day Saint in Norway, the Land of the Midnight Sun, has required sacrifice. Norwegian taxes support the state Lutheran Church, which conducts all marriages and funerals. The Church of Jesus Christ of Latter-day Saints did not receive official recognition until 1991, and its members were often considered strange.

Arne Bakken symbolizes the faith of the modern Norwegian Saints under such adversity. From 1940 Brother Bakken attended meetings with his wife, but his stubbornness kept him from being baptized until 1960. Once committed, he dived into service. He was called as branch president within a year and then as a counselor to Norway's mission president, traveling throughout the country.

The story of his own twenty-year resistance to the Church softened the hearts of those who wavered, especially the less active and non-members whose spouses were members. As a home teacher, he faithfully visited one obdurate member for four years until the man finally invited him in. After becoming Arne's friend, the man returned to church and eventually served as a branch president. Brother Bakkan obtained more than six thousand names of his ancestors to take to the temple. When the Stockholm Sweden Temple was completed in 1985, he was called as the first counselor in the temple presidency, serving despite severe health problems, discovered to be cancer. "Arne Bakken died on 11 October 1986, but Church members still talk of his influence—the way he fellowshipped them, encouraged them, helped them. They remember the proud Norwegian who humbled himself before God and served Him throughout his life."[22]

Church interests in Norway were furthered by innovative uses of the media. In 1989 the Norwegian government's council of physicians used the Church's documentary, *Tobacco, the Winnable War*, to educate citizens about the harmful effects of tobacco. The references to the Church in the production helped missionary efforts.[23] That same year a media advertisement offered Norwegians free copies of the Book of Mormon.

Norway was no longer a poor nation; indeed most citizens owned not only their own home but a summer cottage as well. As often happens with prosperity, citizens had turned from religion, describing themselves as free thinkers who were happy and successful without God and religion. Latter-day Saint missionaries generally found receptive spirits only among third-world refugees in Norway and young people who had not been blinded by their parents' success and who chose not to be confirmed in the Lutheran Church.[24]

The number of Saints in Norway, a country of more than four million people, reached approximately 4,300 by 1996. The Oslo Norway Stake was created in 1977, and by 1996 there were also three districts, one entirely within the Arctic Circle.

Sweden

Sweden, the largest and most populous of the Nordic countries, also had the highest number of Latter-day Saints. Sweden's population is nearly nine million, half of whom live in the southern quarter of the country. Church membership in 1996 was more than 8,300, due in part to the Sweden Stockholm Mission, the highest baptizing mission in the Nordic countries. The Stockholm Stake was created in 1975, the Goteburg Stake in 1977, and the Stockholm South Stake in 1995.

Saints in Sweden have faced the same challenges in the modern period as in other Scandinavian countries. Every child born in the country was automatically registered in the Lutheran Church, despite the general indifference to religion. "People here are secular, affluent, and think they don't need God," explained President Swen L. Karlsson of the Stockholm Stake in 1987.[25] The sexual revolution that swept the western world in the 1960s and 1970s hit Sweden especially hard. Chastity became an anomaly. Topless beaches were the norm, sexuality was open and publicly acceptable, and birth control devices were freely distributed to all ages. Almost all young adults lived together before marriage. Most marriages in Sweden, if they took place at all, occurred after years of living together and out-of-wedlock births of children.

Tithing and the Word of Wisdom were also challenges for investigators in Sweden. High taxes in the Swedish socialist state made an additional 10 percent a significant burden, and the national habit of coffee- and tea-drinking kept some people from joining the Church. Yet despite these obstacles, the Church was vibrant in Sweden and since the mid 1980s has taken on new life, largely due to three phenomena. The first was the triumph of three young Swedish Church members—all brothers—at the renowned European Music Festival. Per, Richard, and Louis Herrey let their instant fame be a vehicle to honor and publicize the Church. Per, who had already served a mission in Chile, said: "We are entertainers, but first we are Latter-day Saints. Our greatest dream is that we may somehow bless the Church with our talents."[26]

The second was the dedication of the Stockholm Sweden Temple in the suburb of Västerhaninge. Since President Spencer W. Kimball's announcement in 1981, the temple project proceeded exceptionally

The Stockholm Sweden Temple, dedicated in 1985

smoothly from start to finish, experiencing none of the usual opposition. Elder Thomas S. Monson, whose ancestry is Swedish, broke ground in 1984, and the following year President Gordon B. Hinckley dedicated the temple. More than 47,000 visitors had filed through the building during its open house, and numerous people, especially from the temple's vicinity, had filled out referral cards. "Bless this nation where is found thy temple, and its sister nations. . . . Save [them] from war and oppression, and may their people look to thee and open their doors and hearts to thy messengers of eternal truth," appealed President Hinckley in his prayer. "May the dedication of this temple usher in a new era for thy work in all of Scandinavia and Finland."[27]

Västerhaninge became a mecca for Church members. Many chose to settle near the temple. "Latter-day Saints make up 1.4 percent of the population, which gives them stature in local government, housing projects, and political groups. Instead of being the only Mormons in their schools, many young Latter-day Saints have two or three member friends in their classes. Teachers are aware of Church standards and open-minded about LDS ideals."[28] Sister Kajsa Wennerlund spoke out in the early 1980s about improving public moral standards. "Her ideas and concerns led to

President Gordon B. Hinckley and Elder Thomas S. Monson at the capstone-laying ceremony at the Stockholm Sweden Temple

her being elected to the Västerhaninge city council. There, she has continued to champion higher standards, a cause that has resulted in considerable media exposure."[29]

The grounds of the Stockholm Sweden Temple were the site of an historic event in 1995. President Thomas S. Monson hosted a visit there by King Carl XVI Gustaf and Queen Silvia of Sweden. Their visit was part of the tradition of "Eriksgata," dating back to the thirteenth century, in which the king travels throughout the country to be met by its citizens. These visits were filmed by Swedish television.[30]

The third public relations boon was President Ronald Reagan's 1986 appointment of Church member Gregory Newell as United States ambassador to Sweden. At age thirty-six, Brother Newell, a former assistant secretary of state, was the United States' youngest ambassador. Not only did the diplomat receive rave reviews in Sweden's newspapers for his adept improving of relations between the United States and Sweden, but Brother Newell, his large family, and the Church became a popular subject in the media as well. The Newell family of five small children was considered extremely large compared to the usual Swedish family of

Gregory Newell, United States ambassador to Sweden, and his family

at most two children. During Brother Newell's three-year stay, the mission held firesides in all the large cities throughout Sweden. Brother Newell spoke on family values; his wife, Candilyn, a concert pianist, performed; and the whole family sang. After these firesides numerous people were interested to hear the gospel through missionary lessons. In 1989, the year of the Newells' scheduled departure from Sweden, more than two thousand newspaper articles appeared on his family and the Church. Another thirty-five hundred articles dealt solely with Ambassador Newell's political efforts. Shortly before he left the country, a woman approached him and exclaimed, "I know who you are. You are the family ambassador."[31]

In the late 1980s, Sweden accepted political refugees from South and Central America, especially from Chile. Because some of these refugees were Church members, Spanish-speaking branches were set up for them. Missionaries learned Spanish to proselyte among the other refugees and in the process also found and taught refugees from eastern Europe, the Middle East, and Africa.

In 1990 the Swedish mission received its first native president, Bo Wennerlund. For three decades, President Wennerlund had held leadership positions in the Church in Sweden, serving as branch and district president, and chairman of the Stockholm Sweden Temple Committee. As the Church's public communications director in 1989, Brother Wennerlund wrote an article for a prominent newspaper defending the Church's programs and principles against a previous negative editorial. That the paper printed the rebuttal demonstrated the Church's coming of age in Sweden. After his service as mission president, Brother Wennerlund became president of the Stockholm Sweden Temple.

Finland

The 1970s was a decade of relatively rapid growth in Finland with membership reaching 3,800 by 1980. The Helsinki Stake was created in 1977 and the Tampere Stake in 1983. In the 1980s, however, with its national wealth and prominence soaring, Finland did not experience as much missionary success. "Our biggest single obstacle to spreading the gospel in Finland is, ironically enough, our country's high standard of living," explained President Pekka Roto of the Tampere Stake in 1991. "Like many nationalities in the world, Finns are hard-working people who leave too little room in their lives for spiritual things." But "once a Finn becomes converted to the gospel, *sisu* and faith combine to make deeply committed members."[32] *Sisu* is the word Finns use to describe the admirable trait of sticking to a decision once it is made.

President Roto has himself done a great deal for the Church's missionary effort in Finland. A respected physician in his community, he has talked about the Church in the media and helped counter his country's generally negative attitude toward the Church.

Among the faithful Finnish members was Anna-Liisa Rinne, a pediatrician baptized in 1960. "When I returned home from the baptismal service, I thought, 'Well, I have done the right thing in joining this church, but I will never tell anyone.' But when we arrived home, [my son] Heikki changed his clothes and ran to tell all the neighbors that we were Mormons now," Sister Rinne remembered, smiling. That began her long dual career of medicine and missionary work. She filled two formal district mission calls while still in practice as a pediatrician. When she retired, Sister Rinne served as a health missionary to Samoa in 1974, followed immediately by a similar mission to Tonga. In 1979 she accepted a proselyting call to Scotland. Still later she served two temple mission calls in Switzerland and Sweden. While serving she also has worked on the history of the Church in Finland. Reflecting on her life as a single mother, she stated: "In some ways, I have been a very lonely person, but this has forced me to seek Christ for protection. I have had to depend on him many times, and I have always received help from him."[33]

Two other faithful members were Jussi and Raija Kemppainen from Helsinki. Jussi, one of the first native Finns to become a missionary, was converted in 1967 after he stopped the missionaries in the street to tell them how wrong they were. He later attended Brigham Young University for a time but not as an emigrant to America. He had a yearning to go home, where "I don't take the Church for granted." Raija, holding a master's degree in adult education, has earned her neighbors' admiration for dedicating herself to her five children instead of to a career.[34]

The declining population in Finland has been a constant challenge to missionary work. A low birth rate and steady emigration compound the problem. During the 1970s, approximately four times as many people left Finland as came to it.

In 1987 President Ezra Taft Benson visited the Finnish Saints. This was a time of nostalgia for the prophet who in 1946 had opened the Finnish Mission and in 1977 had created the first Finnish stake. More than half the 4,000-plus Finnish members attended the 1987 conference in a Helsinki convention center. "With all my heart, I love you," the prophet said. "It is a great joy to be back in Finland. You are a great people; may it ever be so. We hope missionary work will go forward because of you. We hope this will be a rebirth."[35]

Within a year of President Benson's visit, a rebirth did develop among the Finnish Saints: sharing the gospel with their Russian and Estonian neighbors. First they handed out Bibles and copies of the Book of Mormon to visiting Russians, some of whom they had met in international sporting activities. Then in 1989, designated couples, among them Jussi and Raija Kemppainen, made frequent visits into the Soviet Union to meet with newly baptized Saints. As congregations grew, these faithful Finns trained new members in Vyborg, Leningrad, and Tallinn to worship and to perform the ordinances of the priesthood themselves. Brother Kemppainen as a traveling elder served as the first district president in the Soviet Union. In 1990 the Finland Helsinki East Mission was created to care for Church members in the Soviet Union. "Finland's beacon in the Baltic . . . is more than a light of freedom in a troubled political sea. . . . More even than the gospel light shining into Soviet lives after a long darkness. . . . Finland's beacon shines also for Church members everywhere, reminding us that despite times of darkness and discouragement, a resolute faith eventually penetrates the fog of apathy and even political boundaries."[36]

In 1996 Church population in Finland stood at about 4,500.

The Netherlands

The Church in the Netherlands, crushed by World War II, rebounded to reach maturity in the 1990s, although the growth rate tapered off after 1975 as the nation became more secular and prosperous. Dutch pride in reclaiming much of their land from the sea has proved a stumbling block to missionary efforts. So too have Dutch laws legalizing prostitution and "soft" drugs, the most liberal in the world.

In the modern era, the population in Holland diversified with a sizable influx of nationals from the former Dutch colonies of Suriname in South America and Indonesia in Asia. Missionaries commonly carried copies of the Book of Mormon in three or four different languages when they tracted. Julie Jacobs, born in 1914 in the former Dutch colony of Indonesia, was one of those nationals. She and her husband moved to Holland after World War II so that he could receive better medical treatment for diseases contracted during the war. He later passed away. In 1962 two missionaries knocked at Julie's door. After several visits, the elders urged Julie to pray, and she spent most of one night doing so. "Never had I prayed so sincerely or for so long. And never had I felt God's love and strength as I did on that night." Sister Jacobs became a stalwart Relief Society worker, serving five years as president in The Hague Netherlands Stake. "It wasn't always easy, but during those years I learned to kneel in prayer often to receive the help and inspiration I needed."[37]

Netherlands native Jacob de Jager became a member of the First Quorum of the Seventy in 1976. He and his wife, Bea Lim de Jager, had joined the Church in 1960 while working in Toronto, Canada. They were taught and fellowshipped by Frances Monson, wife of East Canadian

Mission president Thomas S. Monson. Upon his return to Holland and later as a businessman in Indonesia, Brother de Jager served as counselor to three mission presidents and as a regional representative of the Twelve. Elder de Jager's linguistic talents—he speaks five languages— served him well as resident general authority in many different areas of the world.

In 1996 Church membership in the Netherlands was 7,300. Three stakes covered the entire country.

Belgium

One of the smallest European countries is Belgium, nestled among France, Germany, and the Netherlands. Because of its good access to the sea, Belgium is considered the crossroads of Europe. Its capital, Brussels, is a major international business city of the world and headquarters of both the European Union and NATO. The two languages spoken by Belgian citizens—French and Flemish (similar to Dutch)—have always connected Church affairs in Belgium with France and the Netherlands.

The French-speaking Belgians, known as Walloons, reside in the southern part of the country neighboring France, and the Flemish-speaking Belgians, known as the Flemish or the Flemings, live in Flanders, in northern Belgium. Brussels, the capital, has large populations of both peoples. Over the centuries, both groups have maintained a divisive rivalry. Beginning in the 1980s, street signs and important documents were printed in both languages. Both groups were proportionately represented in the nation's parliament. This rivalry between the Walloons and the Flemish was a hindrance for Church leaders trying to integrate all the various nationalities and languages into district and stake unity.

Church growth in Belgium in the modern era has been slow but steady. A boost came in 1963 when the Franco-Belgian Mission was created and brought more missionaries to labor in Belgium itself. In 1965 the completion of a large chapel in Brussels gave the members a sense of permanence and stability. The press and two television stations favorably covered the building's open house. Typifying the multinational character of Brussels, three congregations met in that building— French-speaking, Flemish-speaking, and English-speaking. In recent years, the English congregation has grown with converts from Africa,

Romania, and other eastern European countries. Another international congregation was in Mons, forty miles east of Brussels, where the military headquarters of NATO were located.

One of Belgium's leading converts was Joseph Troffaes, who joined the Church in 1969. Converted by the Book of Mormon and wanting to accept God's desires for him, he testified, "I knew I had to change my life and give up all the bad things I had been doing."[38] A pioneer of the gospel in the Flemish-speaking part of Belgium, he shared his testimony far and wide throughout his country.

New milestones were reached in 1974 with the creation of the Belgium Brussels Mission covering French-speaking Belgium and part of France. The Flemish members and missionary program, which had been part of the Netherlands Mission, were assigned in 1975 to the Belgium Antwerp Mission, but in 1994 missionary work among the Flemings was moved back to the jurisdiction of the Netherlands Amsterdam Mission. In 1977 the first Belgian stake was created in Brussels, and in 1994 the Antwerp Belgium Stake was created for the Fleming members. In 1996 Church membership in Belgium was nearly 5,500.

In 1975 Belgian native Charles Didier, who served as manager of distribution and translation in Frankfurt, was called to the First Quorum of the Seventy at age thirty-nine. A linguist by profession, Elder Didier spoke fluent Flemish, French, German, Spanish, and English. As a general authority, he used each of these languages to serve in diverse areas of the world. In 1992 he was called as one of the Seven Presidents of the Seventy.

Luxembourg

The nation of Luxembourg is smaller than Belgium, covering only 998 square miles. In this multilingual country, Luxemborgoise (a German dialect), German, and French are the most common languages, although many more are spoken. Church leaders did not authorize official missionary work in this tiny nation until the late 1980s.

The Luxembourg Branch was administered by the Belgium Brussels Mission. Members came from throughout the country, some traveling more than an hour to Sunday morning meetings. Truly a melting pot, the branch boasted members from England, Germany, France, Belgium,

Portugal, Denmark, Spain, Romania, Yugoslavia, the United States, Canada, Japan, the Philippines, and several African countries. To share a testimony in sacrament meeting sometimes took forty minutes because of the translations involved. Though members spoke different languages, they communicated through smiles, touch, and translated conversations. Members also met together often on weekend outings and in group home evenings on the Sabbath. In the 1990s, member-missionary contacts have made Luxembourg one of the best baptizing areas of the Belgian mission.[39]

France

In the 1970s, mission boundaries were realigned in France and French-speaking Belgium and Switzerland. Where previously there were three missions—the French, French East, and Franco-Belgian—there were now five missions.

In 1975 France, which had reached 10,000 members, was ready for its first stake, located in Paris. Gerard Giraud-Carrier, its first president, had joined the Church in 1968. Following his labors as stake president, he became France's first native regional representative of the Twelve. In 1987 he pointed out that because the Church had grown in France to more than 20,000 members, the most pressing need was more and better leaders. "Some of our leaders, especially in wards and branches where there aren't many brethren to share the load of priesthood stewardship, are worn out." He added that because French universities do not allow students to interrupt their education for missions, many worthy young men and women completed their missions and upon their return, went to America for their college education. Often they did not return, depriving France of strong leadership.[40] Forty percent of the membership in France in the 1990s is single, and solid young adult programs attract the singles to activities.[41]

A solid building block of the Church in France is its families who joined in the 1960s and have since reared solid second- and third-generation members. An excellent example is the Simonet family of Nancy. Jacquie, the father, had been attending church for years with his family but had not been baptized because of his smoking habit. One night he saw his wife, Marie, weeping over an article about eternal marriage in *L'Etoile,* the Church's French magazine. "My heart was touched as I talked to my wife that night, and I realized that I already knew the gospel was true," Jacquie related. "I love my wife and I knew that I wanted to be with her for eternity. So I threw away my cigarettes and never smoked again." Jacquie was baptized, and a year later the family was sealed in the Swiss Temple. In the 1990s, Brother Simonet served as president of the Bordeaux France Stake.[42]

Also during the decade of the 1960s, missionaries in Nîmes knocked on the door of eighteen-year-old Jacques Faudin, an active Marxist-Leninist atheist. He invited the missionaries in, planning to convince them of atheism. Instead, the elders exhibited a power he did not understand. He read the Book of Mormon and could find no fault with it. Jacques then attended the dedication of the Marseilles chapel and afterwards met Elder Howard W. Hunter of the Quorum of the Twelve, who promised him a testimony if he exercised faith and prayer. "Then one night, after fasting, I received my answer. I knew without any doubt that Joseph Smith was a prophet and that the Book of Mormon was true. I was baptized two days later on 27 July 1968," he related. Jacques promised that from that day forward he would give his life to the Lord. In the 1990s, he was called as regional representative of the Twelve, and he and his wife, Francine, have reared their large family as stalwarts in the gospel.[43]

Cécile Pelous first learned of the Latter-day Saints as a high school graduate. On a tour of America, her group visited several large cities, including Salt Lake City. There they attended the play *Promised Valley,* "and by the end, Cécile found herself standing and singing with audience and cast, tears streaming down her face." When later asked what had been the high point of her trip, "Cécile shocked her French friends by naming Salt Lake City. She told them she had felt something there unlike anything she had felt in other places they had visited. Three years later, two missionaries doing their daily tracting knocked on the door of her family's home in Paris. Cécile, noticing their American accent, asked if they were from Salt Lake City in Utah. When Elder Ed Borrell from Price, Utah, claimed to be from somewhere close by, Cécile consented to talk to them. (She learned later just how far Elder Borrell was stretching the truth.)" Cécile listened, believed, and was baptized. She has since served as a stake Relief Society president in the Paris Stake and each year has used her paid vacation from the Nina Ricci fashion house to work in orphanages in India and Nepal.[44]

Because many French people were interested in family roots, the Church in France began emphasizing a family history message. An exhibit adapted to the European culture has drawn favorable attention to the Church and its message in many areas. Media advertisements starting in the late 1980s about the Book of Mormon also generated public interest.

The French way of life melds high achievement and exquisite leisure. Most French people enjoy philosophizing, socializing, and savoring their world-famous cuisine while valuing their privacy, which makes it difficult for missionaries to find openings for normal proselyting efforts. Much recent missionary success has been among the millions of poorer individuals flooding into France from current and former French possessions in Africa, the Caribbean, and the South Pacific. Many congregations counted more than a third of the members and investigators each Sunday from these other cultures. Integrating converts of other races, religious backgrounds, and cultures has not always been easy.

By 1996 France had three missions headquartered within its boundaries and some missionaries also serving in France from the Belgium Brussels and Switzerland Geneva Missions. Seven French stakes included two in Paris and one each in Nice, Nancy, Bordeaux, Lille, and Lyon. Approximately 26,000 members were on the rolls.

Germany

Germany, fragmented after World War II, emerged as two separate and ideologically opposite states in 1949. The Cold War exacerbated the differences between West and East Germany until it seemed the division would remain permanent. But almost imperceptibly the enmity between East and West Germany softened through the 1970s and 1980s. After the revolution of 1989 and Soviet president Mikhail Gorbachev's refusal to send Red Army troops to quell it, East Germany threw off its Communist yoke. West German politicians, notably Chancellor Helmut Kohl, pushed for unification, which was concluded on 3 October 1990. Once again Germany was united. Again Germany was the most powerful nation in Europe and the European Union. Again Germany was a nation to be reckoned with.

In the 1990s, with the end of the Cold War, the United States began removing its massive military divisions in Germany. The four service-men stakes were no longer needed, and the small remaining American units were annexed to existing German stakes. These American units became instead international wards and branches, fellowshipping refugees from many different cultures.

By this time, the Church in West Germany compared in maturity to the Church in the United Kingdom or the eastern United States. New leadership came from young men and women who grew up in the Church in the 1960s, gained spiritual strength in seminary and institute classes, became better educated than their parents, went on missions, and married other Latter-day Saints. Eventually the number of German-speaking stakes in West Germany increased to ten, growing more from births to members than from converts.

German native F. Enzio Busche was called to the First Quorum of the Seventy in 1977, having served as district president, mission presi-dent's counselor, and Germany's first native regional representative of the Twelve. Leaving his employment in Dortmund as a chief executive officer of a large printing and publishing firm, Elder Busche served in assignments around the world, including twice in his native land, first as president of the Germany Munich Mission and later as first president of the Frankfurt Germany Temple.

The temple in Frankfurt was announced in 1981, but legal compli-cations delayed the completion of it until 1987. That August, Church president Ezra Taft Benson dedicated the temple and spoke of his excite-ment to be again in Germany, where he had experienced powerful spiri-tual outpourings in two previous terms as European Mission president. Heavy media coverage of the dedicatory events signaled a turnaround of attitude toward the Church in Germany. At the dedicatory service, Elder Busche read poignant excerpts from writings of young German soldiers in World War II. "Why have so many people died so young in this coun-try?" he asked. "Could it be because people in tradition become blind, seeing nothing? Are these young people who die so young now willing to listen [to the gospel message in the spirit world]?"[45]

The Frankfurt Germany Temple, dedicated in 1987

In March 1992, Sister Doris Sertel of Nidderau, Germany, represented European women Church members at the Relief Society Sesquicentennial conference. Her experiences with her husband while both were workers in the Frankfurt Germany Temple had strengthened their marriage. "Every time I go to the temple," she explained, "I feel like I am making promises over again. It is almost like getting married once a week when we go to the House of the Lord together." She also pointed out that even though she belonged to a small Relief Society, strength came from sisterhood, not from numbers.[46]

In 1994 Dieter F. Uchtdorf, president of the Mannheim Germany Stake, was called to the Seventy. Elder Uchtdorf had joined the Church at age eight in Zwickau in East Germany and four years later fled with his family to West Germany. As a young adult, he became a fighter pilot for his nation's air force. Later he flew for Lufthansa German Airlines and then became senior vice president of flight operations and chief pilot. As a pilot, Elder Uchtdorf often soared high above the earth. "I see how beautiful the deserts and the jungles and the seas are," he commented. "I marvel at the world's different cultures. Everyone is different, and yet we are the same."[47] Elder Uchtdorf served in the Europe Area presidency as one of eight members of the Seventy who continued part-time employment experimentally while serving as general authorities.

In the late 1980s, a high proportion of the converts in West Germany were guest workers, refugees from third-world countries, or recent immigrants. This trend continued after reunification in 1990, when Church population stood at 32,000 in West Germany. In 1996 Church membership in unified Germany was approximately 37,000.

Switzerland

From the mid 1970s to the 1990s, progress in the missions in Switzerland was relatively slow, perhaps due to Switzerland's development of the highest standard of living in all of Europe. "Things are simply going too well for the Swiss people and they don't want to hear anything about the gospel," related Guido Muller, a Swiss Church historian. "They have the feeling things will go ahead without God." In some years Switzerland had fewer than one hundred baptisms.[48]

The Church in Switzerland has always had an international flavor. As illustrated by the Petit Saconnex Ward in the Geneva Stake, the passing years brought even more diversity. In 1987 the bishop of the ward was German and his wife, Austrian; the first counselor was British and the second counselor Swiss. The executive secretary was American, the clerk Iranian, and the financial clerk Japanese. The ward mission leader was from the island of Mauritius, and the Young Men president from the Philippines. Home and visiting teachers came from Chile, Cambodia, Italy, Portugal, Spain, Japan, Peru, the West Indies, and Ghana. Many languages were used in Church services, especially in prayer. As the years have gone by, all three wards in Geneva became richly internationalized, with even more countries represented: Canada, Ethiopia, Mali, Nigeria, Sri Lanka, Nepal, and Tahiti.[49] The multicultural membership can be explained when one realizes that Geneva has been headquarters for hundreds of such international organizations as the Red Cross and is an official United Nations Organization (UNO) city.

As members matured in the faith, the Church in Switzerland grew stronger. The Saints rejoiced at the rededication of the remodeled Swiss Temple in October 1992. Thousands attended the open house that preceded the dedication. "There was a very loving, kind and calm spirit about the open house," reported Michael Obst, public affairs director for the Europe Area. "People commented time and again about how impressed they were with the happiness that radiated from the tour guides."[50] In 1996 stakes were headquartered in Zürich, Bern, and Geneva, Switzerland. Membership stood at approximately 6,700.

In 1985 Hans B. Ringger was sustained as a member of the First Quorum of the Seventy, the first native of Switzerland to become a general authority. A retired colonel in the Swiss Army, Elder Ringger was also a noted architect and industrial designer who had served in the Church as a bishop and stake president. Upon his call as a general authority Brother Ringger became a counselor in the Europe Area presidency and then, from 1987 to 1993, its president. He was instrumental during this time in opening several eastern European nations to the preaching of the gospel. Later, as a member of the Europe-Mediterranean Area presidency, he was assigned to investigate possibilities for preaching the gospel in the Arab states of northern Africa.

Austria

In 1980 Ezra Taft Benson, president of the Quorum of the Twelve Apostles, created the Vienna Austria Stake. The new stake included all Church members in the Austria Vienna Mission, except those in the Salzburg and Innsbruck areas (assigned to the Germany Munich Mission) and the Vorarlberg Stake (assigned to the Switzerland Zürich Mission). The Vienna Austria Stake included an international ward of expatriates from the United States, Canada, western African nations, Uruguay, Taiwan, the Philippines, Japan, and central and eastern European countries. In 1994 Innsbruck and Salzburg were assigned to the Austria Vienna Mission as the prospects for a stake in western Austria grew brighter.

Missionary productivity in the Austrian Mission continued low, partly because Austria remained predominantly and staunchly Roman Catholic. The nation's growing affluence and highly secular culture also played a part, as in other modern western European nations.

Still, Austrian members became strong as they sacrificed and dedicated themselves to the Lord and his Church. An example is the Kandler family who live in the Austrian Alps. The Kandlers were the first Latter-day Saints in their village of Eugendorf. "Brother Kandler was working as a roofer and a plumber. When the townspeople found out he had joined the Church, his employees quit work, and he lost a contract to re-roof the large cathedral in town. But the stake patriarch told him not to worry, that because he was so brave, the Lord would bless him. The town boycotted him—no more jobs in Eugendorf. But now he's got so much work in neighboring villages and in Salzburg that it doesn't matter." The daughters were at first excluded from the local Catholic schools, but over time the villagers recognized that the Kandler family had not fallen away from God but actually drawn closer to him.[51]

For centuries Vienna was the effective capital of the massive multilingual, multiethnic, and multireligious Austrian Empire. Known as the end of the west and the beginning of the east, this city, along with much of the rest of Austria, has hosted nationals of many countries. In the 1980s and 1990s, new members in Austria came from the central, eastern, and southern European refugee camps near Vienna. Church leaders worked diligently to help these members from numerous languages and cultures fit into the gospel culture.

The Dornbirn Austria Branch of the Zürich Switzerland Stake has exemplified that process. Dornbirn is located near beautiful Lake Constance and the borders of four countries—Austria, Switzerland, Germany, and Liechtenstein. Members of the branch—from several alpine villages and all four countries—strived to downplay national customs and village dialects as they worshipped together each week.

In 1985 the Austria Vienna East Mission, with headquarters in Vienna, was created to be the springboard for missionary work in Hungary, Czechoslovakia, Poland, the Soviet Union, Yugoslavia, Romania, Bulgaria, Greece, Cyprus, and the Middle East. Members came into the Church in those countries, and some even served full-time missions. Also a number of refugees in Austria from the war-torn former Yugoslavia joined the Church. When most of these nations obtained their own missions, the Austria Vienna East Mission was disbanded in 1992. The Austria Vienna Mission took responsibility for missionary work in the former Yugoslavian republics of Slovenia, Croatia, and Serbia.

In 1992 Austrian Latter-day Saints were proud to learn that Austrian Johann Wondra had been called as president of the Frankfurt Germany

Temple. That same year the Austrian Saints also rejoiced to learn of the visit of President Howard W. Hunter of the Twelve to a hill high above Vienna and the Danube River where he officially dedicated Austria for the preaching of the gospel. President Hunter then went on to Linz to conduct a regional conference. In 1996 Church membership in Austria stood at approximately 3,300.

Italy

The Church in Italy, especially in northern Italy, has developed great strength and produced outstanding leaders. For instance, Giuseppe Pasta first heard of the Church as a young college student in Milan in the 1960s. Giuseppe met and was converted by Latter-day Saint missionaries explaining the gospel with portable street displays. His family was devastated. Well-meaning friends presented him a petition with hundreds of signatures begging him to return to the true church. He even had an interview with a Catholic cardinal, who became convinced of Giuseppe's sincere and unshakable faith.

Brother Pasta worked as an executive with Fiat for seventeen years before he was hired to open the Church's first regional office in Italy. As a temple sealer, he has united many of his countrymen and women for eternity in the Swiss Temple. In 1989 he was called as a mission president to his native land.[52]

Another outstanding example of leadership are Vincenzo and Carolina Conforte. Vincenzo, an agnostic because of his family's tragic experiences in World War II, met the missionaries in 1975. At first Vincenzo harassed the elders and blew smoke in their faces while they tried to teach him. Gradually his heart and that of his wife softened. They prayed sincerely for guidance, and finding answers through reading the Book of Mormon, they became convinced of the truthfulness of the restored gospel. They were baptized, and a year later Brother Conforte was called as branch president. He strived to motivate others to overcome bad habits as he had done. Later he served as counselor to the mission president, as district president, as Italy Catania Mission president from 1986 to 1989, and then as Italy Padova Mission president from 1990 to 1992.[53]

On the island of Sicily, Rosario Virgillito and his fiancée faced opposition from their families when they joined the Church in 1984—a common reaction throughout all of southern Italy. Their families were puzzled and hurt that Rosario and his sweetheart wanted to be married in something called a temple in faraway Switzerland instead of having the traditional big church wedding. But the couple did what they knew was right. Rosario has served as elders quorum president in the Catania Branch of the Italy Catania Mission. As a pioneer in his family, he knows his example is crucial. "I can't make a mistake, because my family watches me closely."[54]

In 1988 missionaries from the Catania Mission introduced the gospel to the Mediterranean island nation of Malta. English is spoken in Malta, but the missionaries found they would be more effective if they spoke native Maltese. In 1990 the four missionaries assigned to the island enrolled in community-sponsored Maltese language classes.[55] Missionary work in Malta, later supervised by the Greece Athens Mission, moved forward on more solid footing.

The Church has faced challenges in preaching the gospel in Italy. Many investigators, sincerely interested in the Church, were simply unable to break with powerful religious tradition. Immorality was also a serious problem, as were habits contrary to the Word of Wisdom. Wine and coffee were an ingrained part of the Italian culture. In addition, young Church members found it difficult to find someone to marry within the Church.

At times even missionaries have been a trial to the members. Italian members talk and argue enthusiastically. They enjoy vehemently expressing their feelings and opinions. This cultural trait does not mean they dislike each other or mean to offend, as some missionaries from other cultures may have mistakenly thought. Americans have also at times cringed at the Italian propensity to more colorful clothing styles as well as bolder hairstyles. In Italy, as in the rest of the world, missionaries had to distinguish cultural traits from gospel principles.

The Church in Italy was honored in 1993 when one of its most experienced leaders, Mario V. Vaira, was called as president of the Swiss Temple. Brother Vaira served formerly as stake president and president of the Italy Catania Mission. Another milestone was reached in 1993 when the government granted the Church official legal status after many years of negotiations. This gave the Church certain privileges, including the right to own property and authorization to perform marriages.[56]

Forty missionaries from the Italy Rome Mission on 19 December 1993 experienced a once-in-a-lifetime opportunity to sing at a Christmas Mass at the famed Saint Peter's Basilica in the Vatican. Their singing was broadcast worldwide on Vatican Radio. Mission president C. Gerald Parker acknowledged the help of the Lord in obtaining this invitation and in "helping us to sing beyond our usual abilities."[57]

In 1996 Italy had four missions—headquartered in Milan, Rome, Padova, and Catania—and two stakes, one in Milan and one in Venice. Church membership in Italy stood at approximately 16,000.

Spain

In Spain, The Church of Jesus Christ of Latter-day Saints experienced renewed growth beginning in 1975. With the death that year of dictator Francisco Franco, Spain's constitutional monarchy was restored and numerous liberal policies were introduced. Given more freedom, the people became less rigid, more willing to risk change. Fewer converts were ostracized by their families, friends, and employers when they joined the Church. The kingdom of God entered a golden age in Spain and grew rapidly. A second Spanish mission, the Spain Barcelona Mission, was organized from the Spain Madrid Mission in 1976. The visit of Elders Gordon B. Hinckley and Neal A. Maxwell to King Juan Carlos in 1978 attracted much attention and paved the way for more missionaries to enter the country. In 1992 President Hinckley, this time a member of the First Presidency, again visited King Juan Carlos and presented him with a leather-bound copy of the Book of Mormon.

Spain prospered in the 1980s as a full partner in NATO and the European Community. Unfortunately, as in the rest of western Europe, fewer people in their prosperity turned to God for solutions to their problems. Also, as in many other countries, the social custom of cohabitation before marriage proved a troubling matter for the missionaries to address.

Another challenge for the Church in Spain in 1990 was the restriction of missionary visas. Government authorities discovered that some Africans were entering Spain using missionary visas to find refuge and work, not to preach. In addition, huge numbers of Christian evangelical missionaries were flooding the country. To solve the problem the government cut off visas to missionaries of all denominations. After much negotiation, the number of visas was again raised for Latter-day Saint missionaries.

The Church succeeded comparatively well in the Canary Islands, two provinces of Spain located sixty miles off the coast of northwestern Africa. Generally poorer and more humble than their countrymen, the inhabitants of the Canary Islands are of Spanish, black, and mixed-race heritage. Missionary work began in the Canary Islands in 1979 when the Francisco Pena family was converted through reading the Book of Mormon and the teaching efforts of Jesus Raureir Gomez y Vega, a Canary Islander who had been baptized in Madrid three years earlier. One decade later, the Church had more than 2,000 members on the Canary Islands.[58] In more recent years, the Spain Las Palmas Mission, which covers the Canary Islands, baptized two to three times as many converts as any other of the Spanish missions. A few converts were single men from the African nations of Nigeria, Ghana, and Sierra Leone who had gone to the Canaries to work. Some returned to their homeland and strengthened the Church there.

The Marrero family is an example of the faithfulness of Canary Island Saints. In 1992 their family of eight began a forty-hour trip in their small van to the nearest open temple, near Frankfurt, Germany. Seasickness on the ferry, mechanical failure, rain, and car sickness plagued their journey. But the sacrifices were worth the price, said Raquel, age fourteen: "When at last we saw the Angel Moroni on top, it was such a joy. . . . It was beautiful—even more beautiful because we'd suffered so much to get there." Once united as an eternal family and spending four days in the temple doing work for the dead, the family headed for home. "The trip was a lot like life, really," explained Desiree, age sixteen. "You go through some tough times, and you work really hard, but it is worth it when you make it to the celestial kingdom. We made a lot of sacrifices so that everyone could arrive together."[59]

The Sevilla Spain Mission began sending elders to the Spanish islands off the coast of Morocco, which are inhabited largely by Muslims. Because freedom to preach existed there, unlike in other Islamic areas, the Church was free to experiment with various methods of reaching Muslims.

In 1996 the Church membership in Spain stood at approximately 24,000. Spain had five missions, headquartered in Madrid, Barcelona, Sevilla, Bilbao, and Las Palmas. Four stakes were located in Madrid, Barcelona, Sevilla, and Bilbao. Members looked forward to having a temple, scheduled to be built near Madrid.

Portugal

Portugal has emerged since 1974 as one of the strongest mission fields in the world. Certainly no other western European nation did as well in the 1970s, 1980s, and 1990s. In fact, Portugal achieved a stake in the shortest length of time. Missionaries first entered Portugal in November 1974, and the Lisbon Portugal Stake was created in July 1981, a period of less than seven years.

From 1932 to 1974, Antonio de Oliveira Salazar ruled a fascist government in Portugal that promoted staunch Catholicism and African colonialism. In April 1974, a military coup overthrew the dictatorship, and a new government that gradually became democratic took over. At the same time, three Portuguese African colonies—Angola, Mozambique, and the Cape Verde Islands—rebelled and gained independence. (These nations were the last African countries to achieve independence from European colonial powers.)

Just three weeks before the 1974 coup in Portugal, Church president Spencer W. Kimball had prophesied that the Lord would "open the gates and make possible the proselyting" to nations closed to the gospel.[60] In August President Kimball dispatched the Church's ambassador-at-large, David M. Kennedy, to Lisbon, Portugal's capital. Because of his vast international experience and credentials, Elder Kennedy had valuable contacts within the Portuguese government and was treated with considerable deference. The minister of justice, Salgado Zenha, had served as a diplomat in Washington, D.C., and knew of American religious freedom as well as the LDS Church and its Washington D.C. Temple. Consequently, he granted the Church official recognition immediately and coordinated the effort to have the parliament adopt a statute permitting religious freedom.[61]

Elder Thomas S. Monson and mission president William Grant Bangerter mingle with Saints in Portugal

William Grant Bangerter, who had served as a mission president in Portuguese-speaking Brazil, opened the Portuguese mission in November of that year. Four carefully selected missionaries serving in Brazil accompanied him. The opening of the mission was not announced publicly nor did door-to-door tracting take place in the early months for fear that elements in the government might push for the Church's expulsion. Yet even with these precautions, fifty investigators were converted by July 1975. At that time President Bangerter was called to be a general authority and was replaced in Portugal as mission president by W. Lynn Pinegar, also a former missionary to Portuguese-speaking Brazil.

In April 1975, Elder Thomas S. Monson of the Twelve dedicated Portugal for the preaching of the gospel. He promised that Portugal would experience the same success as Brazil, where so many Portuguese descendants lived. "We recognize, Father, that from this land went navigators and seafaring men in days of yore and that the Portuguese people have had an adventurous spirit, as they trusted in thee, as they looked for lands unknown. Grant that they may trust in thee as they now search for those truths that will lead them to life eternal."[62]

Beginning in late 1975, baptismal success in Portugal exploded as missionaries began teaching the *retornados*, former Portuguese colonists returning to their homeland when they were forced out of Africa by revolutionaries. Economic and psychological disruption, societal alienation, and a quest for religious strength were common traits of these people. "We lost everything we had," recalled Arnaldo Teles Grilo, who became patriarch of the Lisbon Portugal Stake. "And it was a good thing."[63] From 1975 through the late 1980s, half of the many thousands that joined the Church and a large share of the emerging priesthood leaders were *retornados*.[64]

Among the *retornados* who joined the Church were Joaquim Aires, who became a district president, and his wife. Their former mission president, Harold G. Hillam of the Second Quorum of the Seventy, related this story: "They had returned to Portugal unknown and with very few possessions. . . . One day I received a telephone call. President Aires was in the hospital in Coimbra, several hours' travel away. He had suffered a very serious cerebral hemorrhage and . . . [later] as we walked quietly into the hospital room, we found him asleep. . . . He slowly opened his eyes and then looked at me for a moment, and then the tears came to both of our eyes. He then said in a very weak and soft voice, 'I knew you would come. I knew you would come. Would you please give me a blessing.' . . . It was our privilege to pronounce a blessing on him with power and authority of our Father in Heaven.

"As I would meet with the members of the Church from one end of Portugal to the other, [they] would ask, 'How is Brother Aires? Will you please tell him we love him and we're praying for him?' This good man and his wife, who had returned to Portugal almost unknown, now, because of their membership in the Church, had literally thousands who loved them and were concerned about them and remembered him in their prayers." Brother Aires recovered completely. He and Sister Aires later served a full-time mission together.[65]

In 1985 Elder Russell M. Nelson presided over a Lisbon regional conference that Portuguese Saints have long remembered. Elder Nelson said: "As an apostle of the Lord Jesus Christ, I will now make a prophecy. . . . Portugal will be covered from north to south and from east to west with stakes of Zion. Chapels will be built in cities and towns throughout the whole land. And as a consequence of the growth of the kingdom of God, this nation will be exceedingly blessed and will become again a great nation as it was in times of old. . . . And I will be alive to see it."[66]

The Church in Portugal grew by leaps and bounds. In 1978 Church membership reached 1,000. Nine years later there were more than 11,000 members. By 1990 there were 23,000, and in 1996 the total exceeded 34,000. As the Church grew, new meetinghouses—which contributed to proselyting success—were constructed following the Portuguese-inspired designs of Alcino Silva, a Church architect and president of the Porto Stake. The Portuguese flavor of his designs helped the Church appear less American.

In the late 1980s, the number of baptisms accelerated almost too rapidly. Growth exceeded the ability to develop leadership. In addition, not enough attention was being given to baptizing heads of households. So, in the 1990s, more emphasis was placed on properly preparing baptismal candidates and on member retention, reactivation, and leadership development. Strong leaders soon emerged. In recent years, a Portuguese Angolan became a stake president. A federal judge in Lisbon became another stake president, and a Portuguese high priest became mission president in his native land.

Numerous Portuguese young men and women served missions, often at a sacrifice. Universities were unsympathetic to interruption of schooling for religious service, so readmission was difficult. Mandatory military service sometimes cut their missions short.[67]

In 1990 President Gordon B. Hinckley of the First Presidency, Elder Richard G. Scott of the Quorum of the Twelve, and Elder Spencer J. Condie of the Europe Area presidency met with 3,500 people at a regional conference in Lisbon. Portuguese Saints were thrilled at this first visit to Portugal by a member of the First Presidency. They "felt the love of the Brethren and experienced the great blessing of being in the presence of the Lord's anointed."[68]

Portugal was the poorest country in western Europe, and the resultant humility of the people created receptive hearts for the Church's missionary efforts. But since Portugal entered the European Union, its standard of living has risen remarkably, as have materialism and secularization. Even so, the deep religious feelings of the Portuguese have kept many open to the missionaries' message.

An interesting note to the work in Portugal was the baptism of a number of people from Angola who were visiting Portugal for extended periods. They returned to Angola, anxiously awaiting the day when political conditions would allow the gospel to be preached in their African country.

Another happy development was the introduction of the gospel in 1989 to three island chains: the Azores, the Madeira Islands, and the Cape Verde Islands. The inhabitants of all three speak Portuguese, receive their missionaries from Portugal, and have a mission district.

The Azores are eight hundred miles westward in the North Atlantic, and the Madeira Islands are off the coast of Africa. Both are territories of Portugal. The Republic of Cape Verde, independent from Portugal since 1975, consists of a string of ten dry and barren volcanic islands about four hundred miles off the coast of western Africa. The Church had remarkable success in Cape Verde. A returned missionary reported, "Their humility, ability to love, and openness to others is what allows this nation to progress."[69] In September 1994, Elder Dallin H. Oaks of the Twelve dedicated the country for the preaching of the gospel. At that point, there were 2,500 Church members among the population of 350,000. Elder Oaks prayed that the deficiencies of Cape Verde might be overcome—"deficiencies in its commerce, and in its moisture, and in the hope of its people, and in many other things known to thee."[70]

The future in Portugal looks bright. In 1996 there were five stakes in Portugal: two in Lisbon and one each in Porto, Setubal, and Matosinhos. More stakes are planned. Three missions spread the gsopel throughout the small country whose population is less than 11 million. The Portuguese Saints were delighted with the announcement of a temple in nearby Madrid, Spain. In a most pleasing development, the Portuguese national television network granted the Church sixty ten-minute slots to promote the Church and gospel values.

Greece

Greece, once the site of so many converts to the gospel through the apostle Paul, was recently opened to missionaries of the restored gospel, but the pervasive presence of the Greek Orthodox Church in Greek society and government has hindered the work. It is an affront to family and cultural ties to forsake the traditional faith. During the nearly four-hundred-year Turkish occupation of Greece, from 1456 to 1830, Greek Orthodox priests secretly maintained the language, culture, and religion. Understandably, Greek Orthodox Church leaders have considerable influence upon the government and the people.

In 1899, a letter to Church leaders asking for information led Latter-day Saint missionaries to Rigas Profantis, a printer in Athens, and his friend, Nicholas Malavetis, who had started a search for the truth in 1895. President Ferdinand F. Hintze of the Turkish Mission visited the pair in April 1899 and taught them about the gospel. In 1905 Profantis wrote again, this time requesting baptism and adding that he had translated a Church pamphlet into Greek. Three other people were awaiting baptism as well. Missionaries from the Near East Mission baptized them, and the fledgling group continued until 1909 or 1910 when missionaries were withdrawn.[71]

Other early Greek converts to the Church were immigrants who had settled in Salt Lake City in the early twentieth century. In the 1950s, these few Greek-American Saints formed the Hellenic Latter-day Saint Society to foster ties with their ancestral home and prepare the way for missionary work in Greece.

Church leaders made numerous attempts over the years to gain favor with the Greek government. In 1972 Church president Harold B. Lee and Elder Gordon B. Hinckley visited officials in Athens without success. Church ambassador David M. Kennedy later visited the Greek Orthodox archbishop, pointing out that the Greek Orthodox Church enjoyed full religious freedom in the United States, that the LDS Church had sent aid to Greece after a devastating 1953 earthquake, and that the Church was fully recognized by other countries of western Europe.

Further attempts to gain recognition followed. In the mid 1970s, President Spencer W. Kimball decided to send Greek-speaking missionaries to large Greek immigrant populations in New York City and Chicago. In 1977 James Nackos, of Greek extraction, and his wife, Tena, went to Athens as special representatives of the Church to make friends and seek permission from the government to hold meetings. With the aid of a few American Saints stationed in Greece, Elder Nackos baptized six converts, gained respect for the Church, and paved the way for meetings to be held beginning in 1981. A Brigham Young University performing group visited Greece in 1982 and built goodwill. Meanwhile President Ezra Taft Benson of the Twelve visited Greece. Because of his previous United States Cabinet position, he gained audience with high-level officials. Three years later, the Greek ambassador to the United States and other officials met with the First Presidency in Salt Lake City.

The stage was set for sending in missionary couples and eventually young missionaries. In 1985 Elder Russell M. Nelson of the Twelve accompanied by the first Greek-speaking missionaries from the United States, dedicated Greece for the preaching of the gospel. The Austria Vienna Mission and later the Austria Vienna East Mission presidents supervised missionary efforts. The earliest converts found their joy in the gospel tempered by the ostracism of family, friends, and employers.

In July 1990, relationships with the government and the state church had progressed sufficiently that the First Presidency established the Greece Athens Mission. R. Douglas Phillips, a professor of Greek and Latin at Brigham Young University, was called as the first mission president. He organized four branches in Athens (one of them English-speaking) and one in Thessaloniki. But missionaries for the most part continued to feel unwelcome in Greece. "Among the first tasks required of a missionary in Greece, after grappling with the acquisition of a foreign language, is acquainting oneself with the prevailing religious tradition—that of the Greek Orthodox Church," wrote commentator Le Grande W. Smith. "As with nearly any large homogeneous group of people, the Greeks have often been described as insular, parochial, or inbred. In such a society, any outside group is immediately suspect, particularly if viewed as an intruder. The Greeks sense an acute danger in tolerating any kind of evangelical or proselyting efforts from without."[72]

Occasionally police, at the behest of local Greek Orthodox leaders, arrested missionaries. To obtain their release, a lawyer from Athens hired by the Church was sent to invoke the religious freedom law. Often the Greek government refused to grant visas to American missionaries to keep their numbers low. Those with visas had to travel out of country and return to renew their residence permits. The Church's International

Agency in Washington, D.C., worked with Greek diplomats to allow missionaries to remain in Greece in the tenuous situation.

The most ominous arrest of missionaries took place in June 1993 in Thessaloniki. Three missionaries were charged with "proselytism," a criminal offense, defined as attempts to deceive, manipulate, pressure, or bribe someone to change their religion. President Phillips testified at their trial, pointing out that the elders were not professional ministers but rather college students called to serve two years in Greece at their own expense. They loved Greece and the Greek culture, and when they returned to America they would be unofficial ambassadors for Greece. They did no deceiving or pressuring. The judge's verdict was not guilty. President Phillips was pleased. Instead of missionaries incarcerated in jail for several months, the Church lawyer had a precedent-setting case in future legal entanglements.[73]

Another solution to these missionary difficulties occurred when Greece joined the European Union. A Union treaty stipulates that citizens of Union member states have privileges to enter and stay in other Union countries. To take advantage of this agreement, the Church began calling residents of other nations in the European Union—such as Britain, the Netherlands, and France—as missionaries to Greece.

In 1996 some 400 members of the Church resided in Greece. The Greece Athens Mission also supervised missionary work in Egypt and Lebanon and on the island nations of Cyprus and Malta.

Cyprus

Cyprus, located in the eastern Mediterranean about forty miles south of Turkey and sixty miles west of Syria and Lebanon, is an independent nation bitterly divided between Greek and Turkish ethnic groups. Seventy-eight percent of the population is Greek and 18 percent Turkish. For centuries these two groups fought each other for control of the island. In 1878 the Congress of Berlin placed Cyprus under British administration. After World War II the Greek Cypriot population continued its long-standing agitation for union with Greece, which the Turks opposed. Frequently violence broke out. In 1960 Cyprus became an independent republic. In 1974 a military coup led by advocates of Greek union prompted an invasion from Turkey. Since then the island has been partitioned between the Greek and Turkish groups with Turkey ruling the Turkish provinces.

The Nicosia Branch was organized in Cyprus in 1962 for member families in government service. Although the branch was temporarily dissolved twice, it was established to stay in the early 1980s. It became the nucleus for missionary work on the island, which began in 1991 under the supervision of the Greece Athens Mission. In September 1993, Elder Joseph B. Wirthlin of the Twelve dedicated the island from a beautiful hillside near the country's honored Monument of Freedom. In his prayer, Elder Wirthlin petitioned the Lord that the government of Cyprus would "continue to open its doors for our missionaries. . . . We are mindful at this hour of the many conflicts suffered over the years," Elder Wirthlin acknowledged in his prayer, "but we also know that the gospel of Jesus Christ can and will heal the wounds if the people follow the principles of the gospel." Elder Wirthlin noted the island's glorious history as the "crossroads of the early apostles," such as Paul, John, and Barnabas, and as a place of refuge for the persecuted Saints in the early Christian church.[74]

The progress of the Church in western and southern Europe has been more difficult than in other areas of the world. Yet the Church has spared no effort to build the kingdom in each of these countries. European Saints have had to sacrifice extraordinarily to embrace and live the gospel. Perhaps because of this, rather than in spite of it, the Church has developed a bulwark in Europe.

NOTES

1 Peter L. Morley, "The Church in England," in F. LaMond Tullis, ed., *Mormonism: A Faith for All Cultures* (Provo, Utah: Brigham Young University Press, 1978), 59–60.

2 "Member of the Church Elected to Parliament in England," *Church News*, 17 November 1990, 3–4.

3 Yana Ivanov, "The Church in England Post World War II," unpublished paper, Brigham Young University, 1 April 1992.

4 Adrian Gostick, "Kingdom by the Sea," *New Era* 22 (November 1992): 21.

5 Richard M. Romney, "Between Seasons: Growing at the MTC," *New Era* 22 (November 1992): 35.

6 Ibid., 32.

7 W. Steven Crook, "The Church amongst the Africans in London," unpublished paper, Brigham Young University, April 1993.

8 Darcie Lyon Smith, "The Church in Bonnie Scotland," unpublished paper, Brigham Young University, 7 March 1994; Mitchell L. Wasden, "The Church in Scotland," unpublished paper, Brigham Young University, 26 May 1994.

9 "The Church in Northern Europe," *Ensign* 24 (January 1994): 79.

10 Bryan J. Grant, "Ground Broken for Preston Temple," *Church News*, 18 June 1994, 3.

11 Anne A. Perry, "The Contemporary Church," in V. Ben Bloxham et al., eds., *Truth Will Prevail: The Rise of The Church of Jesus Christ of Latter-day Saints in the British Isles 1837–1987* (West Midlands: Corporation of the President of The Church of Jesus Christ of Latter-day Saints, 1987), 439.

12 Much of my information comes from Douglas L. Lamb, "The Church in Ireland," unpublished paper, Brigham Young University, April 1993.

13 Richard M. Romney, "Walls Come Tumbling Down," *New Era* 24 (June 1994): 28–33.

14 Perry, "Contemporary Church," 439; see also "Ireland Dedicated for Proselyting," *Ensign* 16 (February 1986): 76.

15 Giles H. Florence Jr., "Sea, Soil, and Souls in Denmark," *Ensign* 22 (February 1992): 48.

16 J Malan Heslop, "His Life 'Was At an End' Until Future Wife—and Gospel—Came Along," *Church News*, 1 June 1991, 5.

17 Florence, "Sea, Soil, and Souls in Denmark," 49.

18 Henrik Als, "Danish Basketball Star and Future Missionary Vows, 'Never on Sunday,'" *Church News*, 14 August 1993, 7.

19 LeAnn Moody, "Icelanders Commemorate Settling in Spanish Fork," *Herald* (Provo, Utah), 4 August 1989, A10; Kate B. Carter, *The First Icelandic Settlement in America* (Salt Lake City: Daughters of Utah Pioneers, 1964); Julie A. Dockstader, "Member Receives 'Highest Honor' from Iceland for Fostering Heritage," *Church News*, 14 August 1993, 5.

20 Todd Harris, "Gospel Touches Remote Iceland," *Church News*, 6 August 1994, 8.

21 Ibid., 8, 12.

22 Kimberly Jacobs Wagner, "Arne Bakken: Lifting with Love in Norway," *Ensign* 21 (July 1991): 51.

23 "Council Uses LDS Documentary," *Church News*, 25 November 1989, 7.

24 Renee C. Toro, "The Receptivity of the Norwegian People to the

Gospel," unpublished paper, Brigham Young University, 1 April 1992; Kara Schneck, "The LDS Church in Norway," unpublished paper, Brigham Young University, 31 March 1992.

25 John L. Hart, "Sweden: Members Mold Lives to Gospel Ideals, Look to Growth," *Church News*, 21 November 1987, 9.

26 "Look Out, Osmonds—Here Come the Herreys," *Church News*, 27 May 1984, 10.

27 "Saints Enjoying Blessings of Stockholm Temple," *Ensign* 15 (September 1985): 74–75.

28 Richard M. Romney, "Everlasting," *New Era* 21 (March 1991): 23–24.

29 Hart, "Sweden," 10.

30 Gerry Avant, "Royal Couple Visits at Swedish Temple with Pres. Monson," *Church News*, 2 Sept. 1995, 3–4.

31 Mike Cannon, "He Thawed Relations between Nations," *Church News*, 9 September 1989, 10; Kathleen Lubeck, "The Art of Family Life: Gregory J. Newell, United States Ambassador to Sweden," *Ensign* 17 (October 1987): 34–39.

32 Giles H. Florence Jr., "Suomi Finland: A Beacon in the Baltic," *Ensign* 21 (August 1991): 37–38.

33 Marja-Leena Kiviniemi, "Anna-Liisa Rinne: Finding Her Life through Service," *Tambuli* 11 (February 1987): 13–17.

34 "Finland," *Church News*, 3 October 1987, 8.

35 John L. Hart, "Pres. Benson Visits Finland," *Church News*, 23 May 1987, 3.

36 Florence, "Suomi Finland," 41.

37 Ruth Harris Swaner, "Julie Jacobs: Her Lamp Is Shining in Holland," *Tambuli* 11 (May 1987): 8–9.

38 J Malan Heslop, "New Knowledge Leads to New Life," *Church News*, 4 January 1992, 7.

39 Denise Thompson, "The LDS Church in France and Luxembourg," unpublished paper, Brigham Young University, 2 November 1993; Neil Hekking, "My Church Experience in Europe and Africa," unpublished paper, Brigham Young University, 18 October 1994; Roger Duce, "Report on Luxembourg," unpublished paper, Brigham Young University, 10 December 1994.

40 Gerry Avant, "Grand Tradition of France Has Impact on Church Growth," *Church News*, 22 August 1987, 7.

41 "Mediterranean Area: New Challenges and Growth," *Ensign* 22 (October 1992): 79.

42 LaRene Porter Gaunt, "A Blooming in France," *Ensign* 25 (March 1995): 41–42.

43 Ibid., 44.

44 Cécile Pelous, introduction by Michael J. Call to "Love in Abundance: The Disadvantaged Children of India and Nepal," in

Women and Christ: Living the Abundant Life, ed. Dawn Hall Anderson, Susette Fletcher Green, and Marie Cornwall (Salt Lake City: Deseret Book, 1993), 9–160.

45   John L. Hart, "Frankfurt Temple Dedicated," *Church News,* 5 September 1987, 4.

46   Sheridan R. Sheffield, "Gospel Brings Greater Self-Worth and the Strength to Conquer Challenges of Life," *Church News,* 22 February 1992, 6, 10.

47   "Elder Dieter F. Uchtdorf of the Seventy," *Ensign* 24 (May 1994): 109.

48   Sheffield, "Gospel Brings Greater Self-Worth and the Strength to Conquer Challenges of Life."

49   "Ward's a Miniature World Church," *Church News,* 11 July 1987, 10; Petrea Kelly, "Geneva—Unity & Diversity," *Tambuli,* November 1992, 42–48.

50   "Temple Open Houses Attract Thousands," *Church News,* 24 October 1992, 4.

51   Richard M. Romney, "A Close-knit Family," *New Era* 9 (January-February 1979): 27–29.

52   Don L. Searle, "Buon Giorno!" *Ensign* 19 (July 1989): 34.

53   Don L. Searle, "The Book Gave Them Answers," *Ensign* 23 (July 1993): 58–60.

54   Searle, "Buon Giorno!" 35.

55   "Missionaries Study Maltese," *Church News,* 17 November 1990, 7.

56   "Milestone Reached in Italy; Church Gains Legal Status," *Church News,* 12 June 1993, 4.

57   "Missionary Choir Sings in the Vatican," *Church News,* 15 January 1994, 7.

58   "Gospel Takes Wing in Canary Islands," *Church News,* 10 November 1990, 8–10; Gerry Avant and John L. Hart, "Many Are Still Blazing Gospel Trails," *Church News,* 24 July 1993, 7.

59   Lisa A. Johnson, "The Eternal Road Trip," *New Era* 23 (June 1993): 28–31.

60   Spencer W. Kimball, "When the World Will Be Converted," *Ensign* 4 (October 1974): 13.

61   Martin B. Hickman, *David Matthew Kennedy: Banker, Statesman, Churchman* (Salt Lake City: Deseret Book, 1987), 347–50; Nuno F. R. Battaglia, "The International Church: Portugal's Role," unpublished paper, Brigham Young University, 5 October 1990. Another Church member serving in Portugal as a diplomat was Ray E. Caldwell, who had accepted the post of first secretary of the Canadian embassy in Portugal. Elder Caldwell was set apart as group leader over members living in Portugal, which included some American military personnel. In the 1960s and early 1970s,

expatriate members had met in small groups or branches, though the Church was not officially recognized by Portugal.

62 Don L. Searle, "The Saints of Portugal," *Tambuli,* February 1988, 27.

63 Searle, "The Saints of Portugal," 34.

64 Mark L. Grover, "Migration, Social Change, and Mormonism in Portugal," *Journal of Mormon History* 21 (Spring 1995): 65–79.

65 Harold G. Hillam, "No More Strangers and Foreigners," *Ensign* 20 (November 1990): 25.

66 Battaglia, "The International Church: Portugal's Role," 14. Brother Battaglia was Elder Nelson's translator for this address.

67 See, for example, Don L. Searle, "Artur Carvalho: Father, Bishop, Judge," *Tambuli,* October 1988, 32–34; Don L. Searle, "Brotherly Love," *Tambuli,* May 1990, 34–37.

68 "Portugal Visit a First," *Church News,* 29 December 1990, 7.

69 Mark Crane, "A Promised Land," unpublished paper, Brigham Young University, 7 March 1994.

70 "Republic of Cape Verde Dedicated by Apostle," *Church News,* 24 September 1994, 3, 5.

71 *1995–96 Church Almanac* (Salt Lake City: Deseret News, 1994), 237.

72 LeGrande W. Smith, "Trial & Triumph in Thessaloniki: The Challenge of Opening Greece for the Preaching of the Gospel," *Latter-day Digest* 3 (July 1994): 23.

73 Ibid., 29–33.

74 "Elder Wirthlin Dedicates the Island of Cyprus for Preaching of Gospel," *Church News,* 27 November 1993, 3; "Cyprus Dedicated for Preaching of Gospel," *Ensign* 24 (February 1994): 74–75.

CHAPTER 11

Central and Eastern Europe

1986   **ELDER RUSSELL M. NELSON BEGINS VISITING EASTERN EUROPEAN NATIONS**

1987   **MIKHAIL GORBACHEV IMPLEMENTS *GLASNOST* IN SOVIET UNION; AUSTRIA VIENNA EAST MISSION IS CREATED TO DIRECT CHURCH WORK IN EASTERN EUROPE**

FALL 1989   **REVOLUTION BEGINS IN EASTERN EUROPE, INCLUDING THE VELVET REVOLUTION IN CZECHOSLOVAKIA AND THE FALL OF THE BERLIN WALL**

1990   **GERMANY IS REUNITED; MISSIONS ARE OPENED IN POLAND, HUNGARY, AND CZECHOSLOVAKIA; MISSIONARY WORK STARTS IN RUSSIA**

1991   **MISSION IS OPENED IN BULGARIA; RUSSIA OFFICIALLY RECOGNIZES LDS CHURCH; SOVIET UNION IS DISSOLVED INTO A COMMONWEALTH**

1992   **FIRST MISSIONS IN RUSSIA AND A MISSION IN UKRAINE ARE OPENED**

1993   **MISSIONS ARE OPENED IN ROMANIA AND THE BALTIC STATES**

 s anything too hard for the Lord?" asked President Spencer W. Kimball in 1974. "The Lord can do anything he sets his mind to do," President Kimball affirmed as he prophesied the eventual end of the Iron Curtain that had long blocked Church representatives from preaching the gospel in Communist-dominated lands.[1] Now, the Iron Curtain has indeed fallen, and millions of our Heavenly Father's children have heard the gospel in their own tongue.

"During a brief period of weeks, we have witnessed some phenomenal changes in the world, particularly in the Eastern Bloc countries, changes which God-fearing men attribute to the hand of the Almighty in bringing about His glorious purposes to fill the earth with the knowledge of the Lord," declared Elder David B. Haight of the Quorum of the Twelve in 1990. "Walls have come down, gates have opened, and millions of voices have chorused the song of freedom! We rejoice in the dawning of a brighter day."[2]

By 1996 the restored Church had taken firm root in central and eastern Europe. Eight missions were in the former Soviet Union and fifteen in what was formerly the Soviet bloc. In 1990 as the eastern European revolutions were gaining strength, the Church had approximately 350 members (not counting those in East Germany) among a population in eastern Europe of about 350 million. By 1996 Church membership in central and eastern Europe had surpassed 19,000 and was rising rapidly.

Country	Estimated Church 1996 Membership	Approximate 1996 population
Czech Republic	1,300	10,700,000
Slovakia	100	5,400,000
Hungary	2,700	10,500,000
Poland	1,000	38,700,000
Romania	800	23,300,000
Bulgaria	1,000	8,800,000
Albania	400	3,400,000
Russia	5,000	149,800,000
Ukraine	4,000	52,000,000
Armenia	300	3,600,000
Belarus	300	10,500,000
Estonia	700	1,600,000
Latvia	400	2,800,000
Lithuania	400	3,900,000
Slovenia	200	1,900,000
Croatia	300	4,700,000
Serbia	200	9,400,000
Others		20,000,000
Europe East Area Total	19,100	361,000,000

History, Geography, and Politics

Central and eastern Europe after the ending of Communist domination included the nations of Poland; Hungary; the Czech Republic; Slovakia; Romania; Bulgaria; Albania; the Yugoslavian republics of Slovenia, Serbia, Croatia, Bosnia-Herzegovina, Montenegro, and Macedonia (only Serbia and Montenegro have remained united as the country of Yugoslavia); and the former Soviet Union republics of Russia, Ukraine, Belarus, Moldova, Lithuania, Estonia, and Latvia. Two other former Soviet republics—Armenia and Georgia—have largely Christian European populations but are in the Asian continent.

The revolution would not have happened without the rise to power of Mikhail Gorbachev in the Soviet Union in 1985. In 1987 President Gorbachev introduced *glasnost* (openness and political change), *perestroika* (economic restructuring and reform), and gradual democratization that led to wholesale changes in Soviet society. Another factor at work was the economic bankruptcy of the Communist system, which forced the USSR and its allies to reduce military spending. Gorbachev's ideas also greatly influenced eastern European nations, notably Hungary and Poland, who wanted to modernize their economies and impose fewer restrictions upon their citizens. Poland held democratic elections in early 1989, and the Solidarity trade union won a majority of seats in Parliament. Hungary decided in the summer of that year to eliminate the Iron Curtain border with Austria. Thousands of East Germans, learning of the breach, made the long, roundabout journey to Hungary and then through Austria to reach West Germany. Gorbachev did nothing to stop these developments; indeed, he even seemed to encourage them.

In the early fall of 1989, groups in central and eastern European nations, including the Baltic republics within the Soviet Union, began demonstrating on public streets. By late fall the demonstrations had reached such intensity that only one of two possibilities existed: send tanks and air power to crush the separate rebellions or allow the Communist regimes in the satellite states to topple. Gorbachev decided against sending in tanks. One by one the Soviet-dominated governments fell peacefully, except in Romania, where outraged citizens violently deposed the brutal dictator Nicolae Ceausescu. The most symbolic day of the revolution was the breaching of the notorious Berlin Wall on 9 November 1989. The revolution continued through 1990 and 1991. A single Germany once again came into being on 3 October 1990. Democratic governments were established in Poland, Czechoslovakia, Hungary, Bulgaria, and partially in Romania and Albania.

In the summer of 1991, civil war began in Yugoslavia, composed of six republics and numerous disparate ethnic groups, between the republics of Serbia and Croatia. By the end of that year, the European Community had recognized the republics of Slovenia and Croatia. In the spring of 1992 the United States also officially recognized Slovenia and Croatia as well as Bosnia-Herzegovina. United Nations forces attempted to limit fighting in the former Yugoslav republics, yet the fighting escalated, particularly in Bosnia, where neither Serbs nor Croats wanted to give up autonomy within parts of Bosnia. As the war escalated, all three fighting parties—the Bosnian Muslims, the Bosnian Croats, and the Bosnian Serbs—committed atrocities against one another. More than 250,000 were killed in the war. The situation deteriorated, even though the European Union, the United Nations, NATO, and a group representing the United States, Britain, Germany, France, and Russia strived to bring about peace. NATO air strikes in 1995 brought warring parties to the peace table. In 1996 some 60,000 NATO troops began supervising implementation of the peace accord.

In contrast to Yugoslavia, the consequences of revolution in Czechoslovakia were much more peaceful. The Czechs and the Slovaks had come together in a post–World War I coalition in 1919. Both were Slavic peoples, but the union had never been entirely comfortable. The Czechs in the west outnumbered the Slovaks in the east two to one and developed a more industrial society. In 1992 Slovak nationalists won parliamentary elections in the east and led their countrymen to split off peacefully. The Czech Republic and Slovakia became two separate nations on 1 January 1993.

As for the largest and most powerful of the eastern European states, the Soviet Union, President Gorbachev continued to implement gradual economic reforms. The Soviet leadership declared new religious freedoms and inched toward a free market economy and a democratic government. In August 1991, hardline Communist leaders from the military and the secret police (KGB) failed to depose Gorbachev but weakened his political power. The Baltic republics—Lithuania, Latvia, and Estonia—obtained complete independence in September. Russian Federation president Boris Yeltsin replaced Gorbachev as the most popular and powerful government leader, although Gorbachev still served as president of the Soviet Union. In December most republics withdrew from the Soviet Union and, under Yeltsin's direction, created the new Commonwealth of Independent States (CIS). On Christmas Day, Gorbachev resigned as Soviet president: the Union of Soviet Socialist Republics no longer existed. Thereafter chaos and often anarchy reigned throughout most of the new states in the CIS.

President Yeltsin's plans for the Russian Federation were that Russia would rid itself gradually of its nuclear armaments and ally itself with the United States and other western nations. In 1993 Yeltsin's government and economic reforms were opposed by the Communists in the legislature, elected before the revolution. In September Yeltsin dissolved the parliament and called for new elections. A bloody standoff followed from which Yeltsin, supported by the military, eventually emerged victorious. A new constitution and a new parliament were established in December elections. Yet various infighting persisted within the Russian Federation and the other countries of the CIS. The 1995 civil war between Russia and the Muslim province of Chechnya is a case in point. Russia certainly lacked the political stability many citizens longed for, crime became rampant, and many unscrupulous foreigners and the so-called Russian Mafia plundered the country's economic resources. Important presidential elections were scheduled for June 1996.

New Beginnings

The revolutions that began in 1989 opened new doors to The Church of Jesus Christ of Latter-day Saints. Before that time in Communist Europe, the Church's largest concentration of members was in East Germany—almost 3,500, whose roots dated to before World War II. In Czechoslovakia fewer than 200 members had been converted in the decade prior to World War II and just after it.

Starting in 1986, even before the revolutions began, the First Presidency and the Quorum of the Twelve Apostles made preliminary contacts with government leaders in central and eastern Europe to gain legal entry into the various Communist countries. The Church's International Agency in Washington, D.C., greatly assisted their efforts. In 1987 Church leaders created the Austria Vienna East Mission to coordinate all member and missionary contacts with the Eastern Bloc.

Church leaders operated on the basis of scripture: "The Twelve . . . officiate in the name of the Lord, under the direction of the Presidency of the Church . . . to build up the church, and regulate all the affairs of the same in all nations. . . . The [Twelve] . . . call upon the Seventy, when they need assistance, to fill the several calls for preaching and administering the gospel" (D&C 107:33, 38). Before, during, and after the revolutions, Elder Russell M. Nelson of the Twelve and Elder Hans B. Ringger of the Seventy (with the aid of Church legal counsel David Farnsworth from Frankfurt) visited country after country to build relationships and gain legal recognition. "Establish the Church, not just baptize," and "Enter through the front door" were two principles that guided their actions in each nation.[3]

Elder Ringger was retained as Europe Area president for twice the usual term of three years (from 1987 to 1993) to maintain continuity in establishing favorable relationships. He explained that he and his associates felt like pioneers in entering prospective new mission fields, or like Columbus in discovering a new world. They didn't know what to expect; they simply had to step in and discover what was there. Before missionaries entered a new area, the area presidency and a mission president would establish a branch boundary and then send in four to six missionaries with the challenge to build up a branch. At first, the area presidency sent missionaries only into cities, which gave them a wide field of choice. In the former Soviet Union, for example, there were thirty-one cities with a population of more than a million.[4]

Elder Dennis Neuenschwander replaced Elder Ringger as president of the Europe Area in 1993. Elder Neuenschwander, who could speak Russian, Finnish, and German, had considerable previous experience and important government contacts in the various eastern European countries. From 1977 to 1982 he had worked in Europe with genealogical microfilming. Then he was called in 1987 as president of the Austria Vienna East Mission to oversee potential eastern European mission fields. In 1991 he was called to the Seventy and assigned as a counselor to Elder Ringger. Upon his call as a general authority, Elder Neuenschwander assessed the eastern Europeans: "The greatest changes have been in the individual lives of the people. . . . Decades of atheism and repression of spiritual matters could not, did not destroy the people's desire to believe, the desire to do good, the desire to serve and be happy, to feel comfortable in one's family, all of the things the gospel represents.

As the missionaries brought that message into the lives of numerous people, they have responded and responded quickly. There is marvelous growth of the Church throughout eastern Europe. Attendance is high all over."[5]

After the revolutions, the visibility of the Church in eastern Europe was enhanced by the visits of performing groups from Brigham Young University; the assistance of numerous Latter-day Saint expatriate businessmen, diplomats, and educators; and the efforts of volunteer physicians and educators serving as short- or long-term Church humanitarian services missionaries.

Latter-day Saint doctrines and practices that especially appealed to eastern Europeans included new scripture that witnessed of Jesus Christ, the existence of a living prophet, the importance of the family unit, using an eternal perspective to solve personal and national problems, and the quest to live an honest and moral life.[6]

Former Czechoslovakia

Beginning in 1986, Elder Russell M. Nelson of the Twelve and Elder Hans B. Ringger of the Seventy met yearly with government officials in Prague, Czechoslovakia. They always emphasized the continued presence of Latter-day Saints in the country since 1929. "Your request for recognition is still being studied," was the standard answer these brethren received from Communist officials. At one meeting, the chairman of the Council of Religious affairs added that only a Czechoslovakian Church member could make formal application for recognition. "So we went to the home of Brother [Jiři] and Sister [Olga] Šnederfler [the district president and his wife]," related Elder Nelson. "Knowing that other Czechoslovakian leaders and thinkers had been imprisoned or put to death for religious or dissident belief, we told Brother Šnederfler that we, as his Church leaders, could not and would not make that request of him. After contemplating only a brief moment, Brother Šnederfler humbly said, 'I will go! I will do it!' As he spoke, his wife, Olga, shed a tear. They embraced and said, 'We will do whatever is needed. This is for the Lord, and His work is more important than our freedom or life.'"[7]

A few months later, Brother Šnederfler submitted papers applying for recognition of the Church. The secret police subjected him and other Saints to strict surveillance. Although recognition was still not granted, through fasting and prayer, no harm came to Brother Šnederfler.

Then in November 1989, Czechoslovakia's nonviolent Velvet Revolution occurred: millions of citizens took to the streets in Prague and other cities demanding democracy and freedom. Similar demonstrations were taking place throughout all of central and eastern Europe. Well-known patriot Vaclav Havel, a playwright imprisoned by the Communists in February, became head of state by December.

In February 1990, Elder Nelson, Elder Ringger, and Brother Šnederfler visited democratic government officials in Prague to discuss President Šnederfler's application for recognition of the Church submitted two years before. The new government quickly granted recognition "not as a new church, but as a church that was established in the country over 60 years ago." Elder Nelson explained: "This means our members will be able to worship in full dignity as they once did. It means we will be able to buy and sell property. We will look for a place in which the Saints can meet. Missionaries will return again to Czechoslovakia."[8]

After his official meetings in Prague were concluded, Elder Nelson led a group of Czech Saints to Knezi Hora, the spot in the city where Elder John A. Widtsoe had offered a dedicatory prayer in 1929. After songs and testimonies, Elder Nelson offered a prayer of gratitude thanking God for the blessings of freedom and legal recognition that would again allow the gospel to reach the people of Czechoslovakia. Gád Vojkůvka, president of the Brno Branch, closed his testimony with this passage from the Book of Mormon: "I desire that this inequality should be no more in this land, especially among this my people; but I desire that this land be a land of liberty, and every man may enjoy his rights and privileges alike, so long as the Lord sees fit that we may live and inherit the land, yea, even as long as any of our posterity remains upon the face of the land" (Mosiah 29:32).[9] Ironically, the Saints in Prague, the beautiful city of a thousand spires, began to meet in the Kastan, a Communist museum filled with memorabilia of atheistic Communism, which had tried to erase religion from the Czech culture. Previously, anyone professing belief in God, for instance, had not been allowed to attend or teach at the universities.

Before the 1989 revolution, preparations for missionary work in Czechoslovakia had already begun. Two missionaries in Austria began learning Czech while they were teaching Czech people from refugee camps. A Czech convert, who was a member of a branch presidency in Wiener Neustadt, was paid to teach these two elders and four others previously serving in Portugal. Together these missionaries underwent intensive language training as they awaited permission to enter Czechoslovakia. On 2 May 1990 mission president Dennis Neuenschwander of the Austria Vienna East Mission drove them to their new fields. One elder wrote: "The members had fasted on the third Sunday of every month for the return of missionaries. It was a great honor to be the answer to someone's 40-year-old prayers."[10]

Concurrent with official recognition in Czechoslovakia on 1 March 1990 came the announcement in Salt Lake City that a new mission would open on 1 July. The biggest challenge the Church now faced was finding Czech language teachers to train missionaries soon enough to staff a mission. Miraculously, teachers were found. The first president of the new Czechoslovakia Prague Mission was Richard W. Winder, one of the young missionaries to Czechoslovakia in the postwar period forty years earlier. His wife, Barbara Winder, while serving as the Church's general Relief Society president, had visited Czechoslovakia. After the Prague mission opened, nine elders who had served in the Czechoslovak Mission between 1947 and 1950 returned with their wives as couple missionaries.

Success came immediately to the new mission. "We are attracting well-educated people," President Winder commented. "Students, teachers, scientists, people who read well are being taught by the missionaries. One missionary said, 'I can't believe how many people we are baptizing who have titles like doctor or who are engineers.'"[11] Another missionary reported: "In Brno, Elder Streetman and I found that the people were very open and receptive to the gospel message. On Mondays the Brno members would have *skola moudrosti* (school of wisdom) and . . . bring their friends to teach them about religious things. On my first visit to *skola moudrosti* there were about thirty people there, about fifteen members and fifteen of their friends." After the *skola* presentation, a member asked if anyone "would like to stay and hear the first discussion from the missionaries. No one left. . . . Nearly all fifteen of the investigators there that night were baptized in the next two months."[12]

The 1991 Tabernacle Choir visit to Prague prompted Czechoslovak Television to do a documentary. "Because we have no information about the Mormon Church in the Czech Republic," explained Czech news reporter Premysl Cech, "we want to show what Mormons are and what they do." Openly discussing values was a new freedom after the revolution and of great interest to the Czech people. "It's important to know the lifestyle of the Mormons," commented the reporter, "because money and property are not the most important things in life, but other things, such as values and manner of thinking." The documentary was broadcast to more than five million viewers in the Czech Republic and Slovakia in 1993.[13]

In September 1991, Jiři and Olga Šnederfler became president and matron, respectively, of the Freiberg Germany Temple. Their calling honored the courage and devotion of all central and eastern European Saints.

Early in 1992, before the division of Czechoslovakia into two separate nations, missionary work began in the eastern area that became Slovakia. In 1996 missionaries from the Czech Republic Prague Mission continued to serve in a few newly opened cities in Slovakia. Church population for both countries numbered about 1,400.

Hungary

After the official recognition of the Church in 1988, Hungary became one of the Church's most successful European mission fields.[14]

A new era for the gospel in Hungary had begun in 1984. That year Hungarian National Television sent a film crew to Utah to produce a series about the Church. This visit had been precipitated by the Mormon Tabernacle Choir's European tour, telecast in Hungary in 1982. The national television network broadcast its four-part series in November and December 1985. Surveys show that nearly every Hungarian adult viewed at least one program in the series. Soon the Church's missionary department began receiving requests from Hungarians for more information.

One letter followed a less direct route but in so doing answered the prayers of a Utah family, recounted historian Kahlile Mehr: "A Hungarian ear, nose, and throat surgeon, interested by the broadcast, pored through back issues of his professional journals to rediscover an article he assumed had been written by a Latter-day Saint. He wrote the author—Dr. R. Kim Davis of the University of Utah Medical School—asking for information about the Church. The letter was an unexpected but welcome answer to some specific prayers of the Davis family, who had desired to assist in missionary work. They forwarded the letter to the mission president with a picture of their family and their testimony. In February 1986, the mission president began teaching the Gedeon Kereszti family in Ajka, Hungary. That September, the family traveled to Vienna to be baptized."[15]

Later in 1986, a miracle took place. Francis A. Madsen, a bishop in the Washington, D.C., area and an assistant to a United States senator, had numerous contacts with the Hungarian embassy in the United States. Bishop Madsen successfully negotiated with the Hungarian envoys to arrange for their government to invite the Church to apply for possible recognition in Hungary. Two circumstances dovetailed to bring about this unique offer. First, the Communist government in Hungary, taking a more progressive stance toward democratization and economic reforms, decided to initiate friendly relations with groups in the United States. Second, the television special had made the Church a topic of national interest, so the "American" Church of Jesus Christ of Latter-day Saints was a natural choice.

Elder Russell M. Nelson, apostolic supervisor over Europe at the time, went to Budapest, Hungary, in April 1987. Accompanying him were Elder Ringger, Bishop Madsen, and the Hungarian national Miklos Radvanyi. Brother Radvanyi, who had escaped to Germany in the 1970s and there had joined the Church, translated for Elder Nelson. On Easter Sunday, Elder Nelson offered a dedicatory prayer for the Hungarian nation on Mount Gellert in a park in Budapest. "Two days later, Elder Ringger and I met with the chairman of the Council of Religious Affairs, Imre Miklos," explained Elder Nelson. "Our reception at first was a bit tense. It was clear that we were neither welcome nor wanted. Things were not going particularly well. But then I felt impressed to let this leader know that two days prior to this meeting, I had offered a special

Villa in Budapest, Hungary, dedicated in 1989 as a meetinghouse and district headquarters

apostolic prayer for his country and for its people. As this was mentioned, his countenance changed. Now he was listening. A meeting planned for thirty minutes lasted an hour and a half. From that point forward, he became our friend and advocate."[16]

The government desired that a few native Hungarians be Church members before granting official recognition, so negotiations continued quietly for another year. Meanwhile, six missionary representatives—two married couples and two young elders—were granted permission to enter the country on tourist visas. Four more Hungarians were baptized in 1987 and two in the first half of 1988, although the converts went to Vienna for their baptisms to avoid any possibility of offending Hungarian authorities.

In the spring of 1988, Elder Nelson again visited Budapest. This time he completed negotiations, and recognition of the Church was granted on 14 June. Part of the Church delegation were two Hungarian medical doctors serving in Hungary as district president and first counselor, respectively: Gedeon Kereszti and Peter Paul Varga. The presence of these two prestigious Hungarian citizens was a vital factor in the culmination of the negotiations. Elder Nelson related: "[The government

The Feher family—Terezia, Judit, Emese, Jozef, Rita, and Balazs—were early converts in Budapest, Hungary

representatives] are very, very high-minded, high-principled men. The reason that they have granted permission for the Church to function in Hungary is they are fully convinced that this will be a blessing for the people of the land they love."[17] The day after a national news conference featuring Elder Nelson, the first two baptisms were performed in Hungary. Later that evening, Elder Hans P. Ringger, Europe Area president, addressed a fireside attended by eighty-five people. The next day he conducted the first Budapest District conference, which was attended by fifty-seven.[18]

The year 1988 witnessed thirty-four baptisms in Hungary. Attendance at meetings in Budapest multiplied beyond the capacity of the rented apartment near the river, so Church officials purchased a stately villa in a forested area of Budapest. President Thomas S. Monson dedicated this building on 17 October 1989, the same month when peaceful revolution brought democracy to Hungary. President Monson noted: "The Hungarians are a handsome and intelligent people. They are anxious for a knowledge of the truth and they seem to be attracted by the message of the restoration and the plan of salvation particularly."[19]

Elder Russell M. Nelson of the Twelve and Elder Trevor Andreason, a missionary from Utah who spoke fluent Hungarian, were interviewed on Hungarian television after the dedicatory service. Elder Andreason, an immediate hit because of his ability to speak the language, enthralled the interviewer with his experiences. When Elder Nelson referred to his dedicatory prayer of two and a half years previous, in which he had besought the Lord for a better way of life for the Hungarian people, the hostess said, "Thank you! Things have been getting better ever since."[20]

The magnificent meetinghouse aided missionary efforts in Hungary under the direction of President Dennis B. Neuenschwander. The missionaries had their hands full in keeping up with a flood of referrals. By January 1991, approximately 300 baptisms had been performed in Hungary, three times the number performed before World War I. On 1 July 1990 the Church created the Hungary Budapest Mission.

Missionary work continued to prosper. Next to Portugal, Hungary witnessed more baptisms per missionary than any other European nation. Membership doubled from approximately 300 in January 1991 to 600 in January 1992 and then doubled again to 1200 by January 1993. New cities opened to missionaries. At first, a large share of the converts were young single adults, but the Church's emphasis on family solidarity and strong brotherhood and sisterhood resonated with deep-seated Hungarian values, and before long whole families started joining the Church. The two Budapest branches were divided into five in 1992 with emphasis on developing local leadership. By 1994 eighteen branches or groups were organized in fourteen Hungarian cities. In 1992 mission president James L. Wilde indicated that the Church was laboring to fulfill Elder Nelson's prophecy that wards and stakes would soon grace Hungary.[21] Since 1992 an emphasis has been placed on developing local leadership so that a stake can be organized.

The Tabernacle Choir again opened doors in Hungary, this time in person when the Choir visited Budapest as part of its 1991 tour. Before a packed audience at Budapest's Opera House, "Music and the Spoken Word" was broadcast live on 16 June. Hungarian national television rebroadcast several segments during prime time, which strengthened the positive impressions of the Church in Hungary.

Hungarian Saints began attending the Freiberg Germany Temple in 1991, embarking on two or three excursions each year. Seminaries and institutes of religion were begun in 1993, and in 1994 more than 250 students received their first-year certificates of completion. Church membership in Hungary was approximately 2,700 at the beginning of 1996.

Poland

The Poles have valiantly defended their right to exist as a nation and as a free people many, many times. It is no coincidence that the 1989 revolutions began in Poland, a land long noted for its courageous freedom fighters.

In 1986 President Thomas S. Monson, Elder Russell M. Nelson, and Elder Hans B. Ringger met with heads of Polish religious affairs in Warsaw. The brethren expressed two hopes: "for young missionaries to enter Poland, and for permission to buy or build a chapel. Both requests were granted!"[22] Both couples and young missionaries soon entered Poland from the Vienna Austria East Mission.

One retired couple, Juliusz and Dorothy Fussek, accepted a call to Poland for two years with an assignment to help prepare for a future mission in Poland. Juliusz, born in Poland, knew the language, but Dorothy did not. Trusting in the Lord, they undertook their lonely task of finding existing members and teaching some referrals in Warsaw. The two years stretched to five, and their efforts bore rich fruit.

Early in 1989, the Solidarity Union, spearheaded by the charismatic Lech Walesa, demanded and received free elections in Poland. With the victory of the Solidarity party in the parliamentary elections, the revolution was underway. On 16 May, the new government passed a law guaranteeing freedom of conscience and belief in Poland. Eventually Walesa became the elected president of Poland.

This religious freedom law prompted a second visit to Warsaw from President Thomas S. Monson and Elder Russell M. Nelson. The Brethren took with them Elder Fussek to meet with government officials about recognition for the Church. President Monson reported: "[We] met with Minister Adam Wopatka of the Polish government and heard him say, 'Your church is welcome here. You may build your buildings, you may send your missionaries. You are welcome in Poland. This man,' pointing to Juliusz Fussek, 'has served your church well. You can be grateful for his example and his work.'"[23]

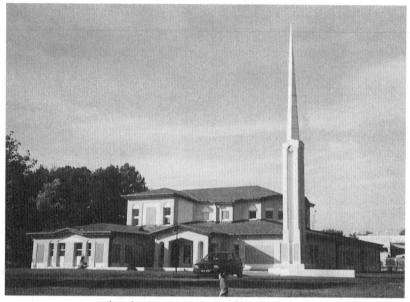

Chapel in Warsaw, Poland, dedicated in 1991

On 15 June 1989, Elder Nelson conducted the ground-breaking ceremony in Warsaw for the first Latter-day Saint meetinghouse in Poland. More than two hundred people attended, including an unusual mix of church and civic officials: several religious affairs ministers; Andrzej Ostrowski, mayor of Warsaw's Wola District; Elder Hans Ringger of the Europe Area presidency; Dennis Neuenschwander, president of the Austria Vienna East Mission; Juliusz Fussek, Latter-day Saint Warsaw presiding elder; and Cieslaw Mazur, branch president. Only three missionary couples and four young elders were serving in Poland at that time.

Conversions came quickly following the declaration of religious liberty in Poland. By the end of 1989, there were more than 100 members, and by the time Poland obtained its own mission on 1 July 1990, the number had doubled. The beautiful, large, Warsaw chapel was dedicated 22 June 1991, and the growth of the Church progressed at a steady pace, reaching 600 by mid 1994. The missionary force increased from sixteen to nearly one hundred during the first three years of the mission's existence. Since 1990 more than a score of Poles have been called on missions to other countries—mainly to the United States, England, and Russia.

The main obstacle converts faced when joining the Church in Poland was the same as in many other nations—social pressure from family and friends to stay with the Catholic Church, despite the LDS Church being viewed favorably by the Polish people. In Poland, as elsewhere, positive exposure came with the 1991 visit of the Tabernacle Choir and the many newspaper articles covering the event.

Though the Church was growing in Poland, the country's economy still struggled. Responding to dire needs, Church Welfare Service workers arrived to serve in a nondenominational consulting company that was helping Poland modernize their agriculture.[24] Early in 1991, the Church's general Relief Society organization donated huge quantities of clothing, quilts, and blankets to Poland. Later in the year, Andrezej Kozakiewicz, assistant to President Lech Walesa, wrote to the Relief Society in Salt Lake City, expressing "heartfelt gratitude" for the generosity of the women's organization. He noted that this effort "scored a 'home run' in supplying much-needed health-care assistance to our people."[25]

Romania

Romania was the only eastern European nation to undergo a bloody revolution in late 1989. An ugly dictatorship had oppressed the citizenry and done nothing to alleviate poverty and its associated health and social problems, which included tens of thousands of young orphans. The dictator, Nicolae Ceausescu, refused to step down and ordered security guards to fire on demonstrators; hundreds were buried in mass graves. Fighting broke out, and irate citizens succeeded in overthrowing the oppressive government.

In February 1990, Elder Russell M. Nelson, Elder Hans B. Ringger, legal counsel David Farnsworth, and temporal affairs director Peter Berkhan visited Romania and spoke with the new Minister of Justice, Teofil Pop. He informed them that religious freedom now existed in Romania. After some discussion, the Church authorities offered massive welfare services to assist the Romanian people. Then the brethren walked to Cismigiu Park where, standing on a small hill, Elder Nelson dedicated Romania for the preaching of the gospel. While traveling through the city in an official vehicle, Brother Berkhan heard the driver say, "Today I have seen an Apostle of Jesus Christ. He has blessed

Romania and now I know the country is saved."[26] Church officials quickly arranged for truckloads of relief supplies donated by European Saints to be sent to the stricken land. "In this humanitarian effort, compassion has known no national boundaries," said Peter Berkhan, the Europe Area temporal affairs director. "Our project was targeted on helping orphans and other children in child-care institutions."[27]

In late February, the first group of European Latter-day Saint physicians arrived in Bucharest, Romania. Meanwhile the Church's humanitarian services department, at the invitation of the Romanian government, called four married couples from the United States as humanitarian missionaries—the first such calling in Church history. They were to provide medical, dental, and social help for the nation's tragically deprived orphaned and handicapped children. These four couples arrived in September 1990 under the auspices of the Austria Vienna East Mission. In addition to health care, the missionary couples also established such successful programs as Special Olympics and art education. Other missionary couples who followed later helped establish much-needed adult programs, such as Alcoholics Anonymous. The Latter-day Saint humanitarian missionaries were only one of nearly two hundred different programs in Romania, most of which were much larger and more extensively funded. Yet local observers gratefully acknowledged the impressive work of the Church members, particularly in terms of long-range benefits.[28]

The first four missionary elders to Romania arrived in December 1990, three from the Italy Padua Mission (Romanian is similar to the Italian language) and one originally assigned to Yugoslavia. Together the couple missionaries and the young elders began proselyting. A much-needed boost to their efforts came from more than one hundred American Latter-day Saint couples who adopted Romanian orphans and shared the gospel in the process with people they came in contact with. A goodly number of the first thirty converts came from this source.[29]

Dr. Glenn K. Lund and his wife, Anne, from Bountiful, Utah, were among the original humanitarian missionaries to Romania. While they were in Bucharest, a local nurse, Constanta Hatu-Tieru, asked Dr. Lund if something could be done to correct her young son's orthopedic problem. Dr. Lund promised to look into the problem when he returned to

Utah. Once home, he arranged for surgery on the young boy's ankle to be performed at Primary Children's Medical Center in Salt Lake City. The son, Dragos, then eleven, traveled alone to Utah, lived with the Lund family, and was operated on by an orthopedic surgeon free of charge. During Dragos's three-month visit to America, he lived the Latter-day Saint lifestyle and learned some of the doctrines, especially in his Blazer B Primary class taught by Brother Lund. When Dragos visited Temple Square, he wrote in the guest book, "I want to be a Mormon." The Lunds suggested that he look up the Church back home in Bucharest. In Bucharest, the missionaries taught Dragos's family of four, and all of them joined the Church. His father, Ioan, became a member of the Bucharest First Branch presidency, his mother was a leader in the Relief Society and Young Women in the infant Church in Romania, and Dragos translated for English-speaking Church leaders visiting Bucharest.[30]

Another early convert was Octavian Vasilescu, a mechanical engineer, who first met Latter-day Saints when a family visiting Romania from California inquired about American church meetings in Bucharest. He had never heard of Mormons or Mormon pioneers, but later he realized he was a pioneer himself: "I am a pioneer in a way because I am one of the first members of the Church in my country. I have to be an example for the others, teach others about the Church and the gospel." Three months after his baptism in March 1991, he was called as the first branch president in his country. In July 1993, Brother Vasilescu and his family visited Utah to receive their sealing ordinances in the Salt Lake Temple.[31]

In 1992 Romanian missionary efforts were placed under the direction of the Hungary Budapest Mission. In December of that year, Romania recognized the Church as the "Liahona Association" and granted it freedom to buy and sell property. The Church planned to gain official recognition once it had a larger membership in Romania.

In 1993 the Romania Bucharest Mission came into being with four branches and 250 members of less than two years Church experience. "Most of the branches have at least a Relief Society and a Young Women organization and priesthood groups," reported James L. Wilde, who had presided from Hungary over the Romanian Saints. He indicated that by early 1993 two native Romanians had been called on full-time missions.[32] By the beginning of 1996, the Church had grown to 800 members in that country.

Bulgaria

Bulgaria, like other Eastern Bloc Communist countries, insisted on complete fealty to the state and its leaders. Atheism was common, although some few people, mostly the elderly, clung to their Bulgarian Orthodox Church traditions. Julia Kiriakov Caswell, a Bulgarian who with her family joined the LDS Church in France, related an experience she had in kindergarten in 1953. Her teacher asked if any of them believed in God. Several raised their hands. The teacher then proposed that the children pray for God to give them each a pile of candy in their right hand. "If God listens to your prayer, He really exists; if He doesn't, there is no God." She ordered the children onto their knees to begin praying. After a few minutes, the teacher exulted: "You see, nothing happened. He is not as powerful as our leader and god, Stalin." The teacher then told the students to kneel again and pray to Stalin for candy, something in short supply in Bulgaria. The school guard silently stole into the room and gave each child candy. "You see," the teacher declared triumphantly, "our god is Stalin. If you need something, pray to him."[33]

The Church of Jesus Christ of Latter-day Saints had to wait for the 1989–90 revolution in Bulgaria before the gospel could be preached in this Communist-held land. In preparation for that time, two Church members with Bulgarian roots had translated the scriptures into Bulgarian. In 1936 Sister Coy in Vermont translated the Book of Mormon, the Doctrine and Covenants, and the Pearl of Great Price; in 1973 Julia Caswell improved and corrected the original translation. These volumes were already on computer when the revolution of 1989 occurred.[34]

The year before the revolution, in 1988, Elders Russell M. Nelson and Hans B. Ringger had visited the head of religious affairs in Sofia, Bulgaria, but with no visible results. They returned to Sofia to meet with government leaders after the 1989–90 revolution in Bulgaria. Elders Nelson and Ringger were aided by Baird King, a returned missionary working in the United States embassy. "The director of the International

Foundation in Bulgaria asked if we could help provide teachers of English," reported Elder Nelson. "We assured him that we could. Capable teachers were called and sent to fulfill that request." Before the two brethren left Bulgaria, they visited the Park Na Svobodata, which means "Park of Liberty," where Elder Nelson dedicated the nation for the preaching of the gospel.[36]

The implementation of the assistance promised by Elder Nelson to the Bulgarian authorities fell to President Dennis Neuenschwander of the Austria Vienna East Mission. This was most appropriate because President Neuenschwander had visited Bulgaria numerous times beginning in 1976 in connection with his work with the Church Genealogical Department.

Two married couples and two sister missionaries were sent to teach English at the Bulgarian National School of Language in Sofia and Smolyan. Their first assignment was to prepare students for college-level tests in English. The *Church News* reported a school director's comments to President Dennis Neuenschwander: "The example to the school by the sister missionaries was such that the 'moral level of our students, faculty and whole town has measurably increased since your sisters arrived.'" Other English-teaching missionaries to Bulgaria followed, and they were warmly received.[37]

Missionaries transferred from German-speaking missions started teaching German to Bulgarian students in early 1990. Other missionaries were sent from Yugoslavia. Their Serbo-Croatian language was similar enough to Bulgarian to overcome the language barrier. Gradually the missionaries introduced gospel concepts into their language lessons. Some students asked for more information and began receiving missionary lessons and attending Sabbath services. The first baptismal services took place in November 1990. A high proportion of the first converts were college-age students from the classes.

One of the first converts who was not a language student was a woman whose granddaughter had joined the Church in Italy. She visited LDS church services to find out for herself what her granddaughter had become involved with. She too was baptized and became one of the first Relief Society teachers in Bulgaria and a translator of lesson materials into her native language.

In June 1991, the Brigham Young University Lamanite Generation performed in Bulgaria and received a great deal of favorable comment and interest. The Bulgarian government granted official recognition to the Church on 10 July 1991, ten days after the Bulgaria Sofia Mission, the 268th in the Church, was created. A faithful expatriate Bulgarian, Kiril Peter Kiriakov, who had joined the Church in France with his family (including his daughter, Julia, mentioned above), was called as the first mission president.

Beginning in 1992, Church humanitarian services sent ophthalmologists and audiologists (eye and ear experts) into Bulgaria on short-term missions to train local doctors and nurses. Humanitarian services also donated intraocular lenses, textbooks for school and civic libraries, Braille typewriters, microfilm machines, and clothing and blankets to orphanages. After visiting these humanitarian projects in Sofia, Elder M. Russell Ballard of the Twelve praised the work. "The increased efforts to be involved in worldwide Christian service has blessed thousands of our Heavenly Father's children," he remarked. "It's a wonderful thing, and surely the Lord must be pleased that His Church is involved in this kind of humanitarian service."[38]

"There are tremendous changes going on in the lives of people," said President Neuenschwander. "Many people don't have Bibles or religious literature. This creates a tremendous curiosity about religious matters." He also stated that Bulgarian government ministers were pleased to have an organization come to their country that represented honesty, morality, and integrity.[39]

Most Bulgarians thought the tenets of The Church of Jesus Christ of Latter-day Saints were extreme, especially the Word of Wisdom. Much of their social life and many of their family traditions involved drinking. Children picked up the habit of smoking at an early age while helping their families on the extensive Bulgarian tobacco farms.[40] But the gospel, once accepted, brings a great deal of hope. "The emptiness of materialism has created tremendous problems in Bulgaria, as it has in many parts of Europe," observed President Neuenschwander. "People are really without a moral and ethical basis to their lives. . . . Now, everyone struggles to reverse that [emptiness], to return to their lives the principles of human dignity and purity, self-respect, and respect for other people."[41]

By 1996 there were more than 1,000 Church members in Bulgaria, and more than ten branches were spread throughout the country.

Albania

Albania, the most backward and impoverished of all European nations, has sometimes been called "the India of Europe." Seventy percent of its population nominally Muslim. In actuality, the country has been highly atheistic, more so than the rest of eastern Europe. Christian denominations were welcomed after revolution finally hit the country in 1991. Massive changes awaited that society, which had been isolated from western civilization for more than forty years.

In April 1991, Elder Dallin H. Oaks, who replaced Elder Russell M. Nelson as the apostle assigned to Europe, visited Tirana, Albania's capital, and negotiated to send Church representatives into that nation. Charone Hellberg Smith, a registered nurse, and her husband, Thales H. Smith, a pediatrician, were two of the first Latter-day Saint humanitarian missionaries sent to Albania. When they arrived in 1992, Charone related, "conditions at the antiquated Russian-built hospital were horrendous. Windows were missing, and it was bitter cold. We found rooms of children swaddled like infants, even the ones who were two or older. Some could not sit or even hold up their heads. All the children avoided eye contact, and I did not see one smile. Everything was gray—the faces, the clothes, the walls. We were overcome but didn't realize we were crying until the doctors showing us around said, 'Please, don't cry.'"[42]

Humanitarian service missionaries provided skills and supplies that were greatly needed. One couple, George and Nancy Niedans, worked as agricultural missionaries. In 1992 the Church sent a huge shipment of medical and hospital equipment. But besides these physical needs, the people needed the hope and comfort the gospel brings. Charone Smith remembered, "We tried to teach many things by example, and I did learn some Albanian so I could communicate. . . . Some of the staff responded to what I taught them; many did not. I was surrounded by apathy and exhaustion. The Albanian women . . . rose very early to get water for their cooking and washing at home; by the time they got to the hospital, they were already tired. One nurse said, 'I know you're disappointed that we don't do more of what you've taught us, but we're so tired.' Some of that exhaustion is depression. They see no way out of their circumstances."[43] Missionary work began later that year, bringing the good news of the gospel to all who would listen.

Missionaries in Albania served at first under the direction of the president of the Austria Vienna Mission. In April 1993, at the national memorial called The Monument of the Heroes, Elder Oaks dedicated Albania for the preaching of the gospel. He prayed that the land would produce in abundance and that Albanian industry would flourish.[44]

During their first year in Albania, the missionaries learned the language through intensive local training. Once they could communicate, they made contacts and baptisms came quickly. After that the elders did not have to find people to teach—the converts brought investigators to them. In the first year, about 100 Albanians joined the Church. By 1996 nearly 400 members were on the rolls.

Beginning in the spring of 1994, missionaries, including the first sister missionaries to Albania, went through Albanian language training at the Missionary Training Center in Provo, Utah. By that time, Albania had produced three full-time missionaries, who served in the United States and helped to translate the Book of Mormon into their native tongue.[45]

Several thousand tons of food packages were prepared in December 1994 by Church welfare services to send to needy families in Albania in time for Christmas.[46] Humanitarian projects of this kind are an indication of the Church's concern for all peoples of the world, and they build the kingdom of God in modern times.

In March 1996, a separate Albanian mission was announced: the Albania Tirana Mission would begin functioning in July 1996.

Beginnings in the Soviet Union

The Soviet Union, one of the two world superpowers during the Cold War, the world's largest nation in area, and the third most populated country in the world, naturally intrigued Latter-day Saints. The Church certainly could not obey the Lord's instructions, "Go ye into all the world, and preach the gospel" (Mark 16:15), until it had penetrated deep into Russia and the other fourteen republics of the former Soviet Union. With the dramatic changes brought about by the 1989 revolutions

Elders Bill McKane and David Reagan, two of the first
missionaries in the modern era to labor in Leningrad

in eastern Europe, hopes arose among Latter-day Saints that the Soviet
Union, too, would accept Church representatives into its vast and populous land.

The Church had long had a translation of the Book of Mormon in the
Russian language. Russian native Andre K. Anastasiou, who had fled to
England during World War I and joined the Church in 1917, had been
assigned this task in 1925 by European Mission president James E.
Talmage. During World War II, Brother Anastasiou served as the acting
British Mission president.

Having learned from the mistakes of the early nineteenth century
and the successes of the 1980s in eastern Europe, Church leaders took a
cautious approach in the Soviet Union. First, as in all other areas of the
world, every action had to be totally above board and within existing
laws. Second, they would go slowly but surely in sending in missionaries
and establishing new branches.

During the mid to late 1980s, a few Soviet citizens became
acquainted with the gospel while visiting other countries or through contacts with United States embassy personnel in Moscow.[47] Then in 1989,
Soviet citizens were allowed to visit Finland and countries in the Eastern

Members of the Leningrad Branch outside their meeting place in June 1990

Bloc. That allowed possible contact with the Church. For instance, the man who eventually became the first president of the Leningrad Branch and his wife found the Church and were baptized on 1 July while in Budapest, Hungary. Missionaries from the Finland Helsinki Mission, noting the receptivity of visiting Russians, began a Russian-speaking proselyting effort at the railway stations. A few Russians were baptized in 1989 after they crossed over the border into Finland.

That same year, Elder Nelson of the Twelve and Elder Ringger of the Seventy made initial visits with Soviet authorities to explain what the Church would eventually like to do in the Soviet Union. The country began to open when Finnish Mission president Steven R. Mecham obtained permission to send missionaries to Tallinn in Estonia and to Leningrad and Vyborg, Russian cities near the Finnish border, in December 1989 and January 1990. Missionaries could only enter the country with expensive tourist visas and had to live in hotels. The first missionaries to labor in Leningrad arrived in December 1989. They held sacrament meeting in their rooms, performed baptisms in a hotel bath house, and discovered that their phone conversations were monitored by the KGB. But they experienced immediate success and became legends to their converts.

In July 1990, the Finland Helsinki East Mission was organized to handle all Russian programs. Gary L. Browning, a professor of Russian at Brigham Young University, was called as president. The Leningrad Branch by then had approximately 100 members, the Tallinn Branch 50, and the Vyborg Branch 25. The sixteen missionaries in the mission focused their entire attention on Russia and welcomed the help of the arriving missionaries trained in the Russian and Estonian languages. President Browning also called experienced Finnish brothers and sisters to set up auxiliaries and teach the Russian Saints how to run a branch. This action freed the missionaries to concentrate on proselyting.

When President Browning first visited the Russian branches, he witnessed "treasured moments of spiritual refreshment and affirmation." Describing an experience in Vyborg, he recalled, "Before my sacrament meeting talk, six little girls, ranging from about three to nine years of age, sang, in Russian, 'I Am a Child of God.' The singing was angelic, as were their radiant, broadly smiling faces. As I watched and listened in awe, my heart filled with 'hosannas' for the blessing of this long-awaited day."[48]

Meanwhile, the Church's standing in the eyes of Soviet officials was growing. Numerous Soviet military and science officers had visited Temple Square and met Church leaders while in Utah on government business. The Church officially (and many Church members individually, including wealthy philanthropist Jon M. Huntsman) had contributed substantially to disaster relief efforts in the Armenian Republic. As the relationship between the United States and the Soviet Union gradually thawed, relationships warmed between the Church and Soviet officials. Elder Russell M. Nelson visited Leningrad in April 1990, met with the city's council for religious affairs, and offered a prayer of rededication at the summer garden beside the Neva River, where Elder Francis M. Lyman of the Twelve had first dedicated Russia for the preaching of the gospel in August 1903. Elder Nelson also dedicated Estonia that April.[49]

On 19 September 1990, Elder Ringger met in Moscow with Evgenii V. Chernetsov of the Russian Council on Religious Affairs. The council approved the Church's application to register the Leningrad Branch,

In this Leningrad park Elder Russell M. Nelson rededicated Russia for the preaching of the gospel

provided that at least twenty adult members were on record in the branch's political district. After the first branch was registered, other registrations became more routine.

In the fall of 1990, the Vienna Austria East Mission sent missionaries to Moscow and Kiev in the Republic of Ukraine. In Moscow the missionaries had an immediate pool of investigators who had been befriended by workers at the United States embassy, but in Kiev the elders had to start from scratch, except for a list of fifteen people who had visited Temple Square over the years. One of them was baptized.[50] The timing of the missionaries' arrival in Kiev was propitious: it coincided with that of Mikhail Gorbachev, who had come from Moscow to depose a disliked, hard-line Communist leader. Anticommunist and pro-Ukrainian demonstrations in support of Gorbachev's actions took place just a few yards away from the first Sabbath Latter-day Saint service in Ukrainian history. No doubt the climate of political change prepared Ukrainian citizens; many were ready to be taught.[51]

The Church continued its quiet progress in the Soviet Union through early 1991. Then in June, the monumentally successful Mormon Tabernacle Choir visit to Europe completely won over the Russians.

Elders Russell M. Nelson (left) and Spencer J. Condie (right) with Gerd Schmidt, mayor of Friedrichsdorf, Germany, the Frankfurt suburb where the Frankfurt Germany Temple is located. The Tabernacle Choir performed in Friedrichsdorf en route to Russia in 1991

Elder Russell M. Nelson described the tour as "part of the Lord's plan to preach the gospel to the people of the world."[52] Concerts in Leningrad and Moscow were highly acclaimed by Soviet journalists, television commentators, and ordinary citizens. After a visit with Elders Nelson and Dallin H. Oaks of the Twelve in Moscow, the vice president of the Russian republic, Alexander Rutskoi, announced publicly that The Church of Jesus Christ of Latter-day Saints was officially recognized throughout the Russian republic, by far the largest of all the republics of the Soviet Union. The Church could now send more missionaries, print and distribute literature, buy property, and construct buildings.[53] At that time, the Church had more than 400 members in the Soviet Union with members residing in Kurgan, Leningrad (soon to be Saint Petersburg), Moscow, Sochi, Vyborg, and Zelenograd, Russia; Tallinn, Estonia; and Kiev, Ukraine.

Two months after the visit of the Tabernacle Choir to Russia, Communist leaders tried on 19 August 1991 to depose President Mikhail Gorbachev. The Church's approximately fifty missionaries, some responsible to the Finland Helsinki East and others to the Austria Vienna East

The Tabernacle Choir in front of Saint Basil's Cathedral on Moscow's Red Square

Mission, stayed out of harm's way during the tumultuous three days that followed. The coup crumbled after the third day, and by year's end, the former superpower had disintegrated into fifteen separate states.

God's almighty hand has been evident in the spread of the gospel to the former Soviet Union. When Elders Nelson and Oaks presented President Ezra Taft Benson with documents attesting the Church's full recognition in Russia, the prophet responded with a smile of great joy. President Benson had visited Moscow in 1959 as United States Secretary of Agriculture and courageously spoke to a people then severely restricted in their religious freedoms: "Our Father in Heaven is not far away. He can be very close to us. God lives, I know that He lives. . . . Time is on the side of truth. God bless you and keep you all the days of your life."[54]

The Russian Federation

In 1992 missionary work carefully moved forward in the new Russian Federation. New members joined the Church nearly every week. Elder M. Russell Ballard reported that he had met in November 1991 in Saint Petersburg with 220 new members and friends of the Church. "We sang together. We prayed. We felt His Spirit. We wept with joy knowing we are brothers and sisters in the gospel of Jesus Christ."[55]

In January 1992, students from Brigham Young University arrived in Russia to set up English classes. Later in the year, fourteen of these students began teaching classes in Voronezh, a city of about a million people some 250 miles south of Moscow. Through their example, friendship-ping, and charitable service projects, the gospel was introduced to numerous young adults, thus setting the stage for the entrance of missionaries into that part of Russia later in the year.

By February 1992, Church membership in Russia reached 750, including more than 300 in Saint Petersburg alone, where several branches were organized. Seven members began translating into Russian lesson manuals, financial handbooks, and other Latter-day Saint publications. One great challenge facing the Russian members was keeping the Sabbath holy. For Russians, Sunday was the only nonworking day for family outings or shopping. They also found it difficult to heed the prophet's counsel to store food. State officials banned "hoarding" because of food shortages in Russia. Yet the Russian members grew stronger as they learned gospel principles and applied newfound values that had been absent under the previous seventy years of Communist rule. During these pioneer years in the former Soviet Union, the Saints had only the Book of Mormon and the Church lesson manual *Gospel Principles* in Russian. When discussions in classes turned to the Doctrine and Covenants, those who read English translated passages or described these modern revelations to the rest of the members.[56]

Sister Irene Maximova, a Russian Relief Society president, voiced the feelings of the Russian Saints: "I want to express gratitude for your prayers [in the rest of the Church]. All members of the Church in Russia feel this. Our faith will help us meet great changes in our country. Your prayers [for the members] in Russia will help us to stay strong in the gospel." Members continually expressed their gratitude for food sent by the German Saints and for the many Church members who visited them in Russia.[57]

On 3 February 1992, the Church opened two missions in Russia: the Russia Saint Petersburg Mission and the Russia Moscow Mission. Both mission presidents, Thomas S. Rogers and Gary L. Browning, had helped pioneer Russian-speaking missionary programs in the Finland Helsinki East or Austria Vienna East Missions, which were discontinued at this time.[58] Also in February, members of the Church in Russia, Estonia, and Ukraine gratefully received thousands of pounds of food and clothing from stakes in Germany and from Church headquarters in Salt Lake City.[59]

In the summer of 1992, three Russian television journalists traveled to Utah to make a documentary about the Church that was expected to reach a viewing audience of 150 million. One of the journalists remarked while in Salt Lake City: "I feel that I'm changing inside myself. I didn't believe in God . . . [but now] I have become maybe three-quarters Mormon. . . . I'm thinking about it hard, because I couldn't believe people could live like this, with their families and with so much love between each other." One married couple from the Russian contingent chose to join the Church.[60]

In late 1992, former Soviet Olympian speed skater Klara Nesterova was baptized in Moscow. Barbara Lockhart, an American speed skater, had become friends with Klara at the 1964 Innsbruck Olympics. More than twenty-five years later, Sister Lockhart introduced her Russian friend Klara to the gospel while serving as an adviser to the Brigham Young University study-abroad program. "In Russia, anyone who has won an Olympic medal is a national hero. Nearly everybody [in the branch] knew who Klara was," reported Sister Lockhart.[61]

Pressured by the powerful Russian Orthodox Church, the Russian Parliament passed a bill in the summer of 1993 forbidding new Christian missionaries to enter the country. That President Yeltsin did not sign the law softened the blow, but the LDS Church, not wanting to jeopardize its legal status, proceeded carefully. Only small groups of missionaries entered the country, and missionaries called to Russia but not yet at the Missionary Training Center were reassigned to other missions. The Russian language training program at the MTC in Provo, Utah, had become the third largest group taught. Only Spanish and Portuguese were larger. But by the fall of 1993, the Russian program had dwindled to nearly nothing. When the Russian Parliament was dissolved in September, the Church again started calling missionaries to Russia.

Besides ongoing aid from concerned Saints in Germany, sixteen tons of clothing and shoes were shipped to the former Soviet Union in the summer of 1993 as part of the Church's worldwide humanitarian efforts. These much-needed items were distributed among members and non-members in Russia, Ukraine, and the Baltic states. Sister Tatiana Akimova explained some of the economic problems facing the Russian people: "Inflation is climbing almost every week, yet salaries have remained low. It is especially difficult for those with large families. Last year the exchange rate was 30 rubles to the dollar; today it is 1,100 to the dollar. Last year's winter coat for an adult cost 4,000 rubles; today it is more than 40,000 rubles. . . . That is more than a month's salary for a teacher or an engineer."[62]

Despite pressing economic problems, groups of Russian Saints found ways to attend the Stockholm Sweden or the Freiberg Germany Temple. "Attending the temple gave us great blessings and warm feelings," exclaimed Sister Maya Lvovskaya from Moscow. "As we received the temple ordinances for ourselves, we were deeply moved and edified. We strongly felt the invisible ties uniting Latter-day Saints all over the world."[63]

Russia Moscow Mission president Gary L. Browning noted in 1993: "The Church is becoming better known. It is creating good friends and making contributions." He also praised American Latter-day Saints in Russia who were working in joint economic ventures with Russians. "They have been a tremendous strength to our mission. They bring experience and they are very devoted and generous with their time."[64] He added, "Virtually all told me at one time or another that they had set aside other appealing professional opportunities to come to Moscow and help build up a new Zion."[65]

Another exciting development has been the relationship built between the Utah Genealogical Society and the Russian Genealogical Society as the Church has strived to gather family history records in the former Soviet Union.[66] This effort has not been easy. Igor V. Sakharov, president of the recently founded Russian Genealogical Society, said: "The Communist regime wanted to eliminate memory because memory was dangerous for the regime. . . . Sometimes, [the government] would eliminate an entire mass of documents. . . . Never have so many people disappeared, because you can kill people by forgetting them. To forget a person is to destroy a person. . . . The result is that people are left without roots. A person without roots isn't complete. He's somewhat ill and maybe even very ill."[67] Sakharov considered the genealogist's work in Russia a matter of spiritual health and willingly cooperated in the search for records.

In 1993 the Moscow mission was divided, and a new mission, headquartered in the Volga River city Samara, extended into the south and east. In 1994 the Church opened two more Russian missions, making a total of five in the country. One was headquartered in Rostov na Donu in the southern Caucasus region of Russia and the second in Novosibirsk on the east side of the Ural Mountains in western Siberia. A Siberian mission was added in 1995.

By 1996 there were more than 5,000 Church members in Russia. To deal with this rapid growth, the Europe Area presidency divided branches once they reached 70 to 100 people and then created new districts as the number of branches multiplied. The huge cities of Moscow and Saint Petersburg, for example, each had more than twenty small branches. This organization allowed for quicker leadership development by mission training councils. Many of the concepts developed in Russia have also been followed in the other former Soviet republics.

One indicator of the rapid maturation of the Church in Russia was the 1995 call of Viacheslav I. Efimov to serve as president of the Russia Yekaterinburg Mission. Brother Efimov, born in Leningrad in 1948, was one of the first to join the Church in Leningrad in 1990. Before his call to be mission president, he had served as a branch president, a district president, and full-time apartment coordinator for the Church in Saint Petersburg.[68]

Ukraine

When Ukraine became a sovereign political state in late 1991, it was the second largest political entity in all of Europe after Russia. Ukraine was often referred to as the "great unknown country of Europe," because of its submersion within Russian hegemony over the previous three centuries.[69]

At the end of June 1991, Howard L. Biddulph, a Russian-speaking Soviet specialist from the University of Victoria in Canada, visited Kiev with his wife, Colleen, as president of the Austria Vienna East Mission. At that time Kiev had eight young elders, a missionary couple, and a branch of thirty-nine members. A leading Ukrainian journalist interviewed President Biddulph and then wrote a magazine article that praised the Church but forecast that the Church would not do well in Ukraine because the people would not like the doctrines of free will, joy, chastity, Word of Wisdom, tithing, and personal self-discipline. Coincidentally, Elder Boyd K. Packer of the Quorum of the Twelve Apostles arrived in Kiev to dedicate the nation for the preaching of the gospel at approximately the same time as the magazine article hit the stands. His prayer was offered at the base of a large monument honoring Prince Vladimir, who had courageously introduced Christianity into Ukraine a thousand years earlier.[70] Elder Packer promised that the message of the Restoration would have a great harvest in Ukraine. Three years later Elder Packer's promise was being fulfilled.

In February 1992, the Church opened the Ukraine Kiev Mission with President Biddulph as president. Missionaries learned Russian, which was still commonly spoken in Kiev and in the Russified eastern and southern portions of the country. They found the Ukrainian people highly receptive to the gospel. Throughout 1992 and into 1993, as numbers of missionaries multiplied, so did the number of converts. Missionaries were told not to tract; they found interested individuals simply by talking to people in the streets, on public transportation, and in schools and universities. Often people just appeared at church meetings because they saw poster invitations. Many people were eager to learn more about western and North American peoples and their religious traditions. At the same time, many Ukrainians felt disfranchised from their Orthodox religion because many Orthodox leaders had catered to the Soviet KGB. Then, in the fall of Communism, the Ukrainian Orthodox Church had split three ways, causing more religious confusion.

By late 1994, LDS Church membership in Ukraine had reached 3,000 with forty branches in eight cities. In Kiev, the 1,800 members were in fifteen branches supervised by three districts. There were already 320 Melchizedek Priesthood holders, and all branch and district leadership positions were filled by local leaders. More than 250 members had gone to the Freiberg Germany Temple for their eternal ordinances. President

Biddulph reported that about three-fourths of the members were active, a remarkable figure given the Church average of less than half. A high proportion of the members came from the educated people of the country.

Typical of the converts in Ukraine were Vyacheslav and Zoya Gulko, a leading nuclear physicist and English teacher, respectively. Both were Jews but had become atheists under Communism. As the eastern European revolutions unfolded, they began seeking for spirituality in their lives. They visited many different Christian churches and finally came to the Latter-day Saints after seeing a poster inviting investigators to LDS Church meetings. After their conversion, Brother Gulko became a district president and Sister Gulko the main translator of the Book of Mormon and Church curriculum materials into Ukrainian.

In 1993 the Ukraine Donetsk Mission opened for the eastern portion of the country. That same year, the national government officially supported the Orthodox faith as the defenders of Ukrainian culture. As a result the Church had to negotiate with the government to maintain foreign missionary visas. The number of North American missionaries dwindled to about thirty by early 1995. Many more Ukrainian missionaries and part-time district missionaries were called.

By 1995 basic Church materials had been translated into the Ukrainian language. Missionaries especially needed these translations in western Ukraine, where the native language was predominant. Also in 1995, a humanitarian shipment of six tons of urgently needed medical supplies was sent by the Church to the Kiev Institute of Cardiovascular Surgery. The gift was suggested by a Utah medical team that had visited the Kiev facility to perform surgeries at no charge.[71]

Armenia

In June 1991, the Republic of Armenia donated land to the Church for an office and worship building in the capital city, Yerevan, in gratitude for efforts by Church members to relieve the suffering caused by the December 1989 earthquake that killed 55,000 people and left half a million homeless. David M. Horne, a building contractor from Salt Lake City, responded to a missionary call to build 6,500 apartments financed by Utah businessman Jon Huntsman. Couple missionaries helped with the construction projects and formed community support groups of Armenians to help one another. In early 1996, Brother Horne was severely burned in a propane explosion. Armenians lined the streets to pay their respects when he was taken by ambulance to the airport to be flown to Utah for treatment. He subsequently died of his injuries.

On 24 June 1991 Armenia was dedicated by Elder Dallin H. Oaks. Elder Russell M. Nelson reported the stirring scene: "He and I stood arm in arm on a peak overlooking the city of Yerevan near the monument representing the mother of Armenia. Not far in the distance, we could see the snow-covered peak of Mount Ararat, where Noah's Ark once had come to rest. (See Gen. 8:4.)"[72]

Conditions in Armenia remained unsettled. The Saints and the missionaries serving there during the winters of 1992–93 and 1993–94 struggled under conditions of anarchy and scarcities of fuel and fresh water. Help came often from Europe Area headquarters in Frankfurt. Yet the Church grew gradually in Yerevan as missionary couples continued their humanitarian service and part-time missionary work. The Bulgaria Sofia Mission was given responsibility for the work in Armenia beginning in November 1993.

Belarus

Formerly Byelorussia, or White Russia, the hilly lowland of Belarus is bordered by Latvia, Lithuania, Ukraine, Russia, and Poland. Its people speak Belarussian and are mostly Russian Orthodox.

Karl Friedrich and Hanna Ruth Bocherding from Hanover, Germany, opened missionary work in Belarus in February 1993 under the direction of the Ukraine Kiev Mission.[73] The first elders arrived a month later on translator and tour guide visas. In December the Church organized the Charitable Society Sophia in Belarus as its first official organization.

The first baptism came in March 1993. By September 1994, 200 people had joined the Church and were organized into four branches. Sixteen humanitarian missionaries were laboring in Minsk, distributing powdered milk, clothing, shoes, food, and toys to needy and ill people. They also taught English classes, visited patients in hospitals, and donated such community service as cleaning parks. Along with their good works, they found people to teach and performed baptisms each month. The first thirty Belarus Saints to prepare for the temple went to the Freiberg Germany Temple in September 1994. Church membership in Belarus had reached more than 300 by 1996.

The Baltic States of Estonia, Latvia, and Lithuania

In July 1993, the Baltic republics received their own mission with headquarters in Riga, Latvia. Elder Russell M. Nelson had dedicated Estonia for the preaching of the gospel in November 1990 about the same time he had rededicated Russia in Leningrad. Missionary progress in Estonia was much farther ahead of the work in the other two Baltic republics. Its capital, Tallinn, had been one of the first cities visited by Finnish missionaries to the Soviet Union in early 1991. Latvia and Lithuania did not receive missionaries until 1992 when missionaries in the Saint Petersburg Mission began proselyting. Elder James E. Faust dedicated Latvia for the preaching of the gospel in March 1993, and Elder M. Russell Ballard dedicated Lithuania in May of the same year.

The three Baltic republics refused to join the Russian-led Commonwealth of Independent States in late 1991. Their strong nationalistic feelings had been created through centuries of their own cultures and languages. Between World War I and World War II, the three had been separate and sovereign states. The Nazi-Soviet nonaggression pact negotiated by Adolf Hitler with Josef Stalin allowed the Soviet Union to annex the Baltic states in 1940. The Baltic peoples deeply resented the intrusion of Russian people and culture into their lands. Tension continued between the Russians and the native Lithuanians, Latvians, and Estonians, even after the revolutions freed the Baltic republics from direct Russian control.

Elder Faust visited Latvia in 1993 and promised the missionaries: "I prophesy, in your lifetime you will see several stakes organized in the country of Latvia under the Latvian leadership. You are pioneers; you can tell your children about it." In his dedicatory prayer he stated: "We would remind Thee, Father, that recently they have raised their heads in courage and dignity and have sought to overthrow and be relieved of the subjugation and of the oppressive rule of the Communist influence of another country. This has permitted them, in Thy providence, once more to establish their independence in this land as a free people. Father, we acknowledge Thy hand in this release from oppression."[74]

This building housed the first Latter-day Saint meeting
place in Belgrade, Yugoslavia

The Church grew slowly but steadily in Estonia, Latvia, and
Lithuania from 1992 to 1995. Many Russian-speaking missionaries
served in those nations, and other missionaries were enrolled at local
universities to learn each country's native tongues. In 1993 and 1994 separate language branches were established in the larger cities.

In 1994 the lone Lithuanian independent television station and a
radio station and a newspaper featured several programs and articles
about the Church and the missionaries. Missionaries were shown teaching English, playing with children at an orphanage, and sharing the
gospel. "As a result of this media coverage, the Church in Lithuania is
now viewed more positively, misinformation about the Church has been
corrected, and many doors have been opened to the missionaries," said
one elder who was serving an educational mission in Lithuania.[75]

Certain societal patterns made missionary work difficult in all three
of the Baltic republics. For instance, the older people tended to be more
bound by tradition, especially their Lutheran or Orthodox religious faith;
therefore, most Latter-day Saint converts were young adults who were
trying their wings at new careers as well as religions. Also, because
many people worked two or three jobs to make ends meet, missionaries

Elder Jeffrey Moore labors as a missionary in the early 1990s in Ljubljana, Slovenia

scrambled to find times to speak with heads of households. Another unfortunate pattern was the rampant alcoholism that plagued all of the Baltic countries.

Former Yugoslavia

The Austria Vienna East Mission from its creation in 1987 administered the Church's affairs in the Balkans: Yugoslavia, Romania, Bulgaria, and Albania. Bulgaria received its own mission in 1991 and Romania in 1993. Yugoslavia, before its breakup in 1991 and 1992, consisted of six semiautonomous republics that possessed different languages, ethnic groups, religious persuasions, and nationalistic impulses. Civil war broke out in Yugoslavia in June 1991. Soon Slovenia, Croatia, Bosnia-Herzegovina, and Macedonia become independent states. Only Serbia and Montenegro remained of the original six states of Yugoslavia.

The civil war forced all Latter-day Saint representatives to flee the war zones. Only a few missionaries remained in Belgrade, Ljubljana, Zadar, and later Zagreb. In early 1992, Austrian members of the Church sent packets of food, clothing, and blankets to both Serbia and Croatia.

In 1992, after the Vienna East Mission was disbanded, the Austria

Vienna Mission president was given responsibility for the former Yugoslavia and Albania. The missionaries extended the gospel into new cities, creating separate districts in Slovenia, Serbia, and Croatia. In 1993 Elder Dallin H. Oaks held a regional conference in Zagreb, Croatia, to give an apostolic blessing of protection to the people in all their adversities. Ivan Valek, who had served as branch president for ten years, was called as Croatian District president. (Ivan had been converted by Krešimir Cosic when both had played for the Yugoslav National basketball team.)

The civil war continued its horrors. In the fall of 1994, Church humanitarian services sent twenty thousand packages of food and basic medical supplies to Bosnia, Croatia, and Albania. Volunteer workers prepared these packages at bishops storehouses in Utah. In late 1995 a peace accord for Bosnia was worked out under the auspices of the United States in Dayton, Ohio. The deployment of 60,000 NATO troops in 1996 made possible the return of missionaries to the former Yugoslavia.

The 1989 revolutions in eastern Europe were a mixed blessing for the inhabitants of the various nations, several of which came officially into existence only after the revolution. Early euphoria was replaced by widespread disillusionment, skepticism, and, in some cases, considerable bloodshed. But those who accepted the restored gospel of Jesus Christ gained hope and a strong foundation of faith to face their countries' uncertain futures.

NOTES

1 Spencer W. Kimball, "When the World Will Be Converted," *Ensign* 4 (October 1974): 7.

2 David B. Haight, in Conference Report, April 1990, 28.

3 Hans B. Ringger, "Now Is the Day of Europe," address delivered at Brigham Young University, 8 April 1993.

4 Ibid.

5 R. Scott Lloyd, "New Seventy Played Key Role in Thrilling Events of the Church," *Church News*, 18 May 1991, 6.

6 Ringger, "Now Is the Day of Europe."

7 Russell M. Nelson, "Drama on the European Stage," *Ensign* 21 (December 1991): 10–11.

8   "Czechoslovakia Grants Recognition to the Church," *Church News*, 3 March 1990, 3.

9   Memorandum from Russell M. Nelson and Hans B. Ringger to the Council of the First Presidency and the Quorum of the Twelve, 13 February 1990, copy in my possession.

10   Brad Barlow, "My Mission Experience," unpublished paper, Brigham Young University, March 1995.

11   J Malan Heslop and Fae Heslop, "Dawning of New Day," *Church News*, 30 March 1991, 10.

12   Barlow, "My Mission Experience."

13   R. Scott Lloyd, "Czech Broadcasters See Church Close Up," *Church News*, 22 May 1993, 6; "Church, Utah Featured on Czech TV," *Ensign* 23 (August 1993): 80.

14   Information for this section is mostly drawn from Kahlile Mehr, "The Gospel in Hungary—Then and Now," *Ensign* 20 (June 1990): 8–14, and Kahlile Mehr, "The Eastern Edge: LDS Missionary Work in Hungarian Lands," *Dialogue* 24 (Summer 1991): 21–45.

15   Mehr, "The Gospel in Hungary," 13.

16   Nelson, "Drama on the European Stage," 11.

17   Dell Van Orden, "Church Granted Legal Recognition in Hungary," *Church News*, 2 July 1988, 13.

18   Ibid.

19   "Meetinghouse Dedicated in Hungary," *Church News*, 11 November 1989, 3–4.

20   Ibid., 4.

21   President Wilde spoke to a group of Brigham Young University students on 11 October 1992; notes in my possession.

22   Nelson, "Drama on the European Stage," 9.

23   Thomas S. Monson, in Conference Report, April 1992, 70–71.

24   *1995–96 Church Almanac* (Salt Lake City: Deseret News, 1994), 277.

25   "Poland Expresses Thanks for Medical Supplies," *Ensign* 21 (November 1991): 111.

26   Memorandum from Russell M. Nelson and Hans B. Ringger to the Priesthood Executive Council, 13 February 1990, copy in my possession.

27   Gerry Avant, "LDS Humanitarian Relief in Romania," *Church News*, 18 August 1990, 3.

28   Interview with Alvin H. Price, 22 August 1994. Elder Price, a BYU family science professor, and his wife were among the first humanitarian missionaries to Romania, where he also served as the first group leader.

29   Ibid.

30   Quig Nielsen, "Boy Leads His Family into Baptism," *Church News*, 7 November 1992, 11.

31 Gerry Avant and John L. Hart, "Many Are Still Blazing Gospel Trails," *Church News*, 24 July 1993, 6.

32 "Eight New Missions Announced," *Church News*, 6 March 1993, 9.

33 Cited in Deborah A. Vangelov, "The L.D.S. Church in Bulgaria," unpublished paper, Brigham Young University, 31 March 1993.

34 Ibid.

35 This same Brother Neuenschwander was called in 1987 to be president of the Vienna East Mission over the eastern European nations. In 1993 he became president of the Europe Area, which also took in Bulgaria.

36 Nelson, "Drama on the European Stage," 13. Most other information about the Church in Bulgaria comes from Kahlile Mehr, "Keeping Promises: The LDS Church Enters Bulgaria, 1990–1994," *BYU Studies*, forthcoming.

37 "Mission to Be Created in Bulgaria," *Church News*, 18 May 1991, 3.

38 Gerry Avant, "Volunteers Bring Hope to Bulgarian Children," *Church News*, 5 June 1993, 3–4; see also "Health Specialists Volunteer for Service in Bulgaria," *Ensign* 23 (September 1993): 74.

39 Avant, "Volunteers Bring Hope to Bulgarian Children," 4.

40 Vangelov, "The L.D.S. Church in Bulgaria."

41 "Mission to be Created in Bulgaria," 3.

42 Charone H. Smith, "Albania, a Labor of Love," *To Rejoice as Women: Talks from the 1994 Women's Conference*, ed. Susette Fletcher Green and Dawn Hall Anderson (Salt Lake City: Deseret Book, 1995), 154, 156.

43 Smith, "Albania," 155–56.

44 "4 European Lands Dedicated," *Church News*, 12 June 1993, 3, 6.

45 Interview with returned missionary Matthew Wirthlin, 28 April 1994, Provo, Utah.

46 "Food Being Shipped to Families in Need," *Church News*, 3 December 1994, 3.

47 Major sources for this section are Gary L. Browning, "Out of Obscurity: The Emergence of The Church of Jesus Christ of Latter-day Saints in 'That Vast Empire of Russia,'" *BYU Studies* 33, no. 4 (1993): 674–88; Jenifer Larson-Hall, "Love & Faith in St. Petersburg," *Ensign* 23 (December 1993): 32–35; Kahlile Mehr, "1989–90: The Curtain Opens," *Ensign* 23 (December 1993): 36–37.

48 Browning, "Out of Obscurity," 680.

49 "Russian Republic Recognizes the Church," *Ensign* 20 (November 1990): 106; Nelson, "Drama on the European Stage," 15.

50 Brian Bradbury, "The Early Days of the Church in What Was the Soviet Union," unpublished paper, 1992.

51   Howard Biddulph, "The Rise of Mormonism in Post-Communist Ukraine," speech delivered at Brigham Young University David M. Kennedy Center, 21 October 1994.

52   Gerry Avant, "Choir Leaves Trail of Joyful Tears," *Church News*, 6 July 1991, 3.

53   Gerry Avant, "Russia: An Opening Door," *Church News*, 13 July 1991, 3–4.

54   *U.S. News and World Report*, 26 October 1959, 76; see also Sheri L. Dew, *Ezra Taft Benson: A Biography* (Salt Lake City: Deseret Book, 1987), 343–44.

55   Lee Davidson, "Temple Lights 'a Beacon to the World,'" *Church News*, 14 December 1991, 6–7.

56   Jan Stout, "'Russians Are Looking for the Truth,'" *Church News*, 15 February 1992, 7; Steve Fidel, "Converts Pioneer Frontier in Russia," *Church News*, 19 September 1992, 11, 13.

57   Ibid.

58   "3 New Missions Established in Russia, Ukraine," *Church News*, 15 February 1992, 3.

59   "LDS Germans Help Russia," *Deseret News*, 6 February 1992, B–1; "Food Sent to Russia," *Ensign* 22 (March 1992): 74; "Humanitarian Relief in Europe," *Church News*, 29 February 1992, 3.

60   "LDS Heritage Inspires Russian TV Journalists," *Church News*, 29 August 1992, 3; "Free Concert Series at Temple Square Assists Missionary Effort," *Ensign* 23 (September 1993): 77.

61   Gerry Avant, "Skaters Carved Warm Friendship on Ice at Olympics 34 Years Ago," *Church News*, 26 February 1994, 11.

62   Mary Kay Stout, "Russian Members Distribute Bales of Clothes and Shoes among LDS, Others," *Church News*, 4 September 1993, 3; "Russian Members Receive, Distribute Clothing, Shoes," *Ensign* 23 (November 1993): 112.

63   "'Our Souls Sang,'" *Church News*, 20 November 1993, 16.

64   "Eight New Missions Announced," *Church News*, 6 March 1993, 9; Hans P. Ringger, "Now Is the Day of Europe."

65   Browning, "Out of Obscurity," 683.

66   John L. Hart, "Russian Genealogy Rises from Ashes," *Church News*, 27 November 1993, 4.

67   Quoted in Deirdre Paulsen, "Russian Women: Gaining Roots, Growing Strong," in *Hearts Knit Together: Talks from the 1995 Women's Conference*, ed. Susette Fletcher Green, Dawn Hall Anderson, Dlora Hall Dalton (Salt Lake City: Deseret Book, 1996), 56–57.

68   "New Mission Presidents," *Church News*, 6 May 1995, 7.

69   Most of the material for this section comes from Biddulph, "The Rise of Mormonism in Post-Communist Ukraine."

70 "Two Republics in USSR Are Dedicated," *Church News,* 28 September 1991, 3.

71 "Medical Gifts Appreciated," *Church News,* 25 March 1995, 7.

72 Nelson, "Drama on the European Stage," 16.

73 My sources are Howard L. Biddulph and a letter from Elder Eddie Miner in Minsk, 17 September 1994.

74 Boris A. Schiel, "The History of the Latvia Riga Mission of The Church of Jesus Christ of Latter-day Saints, June 17, 1992–December 14, 1993," unpublished paper, April 1995, 15–16.

75 "Media Boosts Profile," *Church News,* 9 July 1994, 13.

CHAPTER 12

Looking to the Future

t the beginning of the Restoration, the Savior "committed unto man on the earth" the keys of his kingdom and thus mandated that "the gospel [would] roll forth unto the ends of the earth, as the stone which is cut out of the mountain without hands shall roll forth, until it has filled the whole earth" (D&C 65:2). The Lord has also promised that Zion will rejoice in the last days, even as the wicked will mourn. Zion, defined in the Doctrine and Covenants as it pertains to the Lord's people as "the pure in heart," will be nurtured by Deity until she is purified (D&C 97:21). "Zion shall not be moved out of her place, notwithstanding her children are scattered" (D&C 101:17). The Savior promises that those in Zion who become pure in heart will receive their inheritance and with "songs of everlasting joy" will "build up the waste places of Zion" (D&C 101:18).

The "strength of Zion," the Lord has declared, will be in her stakes, which in turn become "holy places" (D&C 101:21–22). The First Presidency, the Twelve, and the Seventy strive with all their might to bless the stakes of Zion and to broaden Zion's borders with new stakes throughout the world. Before Christ comes again, hundreds of additional stakes of Zion will dot the European continent. The ninety stakes that existed in Europe in early 1996 were merely a beginning.

One day the European Saints will reach the peaceful plateau of righteousness described in 4 Nephi: "And it came to pass that there was no contention in the land, because of the love of God which did dwell in the hearts of the people. And there were no envyings, nor strifes, nor tumults, nor whoredoms, nor lyings, nor murders, nor any manner of lasciviousness; and surely there could not be a happier people among all the people who had been created by the hand of God. There were no robbers, nor murderers, neither were there . . . any manner of -ites; but they were in one, the children of Christ, and heirs to the kingdom of God. And how blessed were they! For the Lord did bless them in all their doings" (4 Nephi 1:15–18).

These scriptural promises will not come automatically to the European Saints. Obedience and devotion will be required of the leaders, the members, and the missionaries as they face inevitable challenges and obstacles to this holy work. But the Saints have been blessed with living prophets, who lead the Church under the watchful eye of the Savior of all mankind. President Gordon B. Hinckley, who was sustained as prophet, seer, and revelator for the Lord's church in 1995, has been uniquely prepared to lead the Saints in their quest to build Zion in these last days. Elder Jeffrey R. Holland of the Council of the Twelve shared his assessment of President Hinkley: "Perhaps no man has ever come to the Presidency of the Church who has been so well prepared for the responsibility. Through sixty years of Church administration he has known personally, been taught by, and in one capacity or other served with every President of the Church from Heber J. Grant to Howard W. Hunter. As one of his associates says, 'No man in the history of the Church has traveled so far to so many places in the world with such a single purpose in mind—to preach the gospel, to bless and lift up the Saints, and to foster the redemption of the dead.'"[1]

President Hinckley's motto, forged from the adversities in his own life, illustrates his indomitable spirit: "Keep trying. Be believing. Be happy. Don't get discouraged. Things will work out."[2]

Challenges in Europe

The gospel of Jesus Christ is universal. The application of the saving principles and ordinances of the gospel is the same for all the children of God regardless of where they live on this earth. The performance of ordinances and the style of such meetings as the sacrament meeting are remarkably similar in every land despite language and cultural differences. Those differences, however, pose numerous challenges in disseminating the gospel to every kindred, tongue, and people. The Savior commanded, "Go ye into all the world, and preach the gospel to *every creature*" (Mormon 9:22; emphasis added). The difficulty is that every creature does not have the same background, language, cultural

experiences, and traditions. Even people who live in the same community have differences. Europe, with more than forty separate nations,
multiple languages, and millions of people, is a prime example of cultural diversity. "The largest challenge the Church will face in the next
twenty years will be adapting to the various cultures of the world,"
declared Elder Alexander Morrison of the Seventy in 1994. "This will be
the biggest challenge in our history to date."[3]

Elder Richard P. Lindsay of the Seventy suggested that "the answer
to bridging different cultures is the pure gospel of Christ." The Church's
task, he asserted, is to build "a gospel culture that transcends all boundaries and barriers." Fulfilling that goal does not mean "the denial of
everything in our separate heritages." Indeed, each heritage brings traditions that are beautiful and, when shared, enrich the lives of Latter-day
Saints everywhere. Nonetheless, every culture usually has some traditions that are incompatible with the gospel of Christ. "We must keep the
doctrine pure," Elder Lindsay indicated, "and be willing to change certain traditions that aren't compatible with the gospel."[4]

Developing tolerance will assist members in their quest to reach
"every creature." Elder John K. Carmack of the Seventy explained that
"people deserve to be treated as brothers and sisters because they are all
children of God." He added that "one of the tragedies of war is its ten-
dency to build up in people attitudes of hatred against whole nationalities, races, and cultures. During such times, stereotyping spreads to
epidemic proportions, and the rhetoric gets harsh and ugly." Stereotyping
and intolerance are not easy to root out, but brotherhood depends on it.
As Elder Carmack observed: "Internationally, intolerance between religious and ethnic groups is rising. No nation seems immune from intolerance, and the stakes are high. Peace will never be achieved until most
of us master the attitudes and practices of tolerance."[5]

In 1992 the First Presidency issued a formal statement calling for a
recommitment to tolerance of all races and cultures:

"We reaffirm the longstanding concern of The Church of Jesus
Christ of Latter-day Saints for the well-being and intrinsic worth of all
people. Latter-day Saints believe that 'God is no respecter of persons: But
in every nation he that feareth him, and worketh righteousness, is
accepted with him' (Acts 10:34–35). All men and women are children of

God. It is morally wrong for any person or group to deny anyone his or her inalienable dignity on the tragic and abhorrent theory of racial or cultural superiority. We call upon all people everywhere to recommit themselves to the time-honored ideals of tolerance and mutual respect.

"We sincerely believe that as we acknowledge one another with consideration and compassion we will discover that we can all peacefully coexist despite our deepest differences."[6]

Unfortunately, the continent of Europe provides some of the worst examples of racial unrest, religious animosity, ethnic hatred, intolerance, and mutual distrust in the world. World Wars I and II, conflicts in the former Yugoslavia, Chechnya, and other regions, and many other senseless atrocities in Europe plague our memories.

Even in less shattering confrontations, eliminating intolerance is important. For instance, converts to the Church in western Europe are often not native to the country in which they are baptized. In fact, missionaries frequently find more receptive spirits among displaced peoples than among the English in England, the Dutch in the Netherlands, the French in France, and the Germans in Germany, for example. Consequently, congregations in country after country in Europe have struggled with accepting, fellowshipping, and assimilating new, culturally different members.[7] Young missionaries filled with the Spirit of their calling to reach out to "every creature" have been confused and disappointed when investigators of the main culture and ethnic background have been welcomed with open arms and hearts but people of other colors and cultures have not.

Materialism is another challenge to building Zion in Europe. Excessive concern with temporal possessions rather than with spiritual values usually follows prosperity. A materialistic lifestyle has become the norm throughout most of western Europe, and recently liberated eastern Europeans often follow suit. Latter-day Saint missionaries are turned away by people who feel they already have what they want in life, or that what they really need to be happy is more possessions. Hedonism, the practice of pursuing pleasure as the chief good in life, is also rampant throughout Europe. Pornography, homosexuality, public nudity, prostitution, and general immorality are prevalent. Some Latter-day Saints succumb to the temptations of materialism and pleasure-seeking and fall away.

Europe's sports mania is related to materialism in that it draws people's attention away from God. Soccer, or football, as it is more generally known, is virtually a national religion. Other sports occasionally draw similar fanatical devotion. Of course, sports activities per se are not evil. They often provide rich diversity in human life and useful activities for fun and fellowship in wards, branches, and youth conferences. But taken to an extreme, sports excesses have undermined missionary work and some Church members' devotion to the kingdom.

Another ally of materialism and hedonism is the secularism that has taken over Europe in the twentieth century. Religion is often dismissed as mere superstition or magical thinking. Modern scientific, economic, and political belief systems are the objects of far more dedicated study and respect in modern European society than the values, teachings, and philosophies of the Bible and historical Christianity. Sadly, even the traditional European state churches have become secularized, especially in their ministries, activities, and administration, partly because they have so closely allied themselves with the interests of the states from which they receive tax revenues. God and religious values are of little daily consequence to most Europeans. Both in Europe and the United States, biblical teachings have far less influence on social values than does the media.

Despite these inimical trends, missionaries and members find people in every nation who are good, honest, and kind people. Yet many of these fine people are inhibited by cultural and religious traditions from seriously investigating the restored gospel of Jesus Christ. Cooperative humanitarian service and mutual understanding and tolerance are helping to bridge those differences. Community service by missionaries, quorums, and auxiliary groups not only is its own reward but furthers acceptance of the Latter-day Saints. In the past, advertising for the Church delivered in an American cultural package turned away European investigators and distanced our European brothers and sisters; more thoughtful communications have improved the visibility of the Church, its members, and its message of Jesus Christ.

The good works of the Latter-day Saints are the Lord's beacon to a world in darkness. The Lord's anointed—the prophets, seers, and revelators—have repeatedly counseled us to return to bedrock values and to strengthen our families against the confusion and immorality of the latter days. "Like a ship without a compass, society drifts from the family values which anchored us in the past," Elder Boyd K. Packer declared. "We are caught in a current of moral pollution so strong that unless we correct our course, civilization, as we know it, will surely be wrecked to pieces. The standards of the world are constantly adjusted to what is. The standards of the Church are fixed on what ought to be."[8]

Building Zion in Europe

It is incumbent upon Latter-day Saints to learn about the governments and countries in which they live. The Lord's command is explicit in this regard: "Teach ye diligently and my grace shall attend you . . . in all things that pertain unto the kingdom of God, that are expedient for you to understand; of things both in heaven and in the earth, and under the earth; things which have been, things which are, things which must shortly come to pass; things which are at home, things which are abroad; the wars and the perplexities of the nations, and the judgments which are on the land; and a knowledge also of countries and of kingdoms—that ye may be prepared in all things when I shall send you again to magnify the calling whereunto I have called you, and the mission with which I have commissioned you" (D&C 88:78–80). A second witness of this commandment was given to the Prophet Joseph Smith in a later revelation: "And, verily I say unto you, that it is my will that you should hasten to . . . obtain a knowledge of history, and of countries, and of kingdoms, of laws of God and man, and all this for the salvation of Zion" (D&C 93:53).

This knowledge is necessary if people are to actively influence their country for good. Historically, three elements have proved essential for missionaries to effectively carry out their work, for branches to grow into wards and districts into stakes, and for Saints to mature in the gospel. First, religious freedom had to be protected by law. Second, governments and economies had to be stable. And third, the absence of war or serious strife was essential. In the Church's long history, when missionaries have attempted to baptize and build up the kingdom without freedom, stability, and peace, their attempts have invariably been without lasting success.

Another historical key to missionary success has been God's hand in inspiring a religious awakening among a people or society or individuals. The Church's amazing record in England in the 1830s and 1840s coincided with a religious awakening in the country. But the Church can proselyte and build stable branches even if there is not a general interest in religion. That has been the case generally in western Europe, as long as the essential elements of religious freedom, stability in the government and economy, and relative peace in society exist. The Church grew steadily, though not rapidly, in western Europe from the end of World War II through the 1990s.

Perhaps the most dangerous threat to peace in Europe today is brutal nationalism. Throughout the former Soviet Union, for instance, nearly every ethnic group—and there are more than thirty—has violently attacked or defended itself from irrational racial hatred. In central and eastern European countries ethnic feelings are dangerously close to the surface, and in western Europe, acts of violence against foreigners occasionally erupt.

Latter-day Saints in Europe pray in their meetings and in their homes for the help of Almighty God in bringing an end to war on their doorstep and in providing comfort to those in suffering. One service that has captured the imagination of western European Latter-day Saints is preparing welfare packets for refugees in war-torn areas as well as for their brothers and sisters in the gospel suffering in eastern Europe and Russia. Also, from time to time some men and women have accepted calls to go into central and eastern European areas to provide leadership training to the new members. Some medical and other professionals from among western European members have shared their expertise. The credibility of the Church is always heightened by such unselfish service. Many western European members who serve as temple workers have opened their arms and hearts to those from central and eastern Europe who have come to receive their temple blessings.

Latter-day Saints everywhere are learning to transcend human differences of all sorts to unite together as brothers and sisters in Christ. Latter-day Saints who embrace and try to live the doctrine taught by the First Presidency—"as we acknowledge one another with consideration and compassion we will discover that we can all peacefully coexist despite our deepest differences"—will build Zion in all the nations of the earth. Then the kingdom of God will roll forth as prophesied, and Zion will be established in all her beauty.

NOTES

1 Jeffrey R. Holland, "President Gordon B. Hinckley: Stalwart and Brave He Stands," *Ensign* 25 (June 1995): 12–13.

2 Ibid., 12.

3 Alexander W. Morrison, "Women in the Developing World," address delivered at David M. Kennedy Center for International Studies, Brigham Young University, August 1994. Personal notes in my possession.

4 As cited in R. Val Johnson, "South Africa: Land of Good Hope," *Ensign* 23 (February 1993): 34–35.

5 John K. Carmack, *Tolerance* (Salt Lake City: Bookcraft, 1993), 3–4.

6 *Church News*, 24 October 1992, 4.

7 More than half of these new members from different cultures have not been retained. As a rule, new members from different cultures who are Caucasians have been easier to assimilate than blacks or Asians. People who were not from a Christian tradition in the first place, especially Muslims living in Europe, have generally had a difficult time finding fellowship among the Latter-day Saints.

8 "President Packer Addresses Diplomats," *Ensign* 25 (June 1995): 74.

Selected Bibliography

1950 TO THE PRESENT

General

"The Church in Northern Europe." *Ensign* 24 (January 1994): 79–80.

"Church Media-Member Campaign Encourages Growth in Europe." *Ensign* 19 (September 1989): 79–80.

"Conversation with the Europe Area Presidency." *Ensign* 24 (July 1994): 78–79.

Hinckley, Gordon B. "'Here We Build Our Zion.'" *Ensign* 3 (August 1973): 5–9.

"Mediterranean Areas: New Challenges and Growth." *Ensign* 22 (October 1992): 78–79.

Tobler, Douglas F. "The Church in Europe." *Encyclopedia of Mormonism.* Ed. Daniel H. Ludlow. 5 vols. New York: Macmillan, 1991. 2:473.

——. "Update on Western Europe." *Ensign* 6 (August 1976): 30–34.

von Ebengreuth, Immo Luschin. "The Swiss Temple: Spiritual Heart of Europe." *Ensign* 3 (August 1973): 11–12.

Albania

Smith, Charone H. "Albania, a Labor of Love." *To Rejoice as Women: Talks from the 1994 Women's Conference.* Ed. Susette Fletcher Green and Dawn Hall Anderson. Salt Lake City: Deseret Book, 1995. 152–57.

Austria

"Austria." *Ensign* 3 (August 1973): 17–19.

Busche, F. Enzio. "The Church in Germany, Switzerland, and Austria." *Mormonism: A Faith for All Cultures.* Ed. F. Lamond Tullis. Provo: Brigham Young University Press, 1978. 48–51.

Belgium

"Belgium." *Ensign* 3 (August 1973): 19–21.

Didier, Charles A. "The Church in French-Speaking Europe." *Mormonism: A Faith for All Cultures.* Ed. F. Lamond Tullis. Provo: Brigham Young University Press, 1978. 44–48.

Czechoslovakia

Kovářová Olga. "Fruits of Faithfulness: The Saints of Czechoslovakia." *Women Steadfast in Christ: Talks Selected from the 1991 Women's Conference.* Ed. Dawn Hall Anderson and Marie Cornwall. Salt Lake City: Deseret Book, 1991. 134–47.

Mehr, Kahlile. "Czech Saints: A Brighter Day." *Ensign* 24 (August 1994): 46–52.

——. "Enduring Believers: Czechoslovakia and the LDS Church, 1884–1990." *Journal of Mormon History* 18 (Fall 1992): 111–54.

Denmark

"Denmark." *Ensign* 4 (July 1974): 30–32.

Florence, Giles H., Jr. "Sea, Soil, and Souls in Denmark." *Ensign* 22 (February 1992): 44–50.

Wennerlund, Bo G. "The Church in Scandinavia and Finland." *Mormonism: A Faith for All Cultures.* Ed. F. Lamond Tullis. Provo: Brigham Young University Press, 1978. 44–48, 51–57.

England

"British Saints Celebrate 150th Anniversary." *Ensign* 17 (October 1987): 70–75.

"The Church Today in the British Isles." *Ensign* 17 (July 1987): 12–15.

Cuthbert, Derek A. "Breakthrough in Britain." *Ensign* 17 (July 1987): 28–32.

——. *The Second Century: Latter-day Saints in Great Britain, Volume I, 1937–1987.* Cambridge: Cambridge University Press, 1987. 7–193.

Dixon, Derek. "The Saints in the British Isles." *Ensign* 6 (June 1976): 80–84.

Heaton, Tim, Stan Albrecht, and J. Randal Johnson. "The Making of British Saints in Historical Perspective." *BYU Studies* 27 (Spring 1987): 119–35.

Kendle, Roger J. "Preston's Proud Saints." *Ensign* 9 (December 1979): 46–49.

Morley, Peter L. "The Church in England." *Mormonism: A Faith for All Cultures.* Ed. F. Lamond Tullis. Provo: Brigham Young University Press, 1978. 57–64.

Moss, James R. "The Great Awakening." *Truth Will Prevail: The Rise of The Church of Jesus Christ of Latter-day Saints in the British Isles, 1837–1987.* Ed. V. Ben Bloxham, James R. Moss, and Larry C. Porter. West Midlands: Corporation of the President of The Church of Jesus Christ of Latter-day Saints, 1987. 394–423.

Perry, Anne S. "The Contemporary Church." *Truth Will Prevail: The Rise of The Church of Jesus Christ of Latter-day Saints in the British Isles, 1837–1987.* Ed. V. Ben Bloxham, James R. Moss, and Larry C. Porter. West Midlands: Corporation of the President of The Church of Jesus Christ of Latter-day Saints, 1987. 424–41.

——. "'This Is the Truth, and We Will Not Turn Back.'" *Ensign* 17 (July 1987): 44–48.

Finland

"Finland." *Church News.* 3 October 1987, 8.

Florence, Giles H., Jr. "Suomi Finland: A Beacon in the Baltic." *Ensign* 21 (August 1991): 36–41.

Kastianinen, Jouna. "Gospel Spreads Rapidly in Finland." *Church News.* 5 February 1966, 13.

Mitchell, David. "The Saints in Finland." *Ensign* 3 (May 1973): 5–11.

Wennerlund, Bo G. "The Church in Scandinavia and Finland." *Mormonism: A Faith for All Cultures.* Ed. F. Lamond Tullis. Provo: Brigham Young University Press, 1978. 51–57.

France

Avant, Gerry. "Grand Tradition of France Has Impact on Church Growth." *Church News.* 5 September 1987, 3–4.

Didier, Charles A. "The Church in French-Speaking Europe." *Mormonism: A Faith for All Cultures.* Ed. F. Lamond Tullis. Provo: Brigham Young University Press, 1978. 44–48.

"France." *Ensign* 3 (August 1973): 22–24.

Mehr, Kahlile. "The Trial of the French Mission." *Dialogue: A Journal of Mormon Thought* 21 (Fall 1988): 27–45.

Gaunt, LaRene Porter. "A Blooming in France." *Ensign* 25 (March 1995): 40–50.

Wilson, Laurie J. "The Saints in France." *Ensign* 6 (January 1976): 77–81.

Germany

Busche, F. Enzio. "The Church in Germany, Switzerland, and Austria." *Mormonism: A Faith for All Cultures.* Ed. F. Lamond Tullis. Provo: Brigham Young University Press, 1978. 48–51.

"Germany." *Ensign* 3 (August 1973): 25–27.

Hart, John L. "Frankfurt Temple Dedicated." *Church News.* 5 September 1987, 3–4.

"Saints Make Their Mark in Wetzlar, West Germany." *Ensign* 18 (September 1988): 78–79.

Scharffs, Gilbert W. *Mormonism in Germany: A History of The Church of Jesus Christ of Latter-day Saints in Germany between 1840 and 1970.* Salt Lake City: Deseret Book, 1970.

Greece and Cyprus

"Cyprus Dedicated for Preaching of Gospel." *Ensign* 24 (February 1994): 74–75.

Iceland

Dockstader, Julie A. "Member Receives 'Highest Honor' from Iceland for Fostering Heritage." *Church News.* 14 August 1993, 5.

Ireland

"British Saints Celebrate 150th Anniversary." *Ensign* 17 (October 1987): 75.

Card, Orson Scott. "The Saints in Ireland." *Ensign* 8 (February 1978): 44–48.

Dixon, Derek. "The Saints in the British Isles." *Ensign* 6 (June 1976): 80–84.

"First-Ever Regional Conference for Ireland." *Ensign* 16 (November 1986): 103.

Harris, Claudia W. "Mormons on the Warfront." *BYU Studies* 30 (Fall 1990): 7–19.

"Ireland Dedicated for Proselyting." *Ensign* 16 (February 1986): 76.

Murray, Herbert F. "Report from Belfast." *Ensign* 2 (November 1972): 84–86.

Perry, Anne. "'This Is the Truth, and We Will Not Turn Back.'" *Ensign* 17 (July 1987): 44–48.

Italy

"Italy." *Ensign* 3 (August 1973): 27–29.

Jorgensen, Dan C. "The Church in Italy." *Mormonism: A Faith for All Cultures.* Ed. F. Lamond Tullis. Provo: Brigham Young University Press, 1978. 64–65.

"Milestone Reached in Italy; Church Gains Legal Status." *Church News.* 12 June 1993, 4.

Nay, Lori Young. "Catania Italy Saints: Profiles of Faith." *Ensign* 24 (July 1994): 75–76.

Searle, Don L. "Buon Giorno!" *Ensign* 19 (July 1989): 34–39.

Todd, Jay M. "The Saga of the Di Francesca Story." *Ensign* 19 (September 1989): 73.

The Netherlands

"The Netherlands." *Ensign* 3 (August 1973): 29–31.

Warner, Keith C. "History of the Netherlands Mission of The Church of Jesus Christ of Latter-day Saints 1861–1966." Master's thesis. Brigham Young University, 1967.

Norway

"Norway." *Ensign* 4 (July 1974): 32–35.

Wagner, Kimberly Jacobs. "Arne Bakken: Lifting with Love in Norway." *Ensign* 21 (July 1991): 50–51.

Wennerlund, Bo G. "The Church in Scandinavia and Finland." *Mormonism: A Faith for All Cultures.* Ed. F. Lamond Tullis. Provo: Brigham Young University Press, 1978. 51–57.

Portugal

Hillam, Harold G. "No More Strangers and Foreigners." *Ensign* 20 (November 1990): 24–25.

Searle, Don L. "Brotherly Love in Portugal." *Ensign* 19 (August 1989): 66–68.

——. "Discovering Gospel Riches in Portugal." *Ensign* 17 (October 1987): 10–15.

——. "The Saints of Portugal." *Tambuli* (February 1988): 27.

Russia

Florence, Giles H., Jr. "That Sunday in Leningrad." *Ensign* 20 (December 1990): 67–69.

Larson-Hall, Jenifer. "Love and Faith in St. Petersburg." *Ensign* 23 (December 1993): 32–35.

Mehr, Kahlile. "1989–90: The Curtain Opens." *Ensign* 23 (December 1993): 36–37.

"Russian Republic Recognizes the Church." *Ensign* 20 (November 1990): 106.

Paulsen, Dierdre M. "Russian Women: Gaining Roots, Growing Strong." *Hearts Knit Together: Talks from the 1995 Women's Conference.* Ed. Susette Fletcher Green, Dawn Hall Anderson, and Dlora Hall Dalton. Salt Lake City: Deseret Book, 1996.

Scotland

"Aberdeen: Scot by Heritage, Strengthened by the Gospel." *Ensign* 20 (March 1990): 77–78.

"British Saints Celebrate 150th Anniversary." *Ensign* 17 (October 1987): 74–75.

Cuthbert, Muriel. "Strong Saints in Scotland." *Ensign* 8 October 1978): 34–38.

Dixon, Derek. "The Saints in the British Isles." *Ensign* 6 (June 1976): 80–84.

"Missionary Journal: Five Church Leaders Look Back at Their British Isles Mission Experiences." *Ensign* 17 (July 1987): 10–11.

Perry, Anne. "'This Is the Truth, and We Will Not Turn Back.'" *Ensign* 17 (July 1987): 44–48.

Spain

Avant, Gerry, and John L. Hart. "Many Are Still Blazing Gospel Trails." *Church News.* 24 July 1993, 7.

"Gospel Takes Wing in Canary Islands." *Church News.* 10 November 1990, 8–10.

Rivero, Carol Baughman. "The Saints in Barcelona: Faithful Converts." *Ensign* 20 (August 1990): 78–79.

"Spain." *Ensign* 3 (August 1973): 31–32.

Ventura, Betty. "The Saints in Spain." *Ensign* 5 (April 1975): 7–11.

Sweden

Hart, John L. "Sweden: Members Mold Lives to Gospel Ideals, Look to Growth." *Church News.* 21 November 1987, 9.

Lubeck, Kathleen. "The Art of Family Life: Gregory J. Newell, United States Ambassador to Sweden." *Ensign* 17 (October 1987): 34–39.

"Saints Enjoy Blessings of Stockholm Temple." *Ensign* 15 (September 1985): 74–75.

"Sweden." *Ensign* 4 (July 1974): 35–37.

"Swedish Saints: Anticipating a House of the Lord." *Ensign* 15 (July 1985): 78–79.

Wennerlund, Bo G. "The Church in Scandinavia and Finland." *Mormonism: A Faith for All Cultures.* Ed. F. Lamond Tullis. Provo: Brigham Young University Press, 1978. 51–57.

Switzerland

Busche, F. Enzio. "The Church in Germany, Switzerland, and Austria." *Mormonism: A Faith for All Cultures.* Ed. F. Lamond Tullis. Provo: Brigham Young University Press, 1978. 48–51.

Didier, Charles A. "The Church in French-Speaking Europe." *Mormonism: A Faith for All Cultures.* Ed. F. Lamond Tullis. Provo: Brigham Young University Press, 1978. 44–48.

"Geneva—Unity and Diversity." *Tambuli* (November 1992): 42–48.

Kirby, Dale Z. "History of The Church of Jesus Christ of Latter-day Saints in Switzerland." Master's thesis. Brigham Young University, 1971.

"Switzerland." *Ensign* 3 (August 1973): 33–35.

Wales

"British Saints Celebrate 150th Anniversary." *Ensign* 17 (October 1987): 74.

Dixon, Derek. "The Saints in the British Isles." *Ensign* 6 (June 1976): 80–84.

Perry, Anne. "'This Is the Truth, and We Will Not Turn Back.'" *Ensign* 17 (July 1987): 44–48.

1900 TO 1950

General

Babbel, Frederick W. *On Wings of Faith.* Salt Lake City: Bookcraft, 1972.

Boone, David F. "The Worldwide Evacuation of LDS Missionaries at the Beginning of World War II." Master's thesis. Brigham Young University, 1981.

A Labor of Love: The 1946 European Mission of Ezra Taft Benson. Salt Lake City: Deseret Book, 1989.

Walker, Ronald W. "Heber J. Grant's European Mission, 1903–1906." *Journal of Mormon History* 14 (1988): 17–33.

Czechoslovakia

Campora, Olga Kovářová. "Fruits of Faithfulness: The Saints of Czechoslovakia." *Women Steadfast in Christ: Talks Selected from the 1991 Women's Conference.* Ed. Dawn Hall Anderson and Marie Cornwall. Salt Lake City: Deseret Book, 1992. 134–47.

Mehr, Kahlile. "Czech Saints: A Brighter Day." *Ensign* 24 (August 1994): 46–52.

——. "Enduring Believers: Czechoslovakia and the LDS Church, 1884–1990." *Journal of Mormon History* 18 (Fall 1992): 111–54.

Denmark

Christensen, Marius A. "History of the Danish Mission of The Church of Jesus Christ of Latter-day Saints 1850–1964." Master's thesis. Brigham Young University, 1966.

Jenson, Andrew. *History of the Scandinavian Mission.* Salt Lake City: Deseret News Press, 1927.

England

Brown, Hugh B. "Reflections of a Missionary to Great Britain." *Ensign* 1 (September 1971): 8–11.

Cardon, Louis B. "The First World War and the Great Depression, 1914–1939." *Truth Will Prevail: The Rise of The Church of Jesus Christ of Latter-day Saints in the British Isles, 1837–1987.* Ed. V. Ben Bloxham, James R. Moss, and Larry C. Porter. West Midlands: Corporation of the President of The Church of Jesus Christ of Latter-day Saints, 1987. 335–60.

——. "War and Recovery, 1939–1950." *Truth Will Prevail: The Rise of The Church of Jesus Christ of Latter-day Saints in the British Isles, 1837–1987.* Ed. V. Ben Bloxham, James R. Moss, and Larry C. Porter. West Midlands: Corporation of the President of The Church of Jesus Christ of Latter-day Saints, 1987. 361–93.

Cuthbert, Derek A. *The Second Century: Latter-day Saints in Great Britain, Volume I, 1937–1987.* Cambridge: Cambridge University Press, 1987. 1–6.

Evans, Richard L. *A Century of "Mormonism" in Great Britain.* Salt Lake City: Deseret News Press, 1937.

"Missionary Journal: Five Church Leaders Look Back at Their British Isles Mission Experiences." *Ensign* 17 (July 1987): 8–11.

Thorp, Malcolm R. "'The Mormon Peril': The Crusade against the Saints in Britain, 1910–1914." *Journal of Mormon History* 14 (1988): 69–88.

Finland

Mehr, Kahlile. "Johan and Alma Lindlof: Early Saints in Russia." *Ensign* 11 (July 1981): 23–24.

Johansson, C. Fritz. "Wartime Mission in Sweden." *Ensign* 11 (April 1981): 44–45.

France

Marie, Alain. "Leon Fargier: His Faith Wouldn't Go Underground." *Ensign* 21 (September 1991): 29–31.

Germany

Anderson, Jeffrey L. "Mormons and Germany, 1914–1933." Master's thesis. Brigham Young University, 1991.

Dixon, Joseph M. "Mormons in the Third Reich: 1933–1945." *Dialogue: A Journal of Mormon Thought* 7 (Spring 1972).

Holmes, Blair R., and Alan F. Keele. *When Truth Was Treason: German Youth Against Hitler.* Urbana, Ill.: University of Illinois Press, 1995.

Keele, Alan F., and Douglas F. Tobler. "The Führer's New Clothes: Helmuth Hubener and the Mormons in the Third Reich." *Sunstone* 5 (November-December 1980): 20–29.

Mehr, Kahlile. "The Langheinrich Legacy: Record-Gathering in Post-War Germany." *Ensign* 11 (June 1981): 22–25.

Mitchell, Michael. "The Mormons in Wilhelmine, Germany, 1870–1914: Making a Place for a Unwanted American Religion in a Changing German Society." Master's thesis. Brigham Young University, 1994.

Scharffs, Gilbert W. *Mormonism in Germany: A History of The Church of Jesus Christ of Latter-day Saints between 1840–1970.* Salt Lake City: Deseret Book, 1970. 46–151.

Schnibbe, Karl Heinz, with Alan F. Keele and Douglas F. Tobler. *The Price: The True Story of a Mormon Who Defied Hitler.* Salt Lake City: Bookcraft, 1984.

Wobbe, Rudi, and Jerry Borrowman. *Before the Blood Tribunal.* Salt Lake City: Covenant Communications, 1992.

Ireland

Barlow, Brent A. "The Irish Experience." *Truth Will Prevail: The Rise of The Church of Jesus Christ of Latter-day Saints in the British Isles, 1837–1987.* Ed. V. Ben Bloxham, James R. Moss, and Larry C. Porter. West Midlands: Corporation of the President of The Church of Jesus Christ of Latter-day Saints, 1987. 299–331.

The Netherlands

Hartley, William G. "War and Peace and Dutch Potatoes." *Ensign* 8 (July 1978): 19–23.

Warner, Keith C. "History of the Netherlands Mission of The Church of Jesus Christ of Latter-day Saints 1861–1966." Master's thesis. Brigham Young University, 1967.

Norway

Floisand, John. "Inner Peace Can Come in Time of War." *Church News.* 26 February 1994, 7.

Haslam, Gerald M. "The Norwegian Experience with Mormonism, 1842–1920." Doctoral dissertation. Brigham Young University, 1981.

Jenson, Andrew. *History of the Scandinavian Mission.* Salt Lake City: Deseret News Press, 1927.

Russia

Kehr, William Hale. "Missionary to the Balkans: Mischa Markow." *Ensign* 10 (June 1980): 29–32.

Mehr, Kahlile. "Johan and Alma Lindlof: Early Saints in Russia." *Ensign* 11 (July 1981): 23–24.

Sweden

Jenson, Andrew. *History of the Scandinavian Mission.* Salt Lake City: Deseret News Press, 1927.

Johansson, C. Fritz. "Wartime Mission in Sweden." *Ensign* 11 (April 1981): 44–45.

Switzerland

Kirby, Dale Z. "History of The Church of Jesus Christ of Latter-day Saints in Switzerland." Master's thesis. Brigham Young University, 1971.

1830 TO 1900

Belgium

Kehr, William Hale. "Missionary to the Balkans: Mischa Markow." *Ensign* 10 (June 1980): 29–32.

Czechoslovakia

Mehr, Kahlile. "Enduring Believers: Czechoslovakia and the LDS Church, 1884–1990." *Journal of Mormon History* 18 (Fall 1992): 111–54.

Denmark

Jenson, Andrew. *History of the Scandinavian Mission.* Salt Lake City: Deseret News Press, 1927.

Mulder, William. *Homeward to Zion: The Mormon Migration from Scandinavia.* Minneapolis: University of Minnesota Press, 1957.

England

Allen, James B., and Thomas G. Alexander, eds. *Manchester Mormons: The Journal of William Clayton, 1840 to 1842.* Santa Barbara: Peregrine Smith, 1974.

Allen, James B., Ronald K. Esplin, and David J. Whittaker. *Men with a Mission: The Quorum of the Twelve Apostles in the British Isles, 1837–1841.* Salt Lake City: Deseret Book, 1992.

Anderson, Lavina Fielding. "In the Crucible: Early British Saints." *Ensign* 9 (December 1979): 50–55.

Arrington, Leonard J. "Mormon Women in Nineteenth-Century Britain." *BYU Studies* 27 (Winter 1987): 67–84.

Bloxham, V. Ben. "The Apostolic Foundations, 1840–1841." *Truth Will Prevail: The Rise of The Church of Jesus Christ of Latter-day Saints in the British Isles, 1837–1987.* Ed.

V. Ben Bloxham, James R. Moss, and Larry C. Porter. West Midlands: Corporation of the President of The Church of Jesus Christ of Latter-day Saints, 1987. 121–62.

——. "The Call of the Apostles to the British Isles." *Truth Will Prevail: The Rise of The Church of Jesus Christ of Latter-day Saints in the British Isles, 1837–1987.* Ed. V. Ben Bloxham, James R. Moss, and Larry C. Porter. West Midlands: Corporation of the President of The Church of Jesus Christ of Latter-day Saints, 1987. 104–20.

Cannon, Donald Q. "George Q. Cannon and the British Mission." *BYU Studies* 27 (Winter 1987): 97–112.

Cotterill, John. "Midland Saints: The Mormon Mission in the West Midlands 1837–77." Ph.D. thesis. University of Keele, 1985.

Cowan, Richard O. "Church Growth in England, 1841–1914." *Truth Will Prevail: The Rise of The Church of Jesus Christ of Latter-day Saints in the British Isles, 1837–1987.* Ed. V. Ben Bloxham, James R. Moss, and Larry C. Porter. West Midlands: Corporation of the President of The Church of Jesus Christ of Latter-day Saints, 1987. 199–235.

Esplin, Ronald K. "Brigham Young in England." *Ensign* 17 (June 1987): 28–33.

——. "'A Great Work Done in That Land.'" *Ensign* 17 (July 1987): 20–27.

Evans, Richard L. *A Century of "Mormonism" in Great Britain.* Salt Lake City: Deseret News Press, 1937.

Foster, Craig L. "Anti-Mormon Pamphleteering in Great Britain, 1837–1860." Master's thesis. Brigham Young University, 1989.

Godfrey, Kenneth W. "Charles W. Penrose: The English Mission Years." *BYU Studies* 27 (Winter 1987): 113–26.

Harris, Jan G. "Mormons in Victorian Manchester." *BYU Studies* 27 (Winter 1987): 47–56.

Heaton, Tim, Stan Albrecht, and J. Randal Johnson. "The Making of British Saints in Historical Perspective." *BYU Studies* 27 (Spring 1987): 119–135.

Hinckley, Gordon B. "Taking the Gospel to Britain: A Declaration of Vision, Faith, Courage, and Truth." *Ensign* 17 (July 1987): 2–7.

Jensen, Richard L. "The British Gathering to Zion." *Truth Will Prevail: The Rise of The Church of Jesus Christ of Latter-day Saints in the British Isles, 1837–1987.* Ed. V. Ben Bloxham, James R. Moss, and Larry C. Porter. West Midlands: Corporation of the President of The Church of Jesus Christ of Latter-day Saints, 1987. 165–98.

Jensen, Richard L., and Malcolm R. Thorp, eds. *Mormons in Early Victorian Britain.* Salt Lake City: University of Utah Press, 1989.

Jorgenson, Lynn Watkins. *The First London Mormons: 1840–1845.* Master's thesis. Brigham Young University, 1988.

Moss, James R. "The Gospel Restored to England." *Truth Will Prevail: The Rise of The Church of Jesus Christ of Latter-day Saints in the British Isles, 1837–1987.* Ed. V. Ben Bloxham, James R. Moss, and Larry C. Porter. West Midlands: Corporation of the President of The Church of Jesus Christ of Latter-day Saints, 1987. 71–103.

——. "The Kingdom Builders." *Ensign* 9 (December 1979): 26–31.

Moss, James R., and Lavelle R. Moss. "Names and Places: Locales of British LDS Interest." *Ensign* 17 (July 1987): 16–18.

Smith, Paul Thomas. "Among Family and Friends: John Taylor's Mission to the British Isles." *Ensign* 17 (March 1987): 36–41.

Thorp, Malcolm R. "The Religious Backgrounds of Mormon Converts in Britain, 1837–52." *Journal of Mormon History* 4 (1977): 51–65.

——. *Sectarian Violence in Early Victorian Britain: The Mormon Experience, 1837–1860.* Manchester, England: Bulletin of the John Rylands University Library of Manchester, 1988.

——. "The Setting for the Restoration in Britain: Political, Social, and Economic Conditions." *Truth Will Prevail: The Rise of The Church of Jesus Christ of Latter-day Saints in the British Isles, 1837–1987.* Ed. V. Ben Bloxham, James R. Moss, and Larry C. Porter. West Midlands: Corporation of the President of The Church of Jesus Christ of Latter-day Saints, 1987. 44–70.

Tobler, Douglas F. "Truth Prevailing—The Significance of the Nineteenth-Century LDS Experience in Britain." *Ensign* 17 (July 1987): 33–37.

Van Orden, Bruce A. "The Decline in Convert Baptisms and Member Emigration from the British Mission after 1870." *BYU Studies* 27 (Spring 1987): 97–105.

Walker, Ronald W. "Cradling Mormonism: The Rise of the Gospel in Early Victorian England." *BYU Studies* 27 (Winter 1987): 25–36.

Whittaker, David J. "Harvest in Herefordshire." *Ensign* 17 (January 1987): 46–51.

Germany

Mitchell, Michael. "The Mormons in Wilhelmine, Germany, 1870–1914: Making a Place for a Unwanted American Religion in a Changing German Society." Master's thesis. Brigham Young University, 1994.

Scharffs, Gilbert W. *Mormonism in Germany: A History of The Church of Jesus Christ of Latter-day Saints in Germany between 1840 and 1970.* Salt Lake City: Deseret Book, 1970. 1–49.

Ireland

Barlow, Brent A. "The Irish Experience." *Truth Will Prevail: The Rise of The Church of Jesus Christ of Latter-day Saints in the British Isles, 1837–1987.* Ed. V. Ben Bloxham, James R. Moss, and Larry C. Porter. West Midlands: Corporation of the President of The Church of Jesus Christ of Latter-day Saints, 1987. 299–331.

Italy

Christiansen, James R. "Early Missionary Work in Italy and Switzerland." *Ensign* 12 (August 1982): 35–46.

The Netherlands

Warner, Keith C. "History of the Netherlands Mission of The Church of Jesus Christ of Latter-day Saints 1861–1966." Master's thesis. Brigham Young University, 1967.

Norway

Haslam, Gerald M. "The Norwegian Experience with Mormonism, 1842–1920." Dissertation. Brigham Young University, 1981.

Jenson, Andrew. *History of the Scandinavian Mission.* Salt Lake City: Deseret News Press, 1927.

Mulder, William. *Homeward to Zion: The Mormon Migration from Scandinavia.* Minneapolis: University of Minnesota Press, 1957.

Russia

Mehr, Kahlile. "Johan and Alma Lindlof: Early Saints in Russia." *Ensign* 11 (July 1981): 23–24.

Scotland

Buchanan, Frederick S. "The Ebb and Flow of the Church in Scotland." *Truth Will Prevail: The Rise of The Church of Jesus Christ of Latter-day Saints in the British Isles, 1837–1987.* Ed. V. Ben Bloxham, James R. Moss, and Larry C. Porter. West Midlands: Corporation of the President of The Church of Jesus Christ of Latter-day Saints, 1987. 268–98.

——. "The Ebb and Flow of Mormonism in Scotland, 1840–1900." *BYU Studies* 27 (Spring 1987): 27–52.

England, Breck. "Gospel Seeds in Scottish Soil." *Ensign* 17 (February 1987): 26–31.

Sweden

Jenson, Andrew. *History of the Scandinavian Mission.* Salt Lake City: Deseret News Press, 1927.

Mulder, William. *Homeward to Zion: The Mormon Migration from Scandinavia.* Minneapolis: University of Minnesota Press, 1957.

Switzerland

Christianson, James R. "Early Missionary Work in Italy and Switzerland." *Ensign* 12 (August 1982): 35–46.

Kirby, Dale Z. "History of The Church of Jesus Christ of Latter-day Saints in Switzerland." Master's thesis. Brigham Young University, 1971.

Wales

Davies, Douglas James. *Mormon Spirituality: Latter-day Saints in Wales and Zion.* Nottingham: University of Nottingham, 1987.

Dennis, Ronald D. "Dan Jones, Welshman: Taking the Gospel Home." *Ensign* 17 (April 1987): 50–56.

——. "The Reverend W. R. Davies vs. Captain Dan Jones." *BYU Studies* 27 (Spring 1987): 53–65.

——. "The Welsh and the Gospel." *Truth Will Prevail: The Rise of The Church of Jesus Christ of Latter-day Saints in the British Isles, 1837–1987.* Ed. V. Ben Bloxham, James R. Moss, and Larry C. Porter. West Midlands: Corporation of the President of The Church of Jesus Christ of Latter-day Saints, 1987. 236–67.

Hinckley, Gordon B. "The Thing of Most Worth." *Ensign* 23 (September 1993): 2–7.

Index